J Overall potential for abuse and Toxicity	K Reasons drug is sought by users (drug effects and social factors)	L Usual short-term effects (psychological, pharmacological, social)	M Usual long-term effects (psychological, pharmacological, social)	N Form of legal regulation and control
High	To relax. To escape from tensions, problems and inhibitions. To get "high" (euphoria), seeking manhood or rebelling (particularly those under 21). Social custom and conformity. Massive advertising and promotion. Ready availability.	CNS depressant. Relaxation (sedation). Euphoria. Drowsiness. Impaired judgment, reaction time, coordination and emotional control. Frequent aggressive behavior and driving accidents.	Diversion of energy and money from more creative and productive pursuits. Habituation. Possible obesity with chronic excessive use. Irreversible damage to brain and liver, addiction with severe withdrawal illness. (D.T.s) with heavy use. Many deaths.	Available and advertised without limitation in many forms with only minimal regulation by age (21, or 18), hours of sale, location, taxation, ban on bootlegging and driving laws. Some "black market" for those under age and those evading taxes. Minimal penalties.
Very Minimal	For a "pick-up" or stimulation. "Taking a Break". Social custom and low cost. Advertising. Ready availability.	CNS stimulant. Increased alertness. Reduction of fatigue.	Sometimes insomnia, restlessness, or gastric irritation. Habituation.	Available and advertised without limit with no regulation for children or adults.
High	For a "pick-up" or stimulation. "Taking a Break". Social custom. Advertising. Ready availability.	CNS stimulant. Relaxation (or distraction) from the process of smoking.	Lung (and other) cancer, heart and blood vessel disease, cough, etc. Higher death mortality. Many deaths. Habituation. Diversion of energy and money. Air pollution. Fire.	Available and advertised without limit with only minimal regulation by age, taxation, and labeling of packages.
High	To relax or sleep. To get "high" (euphoria). Widely prescribed by physicians, both for specific and nonspecific complaints. General climate encouraging taking pills for everything.	CNS depressants. Sleep induction. Relaxation (sedation). Sometimes euphoria. Drowsiness. Impaired judgment, reaction time, coordination and emotional control. Relief of anxiety-tension. Muscle relaxation.	Irritability, weight loss, addiction with severe withdrawal illness (like D.T.s). Diversion of energy and money. Habituation, addiction.	Available in large amounts by ordinary medical prescription which can be repeatedly refilled or can be obtained from more than one physician. Widely advertised and "detailed" to M.D.s and pharmacists. Other manufacture, sale or possession prohibited under federal drug abuse and similar state (dangerous) drug laws. Moderate penalties. Widespread illicit traffic.
High	For stimulation and relief of fatigue. To get "high" (euphoria). General climate encouraging taking pills for everything.	CNS stimulants. Increased alertness, reduction of fatigue, loss of appetite, insomnia, often euphoria.	Restlessness, irritability, weight loss, toxic psychosis (mainly paranoid). Diversion of energy and money. Habituation. Extreme irritability, toxic psychosis.	Amphetamines, same as Sedatives above. Cocaine, same as Narcotics below.
Minimal	Medical (including psychiatric) treatment of anxiety or tension states, alcoholism, psychoses, and other disorders.	Selective CNS depressants. Relaxation, relief of anxiety-tension. Suppression of hallucinations or delusions, improved functioning.	Sometimes drowsiness, dryness of mouth, blurring of vision, skin rash, tremor. Occasionally jaundice, agranulocytosis, or death.	Same as Sedatives above, except not usually included under the special federal or state drug laws. Negligible illicit traffic.
Minimal To Moderate	To get "high" (euphoria). As an escape. To relax. To socialize. To conform to various subcultures which sanction its use. For rebellion. Attraction of behavior labeled as deviant. Availability.	Relaxation, euphoria, increased appetite, some alteration of time perception, possible impairment of judgment and coordination. Mixed CNS depressant-stimulant.	Usually none. Possible diversion of energy and money. Habituation. Occasional acute panic reactions.	Unavailable (although permissible) for ordinary medical prescription. Possession, sale, and cultivation prohibited by state and federal narcotic or marihuana laws. Severe penalties. Widespread illicit traffic.
High	To get "high" (euphoria). As an escape. To avoid withdrawal symptoms. As a substitute for aggressive and sexual drives which cause anxiety. To conform to various subcultures which sanction use. For rebellion.	CNS depressants. Sedation, euphoria, relief of pain, impaired intellectual functioning and coordination.	Constipation, loss of appetite and weight, temporary impotency or sterility. Habituation, addiction with unpleasant and painful withdrawal illness.	Available (except heroin) by special (narcotics) medical prescriptions. Some available by ordinary prescription or over-the-counter. Other manufacture, sale, or possession prohibited under state and federal narcotics laws. Severe penalties. Extensive illicit traffic.
Moderate	Curiosity created by recent widespread publicity. Seeking for meaning and consciousness—expansion. Rebellion. Attraction of behavior recently labeled as deviant. Availability.	Production of visual imagery, increased sensory awareness, anxiety, nausea, impaired coordination; sometimes consciousness-expansion.	Usually none. Sometimes precipitates or intensifies an already existing psychosis; more commonly can produce a panic reaction.	Available only to a few medical researchers (or to members of the Native American Church). Other manufacture, sale or possession prohibited by state dangerous drug or federal drug abuse laws. Moderate penalties. Extensive illicit traffic.
Minimal	Medical (including psychiatric) treatment of depression.	Relief of depression (elevation of mood), stimulation.	Basically the same as Tranquilizers above.	Same as Tranquilizers above.
Moderate To High	Curiosity. To get "high" (euphoria). Thrill seeking. Ready availability.	When used for mind-alteration generally produces a "high" (euphoria) with impaired coordination and judgment.	Variable—some of the substances can seriously damage the liver or kidney and some produce hallucinations.	Generally easily available. Some require prescriptions. In several states glue banned for those under 21.

nly scattered, inadequate health, educational or rehabilitation programs ally prison hospitals) exist for narcotic addicts and alcoholics (usually outnt clinics) with nothing for the others except sometimes prison.

Ⓢ Hashish or Charas is a more concentrated form of the active ingredient THC (Tetrahydrocannabinol) and is consumed in smaller doses analogous to vodka:beer ratios.

DATE DUE

GAYLORD

PRINTED IN U.S.A.

DRUG ABUSE
Data and Debate

Edited by

PAUL H. BLACHLY, M.D.

Professor of Psychiatry
University of Oregon Medical School
Portland, Oregon

CHARLES C THOMAS • PUBLISHER
Springfield • Illinois • U.S.A.

Published and Distributed Throughout the World by
CHARLES C THOMAS · PUBLISHER

BANNERSTONE HOUSE
301-327 East Lawrence Avenue, Springfield, Illinois, U.S.A.
NATCHEZ PLANTATION HOUSE
735 North Atlantic Boulevard, Fort Lauderdale, Florida, U.S.A.

© 1970, by CHARLES C THOMAS · PUBLISHER
Library of Congress Catalog Card No. 78-119970

With THOMAS BOOKS *careful attention is given to all details of
manufacturing and design. It is the Publisher's desire to present books
that are satisfactory as to their physical qualities and artistic possibilities
and appropriate for their particular use.* THOMAS BOOKS *will be true
to those laws of quality that assure a good name and good will.*

Printed in the United States of America
W-2

CONTRIBUTORS

PAUL H. BLACHLY, M.D., is Professor of Psychiatry at the University of Oregon Medical School, Director of the Western Institute of Drug Problems Summer School, and Director of the Methadone Blockade Treatment Program of Heroin Addicts in Portland, Oregon.

ROBERT W. CARRICK, MSW, is the Assistant Chief, Community Services Section, Narcotic Addict Rehabilitation Branch, Division of Narcotic Addiction and Drug Abuse of the National Institute of Mental Health, Chevy Chase, Maryland. Prior to his present position he had extensive casework experience with narcotic addicts.

KENNETH D. GAVER, M.D., is Administrator of the Mental Health Division, Salem, Oregon. As director of all the mental health services in the state, he must fit the needs of treating drug dependent persons into the perspective of overall mental health.

SAMUEL IRWIN, PH.D., is Professor of Pharmacology in Psychiatry at the University of Oregon Medical School, Portland, Oregon. He is particularly active in the development of behavioral measures for psychoactive drugs.

JEROME H. JAFFE, M.D., is Director of the Drug Abuse Program, Department of Mental Health, State of Illinois, and is Associate Professor in the Department of Psychiatry at the University of Chicago. He has done advanced work in experimental psychology and is an authority on the pharmacology of opiate drugs.

RICHARD E. LAHTI, M.D., was first a pharmacist who went on to become a physician. As a general practitioner he has lectured extensively to students regarding problems of drug abuse.

SIDNEY I. LEZAK, J.D., is a United States Attorney. He is responsible for prosecution of persons who violate Federal laws and hence is continually confronted with the problem of disposition of such individuals.

DAVID W. MAURER, PH.D., is Professor of Linguistics at the University of Louisville, Louisville, Kentucky. His published work deals with language in relation to human behavior, especially the argots of professional criminals as they reflect the patterns of criminal behavior. A new edition of his *Narcotics and Narcotic Addiction* has recently been published by Charles C Thomas, Publisher.

JOHN I. MAURER, M.D., was formerly involved with the free clinic in Haight-Ashbury and at the present time is practicing psychiatry at the Cowell Student Health Center at Stanford University.

GLEN D. MELLINGER, PH.D., since 1959 has been associated with Family Research Center, Langley-Porter Neuropsychiatric Institute, most recently as Associate Director. He is particularly interested in the acquisition habits of the general population regarding psychotherapeutic drugs.

RICHARD PHILLIPSON, M.D., is former Director of Army Psychiatry and Consulting Psychiatrist to the British Army and Professor of Military Psychiatry at the Royal Army Medical College, London. More recently he has been involved with individual and group psychotherapy in a clinic for heroin addicts in London, and at the present time is consultant to the National Institute of Mental Health Section on Alcohol and Drug Abuse, Chevy Chase, Maryland.

GEORGE SASLOW, M.D., is Chairman of the Department of Psychiatry of the University of Oregon Medical School, Portland, Oregon. His interest in drug abuse stems from its reflection of social maladaptation.

CONRAD J. SCHWARZ, M.B., CH.B., is a psychiatrist who has been extensively involved in problems of drug abuse by university students in connection with his position on the health service at the University of British Columbia, Vancouver, B. C.

EDWARD M. SCOTT, PH.D., is Clinic Director of the Alcohol and Drug Section of the Mental Health Division, State of Oregon. His extensive activities in group psychotherapy provide him with a unique perspective on this problem.

REGINALD G. SMART, PH.D., is associated with the Alcoholism and

Drug Addiction Research Foundation of Toronto. He is a special lecturer in psychology at York University, Toronto, Canada. He has published extensively on problems of alcohol and drug abuse.

JEAN PAUL SMITH, PH.D., was formerly Chief, Drug Sciences Division, Bureau of Narcotics and Dangerous Drugs, United States Department of Justice. He is now at the Institute for the Study of Human Problems at Stanford University.

JULIAN E. VILLARREAL, M.D., PH.D., has been extensively involved in the analysis and development of new narcotic drugs at the Department of Pharmacology at the University of Michigan, Ann Arbor, Michigan.

ABRAHAM WIKLER, M.D., is Professor of Psychiatry and Pharmacology at the University of Kentucky College of Medicine, Lexington, Kentucky. Since 1942, he has been associated with the NIMH Addiction Research Center at Lexington, Kentucky, most recently as Associate Director and Chief, Section on Experimental Neuropsychiatry.

The team of NATHAN B. EDDY, H. HALBACH, HARRIS ISBELL and MAURICE H. SEEVERS are consultants to the World Health Organization with regard to problems of drug abuse. Their contributions span many decades and their viewpoint is accepted as authoritative.

PREFACE

F ROM THE SOCIOLOGY of addiction to the technology of developing new drugs to mass habits of using over-the-counter drugs, these papers represent the most recent and authoritative thinking about the problems of drug dependence.

They were presented at the Second Annual Western Institute of Drug Problems Summer School held at Portland State University, August 11-14, 1969. The six hundred participants included educators, physicians, nurses, policemen, medical and nursing students, clergymen, publicists, pharmacologists, social workers, psychologists, vocational rehabilitators, youth and school counselors, and drug addicts—a diverse group active in the prevention and treatment of drug dependency.

Our first summer school in 1968 revealed such interest for a short, authoritative course about drug abuse granting academic credit, that we have planned to repeat it each summer for as long as there appears to be a need. Its timing in the second week of August works out well for educators, and the scenic location encourages many to bring their family and combine pleasure with business. Indeed, some have hooked salmon on the same trip on which they learned how people get hooked on drugs!

Digestion of these papers during the meeting was stimulated by both disciplinary and cross-disciplinary small-group discussions, which drew for additional background data upon movies and exhibits available during the lunch and evening periods.

Each author was encouraged to point the way to additional research studies, new legislation, or educational techniques that will help us to improve the present unsatisfactory methods we have for dealing with drug problems and abuse.

The appendix provides factual background material so fundamental to an understanding of drug abuse that we have received permission to reprint it from Dr. Nathan Eddy and Dr. Abraham

Wikler. It also includes an opinion by Dr. Samuel Irwin of the pros and cons regarding legalization of marihuana.

Dr. Jerome Jaffe presented a paper at these meetings comparing the results of treating addicts by three different methods. Because he wished to do further work on this paper, he kindly consented to let us publish in its place his testimony of August 8, 1969, to the United States Senate Special Subcommittee on Alcoholism and Narcotics of the Committee on Labor and Public Welfare. Comprehension of his statement is fundamental to any governmental organization which seeks to make definable inroads into the jungle of drug abuse.

The reader is urged to follow up the references, to correspond with the authors directly regarding specific questions and with the administrator of the Western Institute for Drug Problems Summer School regarding future courses. (See Acknowledgments.)

ACKNOWLEDGMENTS

THE DEVELOPMENT OF THE Western Institute of Drug Problems
Summer School was suggested by its coordinator, Mr. George
Dimas, Administrator, Alcohol and Drug Section, Mental Health
Division, based upon the success of the Utah Summer School on
Alcohol. Its establishment was encouraged by the Alcohol and
Drug Education Advisory Committee appointed by Gov. Tom
McCall and facilitated by Kenneth D. Gaver, M.D., Administrator
of the Mental Health Division. For such an endeavor to be
effective, people must be made aware that such a school exists,
and this was skillfully managed by Mr. Don L. Short, Director
of Communications Services. Dr. Leroy R. Pierson, Director of
Administration at the Division of Continuing Education, provided
the physical facilities of Portland State University and supervised
the bestowal of academic credit. And coordinating it throughout
was Mr. Dimas, Robert R. Wippel, and the Administrative
Secretary, Mrs. Joan Grogan.

The following organizations provided encouragement as
cooperative sponsors:

American Psychiatric Association, Oregon District Branch
Bureau of Narcotics and Dangerous Drugs, U. S. Department
 of Justice
Consumer Protection and Environmental Health Service, De-
 partment of Health, Education and Welfare
Governor's Commission on Children and Youth
Greater Portland Council of Churches
Mental Health Division, Corrections Division
Narcotic Addiction Research Foundation for British Columbia
National Council for Prevention of Drug Abuse Problems
National Association of Social Work
National Association of Student Personnel Administrators
National Institute of Mental Health

National Rehabilitation Association, Oregon Chapter
Northwest Association of Private Colleges and Universities
Oregon Board of Parole and Probation
Oregon Correction Association
Oregon Council of Churches
Oregon Council on Drug Problems
Oregon Dental Association
Oregon Education Association
Oregon Medical Association
Oregon Psychological Association
Oregon Regional Primate Research Center
Oregon School Boards Association
Oregon Social Welfare Association
Oregon State Bar
Oregon State Board of Education
Oregon State Board of Health
Oregon State Board of Pharmacy
Oregon State University, School of Pharmacy
Oregon State Public Welfare Department
Teen Challenge Center
University of Oregon Dental School
University of Oregon Medical School
Vocational Rehabilitation Division
Western Institute Commission for Higher Education

Eli Lilly and Company generously supported the presentation of Julian Villareal, M.D., Ph.D.

The following persons who participated in the organization of the program and the implementation of the small group discussions deserve commendation:

Chairmen and Cochairmen of Special Interest Groups

Chairman	Cochairman	Group
Frank B. Strange, Ph.D.	The Rev. C. T. Abbott, M.A.	Clergy
Neil McNaughton	Robert W. Humburg	Community Action
Mrs. Joan Bergy	Mrs. Anne Basker Mrs. Jean Horner	Education Section
Mrs. Jean Lacey	Mrs. Celia McKinney	Family Unit

David F. Hain
Mrs. Joanne C. Hazel, R.N.
Mrs. Hanna Larson
Mrs. Louise Smith
Ira B. Pauly, M.D.
Wm. F. Hoffstetter
F. Verne Flock

Dennis Brand, Sgt.

Mr. Richard Rumble
G. Joseph Colistro
Edward Scott, Ph.D.
Charles Crawford
A. L. Frost

Law Enforcement
Nurses

School Counselors
Social Work and Welfare
Treatment Section
Vocational Rehabilitation
Youth Counselors

Interdisciplinary Group Meeting Program

Coordinator
Mrs. William Long, Jr.
Program Executive Committee
Anderson, Carl L., Ph.D.
Bergy, Mrs. Joan
Clark, Mrs. Katherine
Gooderham, Clyde W.
Hazel, Mrs. Joanne, R.N.
Henderson, Norman B., Ph.D.
Horner, Mrs. Jean
Johnson, Robert B., M.D.
Keener, Jack E.
McLain, A. G. "Mike"
Meighan, Spence, M.D.
Strange, Frank B., Ph.D.

Correspondence regarding the Western Institute of Drug Problems Summer School should be addressed to P.O. Box 4372, Portland, Oregon 97208.

CONTENTS

DRUG ABUSE
Data and Debate

Chapter One

TODAY'S DRUG PROBLEM:
WHAT'S HAPPENING

KENNETH D. GAVER

W ELCOME TO THOSE of you who use coffee, tea or tobacco, Cheracol® cough syrup, or who have an occasional martini before dinner; welcome drug users. To those of you who have on occasion lent a tranquilizer to a friend or offered your sleeping pills to your neighbor, welcome drug abusers and transgressors of the law. If any of you have been so brave as to smoke pot, shoot "H" or pop a cap of acid, well, welcome drug abusers and committers of felonies. I guess that includes all of us because drug use is universal amongst human beings.

I think you will hear a number of themes being recurrently echoed. Some of those themes will be the following: drugs and the use of drugs are really a part of the totality of man's history; drug abuse is part and parcel of social change, part of the great social upheaval in Western and especially in American society; drug abuse is tied to youthful alienation and youthful rebellion, part of which certainly characterizes the current social upheaval; drug abuse is simply one parameter of the broad and multi-dimensional parameters of social change characterized by dramatic actions which you read about in the newspaper, hear about on television, and unquestionably take part in yourself.

Some of these parameters of social change are the great civil rights movement of the last decade or two, the kind of unrest and turmoil in the urban ghetto which we read a great deal about two years ago but which is back-paged now, the plight of the city, the rising crime and delinquency rate, the intense antiwar sentiment of certain segments of our society,

3

unrest on the campus, violence on the campus, and the new social animals, the "hippies," the "hopheads," the "acidheads."

You may also hear that drugs are but an ephemeral substitute for truly living life. Some may say that drugs are a search for instant bliss, and Dr. Blachly may tell you that drugs are people substitutes and that drug abuse is a special form of the general phenomenon of seduction.

Another theme that seems to run throughout this conference is that there is really nothing new under the sun, although there is a great deal that has been influenced by technology. Youthful rebellion and alienation are hardly new. They were written of four thousand years ago in ancient Egypt. Aristotle wrote of the rebelliousness of youth and their lack of respect for their elders. The emperor of China a few centuries ago was deeply concerned about his youthful generation. All of us in our lifetime undoubtedly have heard the saying that youth is going to Hell in a hurry. That part is not new. You will also hear about experiments. If you look, you will see that there have been great experiments in drugs, and some of them failed. Alcohol is a drug. There was the great experiment that failed in this country—the great experiment of prohibition.

I had the good fortune to attend the University of California at Berkeley in my undergraduate days. At that time it was a hotbed of Communism. Now it seems to be a hotbed of free speech, free love, free acid. When I was there, the signs all said, "Keep off the grass." Now I understand the signs all say, "Let's get on the grass."

Let me trace for you a little bit of the background of drugs, their use, and some remarks generally upon classifications of drugs. There are, of course, the ethical, pharmacologic agents— drugs properly used for the treatment and cure of various maladies of man. Some of those have become drugs of abuse, of course. There are, for example, the sedative drugs, such as the barbiturates, which are very effective in certain ailments and are properly used in the treatment of such ailments. They are also improperly used in the form of drug abuse. There are, of course, the tranquilizers; the first of those, rauwolfia, came on the American scene perhaps fifteen to seventeen years ago, but interestingly enough had been known for hundreds of years in ancient India. It had one flurry of introduction into Europe a few centuries ago, was lost in antiquity, and then was resurrected as a tranquilizer for the treatment of nervous and mental diseases.

There are ethical drugs of all kinds. There are drugs for treatment of vascular diseases, there are drugs for treatment of infections, there are drugs for relief of pain, there are drugs for almost anything that ails man. As a matter of fact, we have drugs to help us wake up and drugs to help us go to sleep. We have drugs that can stimulate, drugs that can tranquilize. We have drugs that can elevate mood, drugs that can depress mood. We can develop drugs that can increase blood flow through the extremities; there are drugs that can decrease blood flow through the extremities. There are drugs that can speed up the heart; there are drugs that can slow down the heart.

You could go on with an enormous list of drugs. There are drugs, ethical ones or near ethical ones, for almost anything. We hear stories of the notorious cantharides, or Spanish fly, which allegedly stimulates the sexual excitement. We also hear stories of the supposed use of saltpeter in the food of young men to keep down their sexual drive. I might add that cantharides seems to sell better than saltpeter.

So we have drugs, or at least we have myths about drugs which can create or enhance virtually every mood or activity known to mankind. And drugs, particularly the drugs of abuse, and the drugs of dependence, have a long history. The opiate drugs, of which heroin is the most outstanding example, are referred to in Sumerian tablets of three or four thousand years B.C. Hesiod in the eighth century B.C. mentions the town of Necome near Corinth, Greece. The name literally means the town of the poppy from which the opiate drugs are derived. Herodotus and Hippocrates mentioned the therapeutic use of opium in the fourth century B.C.

Paracelsus developed the first medicinal opiate preparation in modern times—a drug called laudanum—in the sixteenth century. And indeed, if you read the historical accounts of the medical care afforded wounded soldiers during the Civil War in this country, you find references to the administration of laudanum for the relief of pain.

It is thought that opium smoking was identified as a technique of intake of the drug toward the end of the seventeenth century. That gives it a history of some three hundred years. There is ample verification of the first opium war, 1839-1842, between Great Britain and China over China's banning of the importation of opium by the British, a lucrative trade, I might add. In 1906 China found it necessary to ban the growth of the poppy. Now there are very many derivatives of opium in forms that you may be familiar with, such as opium itself, laudanum which I mentioned, codeine, morphine, and the drug heroin, which is a drug of choice for the person who really wants to get hooked, but which is strictly illegal, entirely a black-market drug, and cannot be purchased legally anywhere in these United States.

You will hear of the heroin addict whose habit is so great that in everyday parlance he has to steal two color television sets a day to support his habit. I believe that the Portland police arrested a person last year whose heroin habit, if maintained at the current level and purchased at the going price on the street, would have cost him $68,000 a year for the drug alone. Heroin becomes vitally important in the economy of our community because of its importance in crimes against property committed in order to obtain the money for the purchase of the drug.

In addition to the naturally occurring or derived opiates, there are many synthetic opiate-type drugs. One commonly used in medical practice, which may have been administered to ladies during childbirth, is a drug called Demerol®—a very effective synthetic opiate type drug. It can also be a drug of abuse. I recall early in my medical career a man who had taught me one of the medical specialties went next year to Lexington, Kentucky, because in the course of his practice he had become addicted to Demerol, which was readily available to him in his surgical practice. It was really a very great tragedy.

The next of the major drugs of abuse or dependence are the cocaine drugs, derived from the coca leaves. These are believed to have originated in the region of Machu Yunga in the former High Peru, now Bolivia. An Incan about A.D. 1230 is responsible for spreading the use of the coca leaf, which has been widespread amongst the native inhabitants of this region. In 1857, Karl Von Scartzer brought back coca leaves from a trip to Peru, and from them he isolated cocaine, which was the first true anesthetic used in medicine. At one time Sigmund Freud was an ardent advocate of the use of cocaine because of the strong psychic effects which are produced. Gradually, it was recognized that cocaine was a drug of monstrous abuse, and at the time of the passage of the Harrison Narcotic Act in this country in 1914, there were believed to be tens of thousands of cocaine dependent persons in these United States.

The next group of drugs are those which are commonly referred to as the hallucinogenic drugs. The one about which you have heard the most is, of course, LSD, lysergic acid diethylamide. It is a drug of modern technologic innovation. LSD was synthesized in 1937. In about 1943 Hoffman accidentally discovered the hallucinogenic properties of this drug and published some interesting early articles on the subject. I recall that in 1952, some seventeen years ago, when I was at the National Naval Medical Center, LSD was being investigated systematically because of its hallucinogenic and perception altering capabilities. This drug became popularized through the interest of intellectuals, including some of fame and some of infamy. In addition to what you have heard about LSD, you should know that there are forty-seven plants indigenous to the Western Hemisphere from which we can derive drugs with hallucinogenic properties—forty-seven known plants. One of these is the drug peyote. Peyote has been known for some time, particularly in the southwest part of the United States and Mexico. The Huachicol Indians of the Sierra Madre used it extensively. Fray wrote about the use of peyote in the sixteenth century. Furthermore, peyote is legally used, at least as far as the supreme courts of the States of New Mexico and Arizona are concerned, in the religious ceremonies of the Native American Church, an indigenous church of Southwestern American Indians, some 200,000 strong. Peyote is used as a part of the religious service amongst this group.

Another hallucinogenic drug is psilocybin, derived from the so-called sacred mushrooms of Mexico, and mentioned by many writers. There is a variety of others which will be mentioned later.

The next group of drugs of abuse and dependence is referred to as cannabis, commonly known as marihuana. Cannabis has a history dating back before the time of Christ. The hemp plant from which it is derived was botanically described six hundred years B.C. In about the second century A.D. Chinese writings refer to the intoxicant qualities of the extract of the hemp plant. Cannabis is known to have been used extensively in India the first nine or ten centuries A.D. It is believed to have been introduced into the Western Hemisphere some time in about the fifteenth century. It has come on the American scene in the twentieth century. There have been about three waves of interest in the use of marihuana, one following World War I, another wave of interest in about the 1940's, and a third wave of interest which is current. It was of sufficient concern that the Mayor's Commission to study cannabis was established in New York City in the 1940's, and a voluminous report on the use, misuse, and abuse of marihuana was published as the *Mayor's Commission Report* in 1944. It did contain some limited clinical research information, the kind of information sorely lacking in the literature for the next twenty years or so.

Cannabis as a drug of common usage has become increasingly popular. The *Oregon Statesman* a year ago, August 10, 1968, stated as follows: "The extent of the growing marihuana problem can be gauged when one considers that confiscation of about 100 pounds a year in the United States Customs Service has been normal for years, but last year 67,360 pounds was seized. This degree of escalation requires a re-evaluation of measures being used to counter it."

The next group of drugs commonly subject to abuse are the barbiturate drugs—the red devils, the blue devils, the yellow jackets, Nembutal®, Seconal®, the barbitals. Many of these are drugs of proper medicinal use. Many of you unquestionably received them at one time or another. You may even have them in your medicine cabinet at home today. But they have also been adopted as drugs of kicks, drugs of abuse, by those interested in experimenting with various drugs. These also are synthetic drugs, drugs of modern technology, developed during the 1930's.

Speed, or the stimulant drugs produce a sense of brightness, alertness, and ability to concentrate when taken in small dosages. When taken in large dosages, they may produce overreactivity, distortions of perception, and at times, gross loss of impulse control.

Still one more group of drugs of abuse are those drugs referred to as the intoxicant inhalants, of which airplane glue is the one commonly used. But virtually any fat solvent, such as gasoline, paint thinners, airplane glue, and a vast array of products now on the market for various purposes, can be adopted for the purposes of intoxication by inhalation.

To understand the background of the use and abuse of drugs today, we need to take a look at some of the nonabuse aspects of drug use today. We are bombarded daily in the commercial channels with information about drugs. We have seen the great aspirin duel. Which aspirin is better? Is one aspirin better than another aspirin? Or, "this drug has not one, not two, but three pain relieving agents." Then there is the great antiacid controversy. Which antiacid does best when you have had a bad pizza? And if you watch television or listen to the radio, or read the popular magazines, you will find that there are all sorts of antiacids that are available, each one allegedly better than any others. Then there are the drugs that "pick you up." There is a current radio commercial that says even if you have had a day's rest and you are driving along the highway and you become sleepy, the makers of No-Doz® urge you to pull off the highway, rest and take a No-Doz. It supposedly contains the strongest stimulant available without a prescription (caffein). We also have Sleep-Eze® that you can hear about and read about. We also have the drugs to relieve hay fever—Contac® and what have you, drugs to give you comfort and relief from the miseries of allergic states.

This is the commercial market, and it is a market which directs itself not just to adults. It is a program of cultivating a desire for drugs and a use of drugs, albeit for allegedly desirable reasons. It directs itself at all segments of the society, and it says basically, "You need drugs, you should use drugs, and you should especially use our drug." Now it does not say, "You need LSD, you should use my brand of LSD because it's purer than

Brand Y of LSD," but the stage is set by the commercial approach to the sale of drugs. I am not saying that this is not ethical. I am simply saying that we have to be knowledgeable about the impact of modern mass media upon people's receptivity to drugs.

In addition to the pill culture induced by modern advertising, we must frankly state that there is a pill culture which is aided and abetted by modern technologic medicine and pharmacy. It is an ethical process, but it is nevertheless conducive to a readiness, a willingness to use drugs for various purposes.

And there are the common everyday drugs, about which there is not any particular advertising for the drug effect, but which all have pharmacological effects. The coffee companies do not talk about their drug effect, and yet caffeine is a drug which has a stimulant effect. Few tea advertisements mention anything about the pharmacologic properties of tea. But tea does have pharmacologic properties as do all the cola drinks. The tobacco makers do not mention the effects of nicotine on the central nervous system nor on the blood vessels of the legs or heart. But those are pharmacologic actions brought about by the inhalation of tobacco smoke. Instead, they talk about tobacco in terms of whether it will make you look like a cowboy or a sailor, or whether you can burn somebody else's trouser leg when you are polishing his shoes because they have made the cigarette longer. They talk about it in terms of usage for pleasure, not usage for the pharmacologic effect.

Alcohol is the great tranquilizer. It is every man's drug of abuse. It too has been known since the dawn of history. We now estimate there are five to six million full-time practicing alcoholics in these United States. We estimate there are in the neighborhood of 53,000 such persons in the state of Oregon. They account for about one fifth of all of the admissions to our state mental hospitals. In the city of Portland, alcohol users account for about 67 percent of all the arrests. Persons who have used alcohol to the point of intoxication account for approximately one half of all deaths on the highway in this state and in other states. So, alcohol and the consequences of alcohol use and abuse constitute an enormous social, economic, law enforcement, and medical problem.

Now, what is the extent of the problem with the illegal drugs, or the drugs of abuse? You have heard all kinds of estimates about how many people have tried pot. A year or two ago one of the experts in San Francisco said he was quite convinced that at least one in ten adults in the city of San Francisco had at one time or another used marihuana. It was supposed to have been a fact that some 22 to 40 percent of the students at our Lake Oswego High School supposedly had used marihuana. That is a disputable figure. Nevertheless, it is true that marihuana has been used extensively, not only by the college, high school and junior high school population, but by the adult population of this country.

As to the opiates, the conservative estimate is that there are from fifty to sixty thousand heroin addicts in the United States. However, most figures range upward from 200,000. In California the estimates I heard a couple of years ago were 18 to 22 thousand addicts. If we had as many in Oregon as California does, we would have one tenth of that, or 1800 to 2200 addicts. Actually we do not know how many there are in Oregon. We conservatively estimate there may be 150 to 300. In addition to that, there are evidently many more who occasionally have experimented with heroin.

In southeast Asia there may be somewhere between 300,000 and 350,000 heroin addicts. In Hong Kong alone it is said that there are 80,000 to 100,000 addicts. Heroin is a constant menace because of the enormous criminal syndication and the vast economic consequences of having a habit. As a result, every civilized nation in this world has joined together in a treaty attempting to control the traffic of heroin.

I have made reference to social change and to the drug phenomenon and to technology. Certainly these things are at least in part interrelated. Most of us would agree that technologic change is escalating geometrically in this country. And when you have such rapid technologic advance, you create new possibilities, and when you have new possibilities, you alter the mix of choices available to the individual. When you have technologic change, new possibilities and a new mix of choices, you must then find new social approaches, new organizations of human effort, to handle this new mix of choices. Therefore, social change must accompany technologic change. Further, whenever the mix of choices is altered, there are equally as many opportunities offered to the individual to make a mistake as there are opportunities to make the proper adaptive response. So technology does not necessarily bring about favorable social change. It just gives you the possibility to be just as wrong as you are right—but in a new way.

America certainly is in upheaval. We know that there is tremendous technologic change in this country. We know that there is great social change. We know that the technology of drug manufacture and the technology of medicine are rapidly advancing. The drug problem has been facilitated by technologic sophistication and contributing to great social change.

This conference perhaps will open your eyes. I hope it will broaden your perspective, and assist you in finding the answers or the means to deal soberly and thoughtfully with a rather frightening but certainly fascinating bit of the contemporary American scene.

At this conference we are not going to promise you answers. You will not sally forth with the means at hand to right all wrong thinking, to lead all wayward youth back to the straight and narrow; you will not leave here with the knowledge and the skill to interdict the illegal drug traffic, secure the addict, to persuade the teen-ager not to experiment with acid or to try pot. But you should leave with much more knowledge and much more depth about this enormous thing called drug abuse.

I hope, myself, that you will leave here bearing carefully in your minds and in your hearts that drugs and the abuse of drugs are not discrete topics which can be grasped or studied outside the context of the society within which they exist. Nor can drugs and their abuse be comprehended without a knowledge and a compassion for the single, indispensable component of the drug abuse problem, the human being, who knowingly or unknowingly makes the decision to alter himself, to alter his senses of perception of the world, to somehow for better or for worse, to bring about a change in his world or in his life as he lives it, through drugs.

Lastly, I hope you will leave here with one idea firmly implanted in your mind. That idea is that man has always used drugs. Man uses drugs extensively today, and he will undoubtedly continue to use drugs. Man can use his drugs wisely or unwisely, but no matter which way he uses them, he is going to use them, and sometimes abuse them. So drugs, like mankind, seem to be here to stay.

Chapter Two

THE SUBCULTURE OF THE CRIMINAL NARCOTIC ADDICT

DAVID W. MAURER

PROFESSIONAL CRIME AS A CULTURAL PHENOMENON

IF WE ARE GOING to discuss the nature of the subculture of the criminal narcotic addict, perhaps we should preface our remarks by some notes on the nature of criminal subcultures in general. I should add that my view of professional crime differs somewhat from the conventional views now prevalent which explain this troublesome aspect of modern life in moral or legal or psychological terms. Research has convinced me that professional crime is largely a cultural phenomenon, that the specialized subcultures of professional crime are very ancient, worldwide in incidence, and that they are inevitably parasitic on the dominant culture. Professional crime is not to be dismissed as a mere violation of the law; it is a very well established way of life within partially closed subcultures where criminal technology has been honed to a very fine degre of perfection.

Parenthetically, I should note that my work, while primarily linguistic, also cuts across the fields of sociology, abnormal psychology, anthropology, and criminology. I regard language as a living thing, like a plant or an animal. It not only changes as a result of cultural stimuli, but it deeply affects the way in which people see and understand the world about them, and language itself often determines cultural change. Years ago I realized that you cannot study language in a vacuum; it cannot be interpreted exclusively in terms of itself. Language triggers behavior, which in turn reflects language and is influenced by it.

In relation to the criminal subcultures, language becomes one of the keys to understanding the behavior pattern within any

14

given subculture. It is an important factor in understanding the psychology of the professional criminal and is one means of understanding the nature of crime itself, about which we know all too little, I can assure you. It is largely semisecret or highly restricted in usage. And, of course, investigation uncovers large bodies of uncharted language used within the subcultures, a little of which language filters out and into the dominant culture in the form of slang. This work has led me to an attempt to clarify some of the underlying dynamics of language formation and growth, and the criminal subcultures make a good laboratory to work in, because they have been isolated from the dominant culture—along with the standardizing influences of print—for hundreds of years. Here language has been largely dependent on oral tradition and a behavior pattern in many ways dia-metrically opposed to that of the dominant culture. This research cannot be done on an armchair basis; it must be done, as I am sure you realize, by working in close contact with the people involved and the language they speak.

I have already mentioned the dominant culture. Briefly, I define this as the part of our society which writes the laws, controls the educational system, operates the economy of produc-tion and distribution, builds the roads, operates public institutions, provides for defense, and enforces the law insofar as this is possible. In short, it involves the cooperation of millions of people—both the governed and the governing—in order to pro-duce a viable society. There are multitudes of subcultures within and about this dominant culture. Most of them are occupational, social, religious, professional, or connected with recreation or sports. Practically all of these subcultures conform to the pattern of life in the dominant culture in most behavioral indices—except those which involve the particular activity which characterizes them and accounts for their existence; most of them exhibit some linguistic differences which set them off from the dominant culture. Only a minority of these subcultures are devoted exclusively to professional crime; however, even so, these sub-cultures are quite numerous in Western civilization, and they are old, well organized, and highly effective technologically in preying upon the dominant culture. They differ in some very important ways from the dominant culture. By and large, the law of the dominant culture hardly touches them. They invaded Europe from the Near East in the Middle Ages, and for centuries practiced their craft for very small pickings. With the discovery of the New World, they either migrated or were deported to the Americas where in an economy of abundance they have prospered beyond anything their ancestors in the Old World ever envisioned. Today the most prosperous as well as the most powerful of these subcultures is the Mafia, which, incidentally, controls the wholesale contraband drug traffic in the United States and Canada.

Strangely enough, our legal and judicial systems do not differentiate between the professional and the amateur criminal. The professional works at crime as a business; often he has never done anything else for a living. If he knows any legitimate craft, he usually learned it in prison. He has status as a professional and is usually known among a considerable circle of other professionals in his class. He has access to the very sophisticated *modus operandi* developed over the centuries by experts in his subculture. He knows what the established channels are for buying the police protection, which all rackets must have to survive, and he uses these channels effectively when he needs them. He repeats his crime over and over again, relying on his skill to keep from getting caught and, if caught, relying on *the fix* to protect him. If the case is too tough, or *the fix* curdles, or, as is seldom the case, he lacks the money to fight in court, he may do time. This carries no stigma in his subculture unless it is the result of ineptitude or lack of professional ethics; it is simply an occupational hazard. He pays the price for only one crime out of a veritable multitude.

However, the professional does little time in prison. His record almost inevitably shows many arrests and few convictions. In fact, some of the top professionals in many rackets have never done time in prison. I would estimate that the professional constitutes less than 10 percent of our convict population, with the percentage varying, of course, from prison to prison and from locality to locality. Incidentally, he accounts for perhaps 90 percent of the major crime, though in very recent years his amateur imitators are whittling this percentage away.

The professional bears certain marks of his subculture. He feels no guilt for preying on the dominant culture. He rejects the moral and ethical system of the dominant culture, but conforms rather closely to the code of his own subculture, which incidentally is enforced much more rigidly than the laws of the dominant culture. There is no provision for probation or parole in the Mafia; there is only death or ostracism. The professional differs in other ways from the behavior pattern of the dominant culture, but time does not permit our examining these here. But we should note that he has grown up with, or acquired, certain significant attitudes toward the laws, the customs, the values of the dominant culture, as well as certain liaisons and connections with other criminal subcultures. And he carries with him a permanent identification card in the form of his knowledge of the semisecret argot spoken by all members of his subculture. While he was probably born into this culture, he may have been recruited somewhere along the line. In short, he is a member of a parasitic subculture which preys systematically on the dominant culture. He may *pack the racket in* because of pressures, or old age, or disability, but he seldom, if ever, reforms.

The amateur criminal, by way of contrast, is a member of the dominant culture gone wrong. He practices crime only occasionally—and frequently is caught early in his career. Sooner or later he usually does some time for his acts. Often he becomes a recidivist. He develops his own technology—often extremely crude—or imitates what he thinks are professional methods. Often he learns things in prison from others who are more experienced. He has no idea how to operate under police protection or how to use the national and international network of connections which are available to the professional. While he may team up with other amateurs in crime, he has no effective knowledge of mob organization and all that it implies. He does not know the argot of any branch of professionals, though it is not uncommon for him to develop some kind of limited special vocabulary, often based on the argot spoken in prison. He may be employed part-time or full-time legitimately, and it is not unusual for his crimes to be connected with or committed against the people with whom or for whom he works. Basically he is a member of the dominant culture and conforms to most of its cultural indices. He feels shame and guilt if he is caught, and inevitably experiences some degree of ostracism if he does time in prison. He accounts, roughly, for some 90 percent of our prison populations.

The amateur is subject to reform through rehabilitation—though he gets precious little of it in our modern penal system, which presently tends toward being a kind of expensive, government-financed tutorial system for inept criminal washouts. And until we take a more realistic view of crime as a culturally conditioned form of behavior, our penal system will inevitably expand in size while its ineffectiveness increases. Meanwhile, professional crime flourishes as it has in no other culture and at no known time in the past, while amateur crime is running it a very close second.

Past civilizations have had varying approaches to the control of crime, but none of them have been very effective. In the early days, personal vengeance was relied upon to control rebels against the code of the dominant culture. Ostracism or banishment were once in favor. The Code of Hammurabi developed the personalized causation of crime into a system of compensation of those injured or damaged by crime, a technique which might well be restudied by modern criminologists. Christianity favored demon possession as an explanation for crime, and this theory lurks still beneath the surface of some of our more modern approaches to crime. Indeed, the theories based on the conflict between free will and predestination (which we label *determinism* today) die hard. Banishment, eventually expanding into mass deportation, gave Europe some respite from the criminal subcultures which had moved in during the Middle Ages, and the deportation of these subcultures over a period of some four hundred years helps to explain the relatively low rate of professional crime in Europe and the relatively high rate in America. It is interesting to note, by the way, that the criminal argot used in the Colonies and later in the United States followed British criminal usage closely until around the 1800's, when American argots began to develop somewhat independently; many older British terms are still actively used in the United States. In

Latin America, likewise, and especially Mexico, examples of the older Spanish argots from the seventeenth and eighteenth centuries are preserved in the *caló*, which is used widely by criminal subcultures, that differ somewhat from those found in the United States and Canada but which still follow crime as a way of life.

In the late nineteenth century men like Bentham, Beccaria, Isaac Ray, Lombroso, and Freud began as best they could to apply some aspects of science to crime, but they still did not recognize the difference between the professional and the amateur. Within our own generation, the thinking of criminologists has been much influenced by such men as Hooton (who carefully correlates physical measurements with the types of criminals found in prisons, thus presenting a meticulous cross-section of criminal dropouts) and Rorschach, that subtle pornographer who knows so well how to hide dirty pictures in the ink blots. These men show us a good deal about themselves and their methods but very little about the nature of crime itself. We also have tardy recognition of some of the social scientists, and we see the beginnings of a concept that professional crime is primarily a social phenomenon and only secondarily an individual problem. The discovery that a criminal cannot be studied effectively separate from his culture matrix will undoubtedly have a profound influence on our thinking—and hopefully on our laws—during the next generation. However, our attitudes are still largely dominated by Freudian concepts, and a classic example of this approach can be seen in Dr. Gregory Zilboorg's *The Psychology of the Criminal Act and Punishment,* a work replete with the application of Freudian tenets and sadly lacking in an understanding of professional criminals.

In this connection, I suggest that we go beyond the armchair research of modern psychology and psychiatry and look to the behavior pattern for some cues. I call your attention to several points, briefly stated and without the elaboration which might make them more convincing. First, professional criminals do not, as is usually assumed, experience guilt feelings as a result of robbing a member of the dominant culture by whatever means their subculture uses as a specialty. They have been doing this for centuries. It is their way of life. While they might experience guilt feelings if they stole from members of their own subculture, the dominant culture is simply a place where they go to practice their craft. Guilt is not a factor, though some professionals learn in prison, to simulate it in order to influence the parole board.

Second, I suspect that we can rule out many of the Freudian motives for crime, at least in the case of the professionals, with whom crime is a simple act of economic survival. For example, the association of the act of theft with the sensations of the sex act may possibly apply in some cases of kleptomania, but becomes ridiculous when we apply it to professional thieves. In fact, I have caused skilled pickpockets to roar with laughter by reading to them passages from psychiatric works equating theft with sex. The mind of a pickpocket, who might steal fifty or sixty wallets in a good day's work, simply boggles at the thought of such a libidinal extravaganza.

Third, I doubt that a professional criminal who grows up in a criminal subculture can be brought into the dominant culture by way of psychiatry intended to resolve conflicts derived from the dominant culture. While there may be individual or exceptional cases, I do not believe these to be typical. People do not change cultures via psychiatry. Old-time Sioux Indians cannot be brought from the Stone Age into modern American culture with psychotherapy; specifically, I suggest that any psychiatrist who tried to give a group of old-time Sioux insight into the feelings of guilt they should have experienced as a result of the Custer Massacre would have had rough going indeed. Psychotherapy directed at a group of *mafiosi* would probably be equally disappointing, even though the Mafia is much closer to modern American culture than is the Sioux. However, it might be an interesting experiment —if some established *capos* could be persuaded to cooperate.

Fourth, the professional may suffer as a result of major conflicts with the values of his own subculture. We can see occasional examples of this condition in the areas of large prisons where professionals turned informer are isolated for their own safety; often they manifest a kind of fatalistic apathy, and await death with indifference. I have never seen one restored to his normal, hustling self by psychiatric treatment. And informing is only one of many violations of the code of the subculture which might cause emotional problems, though it is the one which is most likely to be observed by members of the dominant culture. I suspect that professionals with various problems within their own subculture might profit from psychiatry—if they found a psychiatrist wise enough in the way of life within the subculture. But where does one find such a psychiatrist? And would his ethics permit him to restore an ailing professional bankrobber to full operating efficiency?

Fifth, some professional criminals do develop conflicts as a result of being ostracized from the dominant culture. They sometimes wish they were not thieves or stick-up men or burglars, and regret that their children are by and large barred from certain advantages within the dominant culture. A few take care to raise their children outside the subculture in the hope that they can find a place, through education and association, in the dominant culture. Usually, however, frustrations caused by exclusion from the dominant culture only tend to reinforce the values of the subculture, and tighten it against various threats from the dominant culture. Often this isolation is used as a rationalization for increased and intensified criminal activity against the institutions of the dominant culture.

Last, the amateur criminal, who is usually a member of the dominant culture gone astray, may suffer unconscious maladjustments with the behavior pattern of his own culture, which take the form of criminal behavior. This type of criminal may benefit from psychotherapy based on the values of the dominant culture. For example, an employee who steals habitually and compulsively from his employer may be a sick man. A respectable housewife who has an uncontrollable urge to steal merchandise—for which she often has no need —from stores may be suffering from maladjustments within her own culture and probably within her own home. But these are very different types than the professional, who preys on the dominant culture with great skill and a conscience as clear as that of any competent craftsman.

Well, so much for notes on the nature of professional crime viewed as a cultural phenomenon. Now we will look closely at the subculture of the criminal narcotic addict with a view to analyzing it in terms of its place in the so-called underworld, its internal structure, and its relationship to the dominant culture.

THE CRIMINAL ADDICT

The various subcultures of professional criminals referred to in the previous paper constitute what is popularly referred to as "the underworld." Some are very tight in their internal organization, some are not. Some are in the big money, some grind along on a relatively low level of subsistence. Most of them are very old, with their roots in European culture. The degree of prestige they enjoy, both in the underworld and the dominant culture, varies widely from one to another. Many of these subcultures are still migratory, while others have settled down in specific localities; often a given criminal subculture has both a migratory phase and a local phase. All of them know how to purchase varying degrees of protection from the law, and all of them have some mechanisms for protecting their members from the penalties which the amateur usually pays for crime. Some have well-developed systems for caring for members or their dependents when arrest and conviction take place. All are loosely but effectively connected in a professional way, and widespread cooperation can be observed, despite internecine strife which sometimes appears on the surface. The number of individuals involved is impossible to estimate, but there is little doubt that they reach into the hundreds of thousands in the United States at the present time and that they constitute a formidable threat to the institutions of the dominant culture. Unfortunately, the professional criminal has been romanticized irresponsibly in romantic film and fiction, and the image held by the general public has about as close a relation to reality as does the wooden cigar-store Indian to modern anthropology.

It is easy to place the subculture of the criminal narcotic addict in the underworld hierarchy if instead of conventional classifications we use the one observed by criminals themselves, which recognizes four major categories, with many subgroups within each category. The first of these contains all the criminal subcultures utilizing violence or the threat of violence in their operations. They include bank robbers, safecrackers, racketeers of all kinds, stick-up men, and on down to muggers and strong-arm men at the bottom. There is at least one exception in the case of the numbers racket, which belongs to this category, probably because it is syndicated. This category is known as *the heavy,* and specific specialties are called *heavy rackets.*

The second category comprises all the subcultures where the sharp wit or the skilled hand, or both, are dominant; in other words, the rackets where violence is not used. Included here are a multitude of sub classifications ranging from the big-time confidence men at the top, down through short-con men, thieves of all sorts, cat burglars, gamblers of all kinds, to pickpockets, shoplifters, and hanger-bingers near the bottom. This category is known as *the grift,* and individual operators are generally known as *grifters* with special designations according to the particular subculture involved. While it is not unusual for a man to belong to two subgroups, or practice within two—rarely more—it is quite exceptional to find a professional who belongs to both *the grift* and *the heavy.* It is interesting to note that within *the grift* there is a strong cultural resistance to the use of violence of any kind. I have known confidence men who had a total aversion to firearms of any kind, and *class cannons* (topnotch pickpockets) who would not stoop to the use of a razor blade to get at a wallet and had only contempt for any operator who did so. Cat burglars almost never go armed to their work. However, *grifters* readily use violence in fighting among themselves over money or women or prestige, even though professionally it is generally excluded.

The third category is a relatively small one and includes the *lone wolves.* These are highly specialized individuals who, unlike the two types above are not thoroughly organized, though they usually have useful, if indirect, connections with the other two branches. However, they generally work without *mob* support, and without routing protection under *the fix.* On the whole they are highly intelligent men (and occasionally women), superbly skilled in whatever specialty they follow, self-effacing, quiet, and generally solitary in their habits. They are much more likely to have acquaintances in the dominant culture (who are unaware of their criminality) than they are to associate with the underworld. They are rarely found in the criminal *hangouts* where professionals meet in some security to socialize. This group includes such types as *bank heels* (who take cash right through the cashier's window at a bank or other institution), some kinds of jewel thieves, some types of swindlers, blackmail specialists, and others. Because of their habits they are difficult to study and, to the best of my knowledge, differ from the other types in that they do not have a well-developed argot, or professional language.

The last category includes those types who are not basically professionals but have, because of their behavior pattern, been ostracized from the dominant culture and forced into the underworld or its fringes. These include, among others, prostitutes, homosexuals who may make a racket out of their deviation or who are simply forced into this area by ostracism, and narcotic addicts who turn to some form of crime (usually not very skilled) to support their habits. While I do not know of any underworld name for this category, I call them *quasi-criminals*. By and large, they are not fully accepted by other criminal subcultures; in fact they are often exploited by the operators of other rackets on the one hand, and harassed and preyed upon by the police on the other. They are always good subjects for a *shakedown* and, as every detective knows, susceptible to the pressures which make stool pigeons. The dominant culture does not romanticize them, as it does some other types, but marks them with a heavy moral stigma.

Thus, we see that the subculture of the criminal narcotic addict is placed in the least prestigious of the underworld categories, and in the lower levels of that division. Not all narcotic addicts, however, belong to this subculture, and before analyzing it, perhaps we should eliminate several kinds of addicts which will not be considered here. First, there are members of the dominant culture who are addicts and whose habits are maintained, one way or another, by the medical profession. These addicts may have had a history of having been addicted accidentally or carelessly in the course of medical treatment, though currently there may be no need for drugs. Relatively speaking, they are not very numerous. Second, there are those who support their habits through legitimate access to drugs, including physicians, nurses, dentists, veterinarians, pharmacists or persons who work in pharmacies, and so forth. While these addicts are technically criminals in that they violate the law in order to divert drugs for their own use (and sometimes for sale), they are seldom prosecuted in the same way as underworld addicts. There are also many drug users (mainly barbiturates and amphetamines) in the dominant culture who are not officially recognized as addicts. Third, there are medical patients, very numerous indeed, who are being carried through the terminal phases of cancer or other painful diseases with the aid of opiates; in the eyes of the law and society in general they are not regarded as criminals nor treated like other addicts. And, incidentally, those who argue that opiate drugs cause people to commit crimes should take a lesson from these addicts. A great majority of them are enabled to work and carry on an almost normal life up to near the time of death only because they are addicts; the incidence of crime among them is practically nil. Last, there is the large number (no one knows how many, though the Bureau of Narcotics from time to time pulls some very specific figures out of the hat) who turn to crime in order to buy drugs of all kinds. It is with this group that we are concerned. We might hazard a guess that, if we exclude marihuana users—who are hardly to be considered true addicts—this subculture comprises more than 250,000 persons.

This is largely a synthetic subculture. That is, it was created by the dominant culture when the Harrison Narcotic Act was passed in 1914. Before that, there were plenty of addicts, but they were not in any way organized and were distributed freely throughout the dominant culture. All kinds of drugs could be bought freely without prescription; in fact, many country stores stocked morphine and opium in various forms, and for twenty-five cents anyone could purchase what would today be regarded as a phenomenal amount of drugs. It is also true that many physicians used opiates and cocaine rather loosely in the treatment of diseases where these drugs would allay the symptoms without eliminating the cause. Many patent medicines—especially "cures" for tuberculosis—were loaded with opiates, and it came as a shock to thousands of self-made addicts when the unauthorized possession of drugs became a crime. A panic of gigantic proportions set in.

Meanwhile, there was a small coterie of opium smokers in this country and Canada, usually centering around a Chinese community in a large city or even around one lone Chinese laundryman in a small town. The members of this group usually had nothing in common except that they smoked opium, and that they came to the Chinese to get it or to smoke it. While, of course, many smokers were little more than drug-besotted bums, there were also many members of the dominant culture—professional men, successful people in show business, sportsmen, musicians, writers, artists, high-society people and business men—who found nothing wrong with maintaining a moderate habit. There were also some professional criminals who casually smoked with the rest of them. Opium smoking was—and still is, as a matter of fact—regarded as a gentleman's vice, though today only a rich man can maintain a habit which, before 1914, might cost him two or three dollars a day. And opium smoking, though still surviving in some areas, is surely disappearing.

When drugs became illegal, mass withdrawal was inevitable unless drugs could be secured. Addicts were treated as criminals. No rehabilitation was available, and the only facilities for treatment—clinics established by the medical profession—were hounded out of existence by the Treasury Department before any good that they might do could be demonstrated. The trek to the Chinaman began, and soon contraband opium was being eaten, drunk in solution, and taken as pills by thousands of people who had not the slightest idea how to smoke it. Since the Chinese had access to unlimited supplies of opium from China, they did their best to stem the panic. Meanwhile, all sorts of black-market arrangements sprang up for obtaining both morphine and cocaine, which were then the drugs of choice. Heroin, which had just been recently discovered in Germany, was as yet practically unknown to American addicts. As enforcement of the law continued to be ruthless, addicts were forced to turn to illegal sources for drugs, and as the traffic became profitable, other criminal subcultures became interested in it. With the enactment of Prohibition in 1921, a vast smuggling empire was born. The smuggling trade soon found it profitable to include morphine, cocaine, and heroin from European and Latin American sources, supplementing the already burgeoning market in stolen and diverted medical drugs available from domestic sources.

This is not the place to go into a detailed history of the evolution of the drug traffic as big business, but suffice it to say that addicts suddenly discovered that they all had something very important in common, which was the need for a supply of drugs. This compelling need forced them together, established close feelings of loyalty between people who had nothing else in common, developed a sense of mutual protection between addict and addict as well as between addict and dealer, and drove addicts with a noncriminal background to experiment with crime in order to buy drugs, or to attempt to join already established small-time criminal subcultures in order to learn a little about criminal technology. The traffic became very clandestine, and a secret or semisecret language very early appeared, based to a large extent on the terminology—much of it Chinese or adapted from the Chinese—which was used around the *lay-down joints.* The term *opium den* was a journalistic creation and never had any currency in the underworld. So tight was the security maintained in this subculture that penetration by nonaddicts was difficult indeed. At that time I had already explored several other criminal subcultures, and by 1935 I published through Columbia University Press a small study of argot terms used in the narcotic traffic. Victor Folke Nelson, a competent writer then doing a long stretch in Sing Sing, wrote the editor verifying the material and expressing surprise that any outsider could collect even a small amount of the argot. Today, of course, the subculture of the criminal addict has not only expanded tremendously, but has become much more open than it was in those days. The very different subculture of the larger dealers and smugglers, the *big men* of the racket, seldom addicted themselves, has tended to become even tighter in response to the heavy pressures of Federal and state governments, until today it is practically impenetrable.

Since we are concerned here only with the subculture of the

criminal addict, we might take a closer look at it through the application of several cultural indices which are useful in breaking down a larger behavior pattern so that certain aspects of it can be considered while keeping the entire subculture in some sort of perspective. The ten behavioral indices considered are patterns of (1) association, (2) interaction, (3) subsistence, (4) bisexuality, (5) territoriality, (6) temporality, (7) education, (8) recreation or play, (9) defense, and (10) exploitation of resources.

Association ✓

Since the criminal addicts are rejects from the dominant culture, they associate mainly with other rejects—although these are not all necessarily addicts. Since this subculture is not as homogenous as, say, that of pickpockets, who generally associate very closely with other pickpockets, narcotic addicts must accept whatever company they find. And this is heterogenous indeed. There are naturally many individuals from established criminal subcultures—usually of a low order—already sharing the subculture of the addict with their own; thus, a thief who becomes an addict must of necessity share the culture of the criminal addict, even though he still thinks of himself primarily as a thief. There are many small-time operators who made their living in illegal activities before they were addicted, then used their specialties to support the habit. There are shoplifters, small-time thieves of all sorts, shortchange workers, petty gamblers, car thieves, short-con operators of various kinds, minor burglars, prostitutes, and others, who became addicts and then carried their small rackets over into the larger society of addicts. Notably absent, or present only in small numbers, are professionals in the higher echelons of both *the heavy rackets* and *the grift.* Although peddlers are almost universally addicted (in my observation, the mythical legal line between the addict and the peddler simply does not exist), it is unusual for men higher up in the narcotic rackets to be addicted or to associate with addicts in the subculture of addicts.

The great majority of addicts, however, come into the addict subculture with no criminal skills at all, and no status in any criminal subculture, however minor. Most addicts come from the dominant culture, have rejected many of its values, and do not have the rather stable set of values characteristic of other criminal subcultures. They come only in a desperate need for money to buy drugs—reinforced by the ready accessibility of drugs—and they continue to come in impressive numbers. Many retain for a time certain associations in the dominant culture, but these usually dwindle with increasing preoccupation with the habit. This subculture lacks the close-knit and well-defined patterns of association found in other criminal subcultures, and it is held together mainly by the need for drugs, the fact that all members are technically criminals however diverse in their activities, and the pressures from the dominant culture exerted mainly through the law. Thus, while in other criminal subcultures association is based on common skills, established traditions, family connections, and other strong ties, the criminal addicts associate mainly because they have a common problem. This problem, however, constitutes a rather strong bond, and addicts tend to congregate because they are addicts, and for few other reasons. This tendency can be observed even in prison, where addicts—or former addicts—find each other and prefer to associate together. Their conversation centers about drugs, their effects, the methods for getting them, various criminal activities connected with drugs, the possibilities for getting drugs in prison, and plans for obtaining or dealing in drugs after release.

Interaction

The addict interacts on several social levels. First, there is extensive interaction with other addicts, motivated to some extent by the common need mentioned above, but mainly by the knowledge that another addict has drugs, or knows a *connection* for obtaining them. Interaction between addicts may be ruthlessly exploitative, with one addict robbing another of drugs or money, informing on him when it is advantageous, or even murdering him (usually with drugs) in revenge for some real or suspected injury.

Second, addicts interact with other rackets in various ways. Those already members of criminal subcultures interact with their own kind, both those addicted and those who are not. The lower orders of criminals commonly accept addicts on their own rackets and work with them as long as addiction does not cause insurmountable problems; however, there is a notable tendency for addicts on the same racket to work together and nonaddicts to do the same. Many of the better class pickpockets prefer not to work with addicts, while the lower ones of the *pick-up* or *clout-and-lam* variety will accept addicts. As one goes up the scale in criminal skills and prestige, addicts are increasingly excluded from working with nonaddicts, not only because addicts are regarded as unreliable, but because their habits require regular times to *fix*, the carrying of equipment which may endanger the security of *the mob*, and the always hazardous contacts with peddlers in order to keep a supply of drugs. Many upper-order professionals also find the activities of an addict personally repulsive. It is principally the interaction with the drug traffic, absolutely essential to an addict, which limits his interaction largely to those in the drug traffic unless he already has solid connections with an already established criminal subculture before addiction. There is also another kind of interaction with other criminal groups stemming from the fact that some of them tend to exploit the addict in many ways, while the addict is usually powerless to return this exploitation.

Third, there is interaction with the dominant culture, which the addict regards as his major source of funds. Therefore, his interaction is predatory insofar as he is able to effect this, however crude his methods may be. If he is from the dominant culture, his predatory behavior usually starts with his own family, friends, and employer, from whom he steals without conscience. There is also the type of interaction which involves the spread of addiction and sometimes makes it epidemic. He does not hesitate to introduce anyone to drugs if it is to his advantage— the woman with whom he lives, acquaintances from the dominant culture who might later prove helpful as sources of money or drugs, or others. This epidemic spread of drug use can often be observed in high schools. When an addict becomes the supplier to several new addicts, he not only has a source of income, but wields a certain power over them as well.

Last, there is interaction with the law. The addict hates and fears the law because it is a constant threat to what he regards as his security. He generally lacks the well-developed mechanism of *the fix* so effectively used for protection by other criminal subcultures—and especially so by the men who control the drug traffic above the level of peddlers and smaller dealers. Because of this he usually accumulates quite a criminal record—predominantly for petty, nonviolent crime. There is a good deal of truth in his contention that the police generally tend to harass addicts, abuse them, and coerce them into service as stool-pigeons. With the increasing realization of police officials that addiction is primarily a medical problem and only secondarily a police problem, a more enlightened policy is forming which favors treatment and rehabilitation rather than simple punishment which has already demonstrated its ineffectiveness. However, we still have a long way to go in this direction, especially since no sure "cure" for compulsive drug use is known and recidivism is high.

Subsistence

There is no uniform procedure for making a living in the subculture of the addict as there is in all other criminal sub-cultures. If an addict has a criminal trade, he practices it as best he can to support his habit. If he has none, he rapidly turns to some form of crime—usually very crude—on an amateur basis. Thievery and prostitution (both homosexual and hetero-sexual) are usually the first experiments. A heavy percentage of addicts never progress much beyond their first ventures, if of course these *hustles* produce enough to buy the necessary drugs. Heroin, the most frequently used of the so-called hard drugs, varies somewhat in price from area to area, but is remarkably stable in price for a contraband product, which stability reflects a national market handling a controlled quantity of the drug. A heroin addict spends from $25 to $200 per day, with the average perhaps around $40. This money *must* be produced every day (in addition to other living expenses) if the addict is to stave off withdrawal, and he must be prepared to increase this amount as his habit builds up. Also, in the event of a *panic*, prices may become exorbitant. If we accept a recent estimate (The U.S. Bureau of Narcotics) of some 75,000 hard-drug addicts, we see that this number could spend some three million dollars per day for opiates alone, which explains why the underworld is involved in the traffic. In my opinion, the figure of 75,000 hard-drug addicts is a very conservative one.

Most of the funds spent for drugs are taken from the dominant culture in one way or another, which explains why drug addiction is costly to society as a whole. But this is only the cost of one type of drug, and only the first cost. When we add to this basic figure, the costs of law enforcement, the courts, the prison and parole personnel involved, and such rehabilitation programs as are now operating, the cost becomes phenomenal. The greatest cost, however, is in a wastage of human lives and human productivity.

Other drugs cost progressively less, with speed (Methedrine®), the amphetamines, and barbiturates being taken not only by a greater number of addicts (and by every means including the needle in the vein), but also in greater quantities per addict. Several other kinds of drugs are used by criminal addicts, but they will not be discussed here. Lowest in cost, perhaps, is marihuana, which is not considered by many as a truly addicting drug, though marihuana users are well represented within the criminal addict culture. In fact, there are many more marihuana users than all other types of addicts combined. For five or ten dollars the pot smoker can get rather high, and for a twenty-dollar bill he can get thoroughly stoned. While this is not the place to discuss the economics of drug addiction in detail, the figures cited give a glimpse of the general picture.

LSD and other hallucinogens, while several years ago peddled in the criminal addict subculture, now are increasingly rare there since the underworld has apparently discarded them as part of the syndicated drug traffic. LSD users are not entirely acceptable in the addict subculture, and the bulk of the present supply appears to come from various university laboratories or the laboratories of private chemists and is sold to individuals who continue to experiment with it both on and off college campuses.

Some addicts in the criminal subculture hold part-time or

even full-time jobs in the dominant culture or on the fringes thereof. This is especially true of newcomers to the subculture, or addicts who have not yet made the transition from the dominant culture. Thus, a counterman in a restaurant may have his wages as a hedge against insecurity and develop two or three customers for drugs on the side as the source for funds adequate to support his habit. But sooner or later his habit will get out of control, and he will find regular employment difficult, if not impossible. By this time he may well also have a police record and will slip into the criminal side of the subculture without making any pretense at legitimate employment. This happens to most hard-drug addicts who try to maintain an in-between status; eventually they end up in an institution or as skid-row types knows as *boots and shoes, birdcage hypes,* or other less euphonious names. Their degeneration parallels that of skid-row alcoholics.

There are a few members of the addict culture who subsist on money from the outside—usually from home—and may not practice any criminal activity, except insofar as violation of the drug laws are concerned. They simply like the drug culture, perhaps for romantic reasons, and because they are always in contact with a good *connection.* They try to identify with the criminal addict, but do not actually do so. Often they are hippie types. Sometimes they are girls supporting a boyfriend who is more deeply involved than are they. When the affair breaks up, they may drift back into the dominant culture from whence they came or *turn on* fully and move into full-fledged addiction and consistent criminal activity. The above, of course, applies to dabblers with the hard drugs. Thousands of others, mostly marihuana users, flit in and out of the drug culture without ever becoming a permanent part of it.

Bisexuality

By this term I mean the role which sex differentiation plays in the culture. In most true criminal subcultures, there is a definite and established tradition regarding the role of the sexes. On most of the heavy rackets, for instance, the males do all the work and the women are kept carefully out of everything connected with the profession. In fact, the type of women they usually keep are totally ignorant of all professional technology, though they generally, through fear or training, conform to most of the behavior indices of the subculture. The so-called *gun moll* (who shoots her way into and out of all manner of scrapes with her man's *mob*) is, to the best of my knowledge, largely a journalistic fiction. While there are plenty of *gun molls* in the underworld and in the addict's subculture, they have nothing whatever to do with guns. They are simply thief girls of one kind or another, universally nonviolent except where mating is concerned. The fiction may have arisen through a dominant culture misunderstanding of the term *gun*, which is simply a form of *gonif*, an old Yiddish word for "thief." Such celebrated types as Bonnie and Clyde and the women who associated with John Dillinger or Baby-Face Nelson were simply outlaws (probably the last of a colorful breed) who, because of their use of violence, have been associated in the public mind with the true *heavy rackets*. To shift over to the top brackets of *the grift,* the big-time confidence men simply do not use their women in connection with their profession; in fact, their women are usually totally unprepared both socially and intellectually to function on the levels where their men operate. I once made a very thorough study of these interesting operators and found not a single woman known to function as a professional big-time confidence operator, though Eddie Guerin (a famed international operator) did have a very smart thief girl named Chicago May, who once distinguished herself by engineering Eddie's escape from Devil's Island in the 1920's when the French still maintained it as an escape-proof penal colony. However, women do function professionally on some *short-con rackets* on the lower levels. Pickpockets accept women professionals in full equality with men, and there are and have been some very expert female pickpockets who had full mob status and got their equal share of the take, whether or not they were living with a member of the *mob* with which they worked.

I mention these facts simply to illustrate the established position of women in a few of the criminal subcultures. In the subculture of the criminal addict, there actually are no mores governing the position of women, whose only equality is that they, like men, are addicts and have the same pressing needs. If they need drugs, they either develop a *hustle* of their own or find a man who will provide for them. This *hustle* is usually prostitution in some form or some type of thievery such as shoplifting. Where prostitution is involved, a girl often starts out on her own, but she is not long permitted to operate as what is called an *outlaw*. A pimp moves in on her, and she finds herself with two habits to support instead of one. Some pimps maintain a *stable* of several girl addicts who are usually dependent on the pimp as a *connection* and are therefore very much aware of his authority. However, some girls live with men on a common-law basis, with each supporting his habit on a separate *hustle* and finding what comfort they can in each other's company.

Bisexuality is affected in this subculture by the physiological effects of drugs. Opiates, for instance, tend to reduce or obliterate sexual needs and to produce impotence in both sexes. Also, they suppress the menses, which is considered an advantage to prostitutes. However, this is only a tendency and not nearly so universal as the medical literature seems to indicate. I have observed addicts to the opiates in all stages of sexual vigor from what might be considered normal among nonaddicts to complete impotence.

Other drugs have varying degrees of effect on the sex life of addicts, with some, like Methedrine and amphetamines being regarded as aphrodisiacs, though there are other factors, including the psychological, which must be considered here. Methedrine injected into the vein, for instance, can produce sexual orgasm automatically and instantaneously; with some addicts it becomes a substitute for normal sex. The amphetamines are believed to increase sexual powers, but there are some doubts about this on the part of those observing addicts. The barbiturates are often used to delay orgasm and prolong sexual pleasure, some-times for long periods of time. Opium is similarly used, especially where the man is addicted but the woman not; such nonaddict women have been known to wax ecstatic over the prowess of opium-smoking lovers, though the lovers themselves must truly be the Sidney Cartons of the boudoir. Hashish has the reputation in the Near East for increasing virility in the male, but actually eventual impotence is produced. It is so new in America that we cannot yet fully assess its effects. However, its little brother, marihuana, is widely used and is often touted as a mild aphrodisiac or at least a deinhibitor which increases sexual powers; certainly through slowing down the time sense and increasing the sensitivity to all stimuli, marihuana may be augmentative to normal sexual pleasure.

Two other factors should be briefly mentioned in connection with the inconsistent pattern in bisexuality. The first of these is the excess of men over women found in the subculture of the criminal addict. Without going into possible causes for this fact, I simply mention it as another disrupting factor. Despite the depressing effect which some drugs have on human sexual behavior, men and women still pair off even though their sexual activity may be greatly reduced, and companionship becomes a strong motivation for living together. Couples so paired off are usually both addicted, but when the man is addicted and the woman not, the male tends to develop a rather extensive repertoire of substitutes for normal heterosexual activity in order to keep the woman satisfied. The second factor is the rather high incidence of homosexuals (both male and female) who move into the drug culture. Most of these come from the dominant culture, since homosexuals are not common in the professional criminal subcultures, with the exception of lesbians among prostitutes. Many homosexuals, both male and female, develop *hustles* based on their deviation (some involving blackmail) but others turn to thievery and prostitution like other amateurs who need drugs. Many heterosexual addicts are converted to homosexuality (either forcibly or voluntarily) while doing time in jails or prisons.

Territoriality

The addict subculture is usually thought of as an urban phenomenon, and it is true that criminal addicts tend to congregate in large cities and in certain specific large cities. This does not mean that there is any geographical factor involved in addiction insofar as we know, but rather that addicts from all over the country are drawn to these large centers both because drugs are readily available there and because the opportunities for association with other addicts exist there. Also, the kind of crime which addicts practice can often best be accomplished on a regular basis in large population centers. However, all cities of any size have drug subcultures of varying size, which shift both in population and location with changes in the traffic, in law-enforcement activities, and in the kind of life style which addicts favor. There is also a certain social territoriality observable within these cities, with addicts clustering in certain social areas, known popularly as " the drug scene."

However, not all criminal addicts migrate to large cities, and today almost every town has a nucleus of criminal addicts, however small, who live to some extent separate from the dominant culture and practice a *hustle* as best they can. Even in rural areas these nuclei exist, often clustering about a certain type of truck stop where narcotics are available. But the numbers of rural and small-town addicts are relatively small compared to the heavy concentrations found in large cities.

Within the cities a secondary type of territoriality sometimes exists, with certain criminal addicts staking out certain areas for their *hustles,* or for their peddling activities, and driving others from these areas. This is particularly true of addicts who already belong to a criminal subculture, such as pickpockets, where it has been customary for a given *mob* to have exclusive rights in certain areas. Migratory professionals who become addicted usually continue to work on the road, using well-established *connections* both along the way and in the large drug centers. If they are prosperous, and they usually are on a relative scale, they tend to buy drugs in rather large quantities and to carry considerable quantities with them on the road. They often have their social or family contacts in the large drug centers.

There is an interesting linguistic phenomenon in connection with the rather disorganized territoriality of the criminal addict. There is a very large body of argot used by criminal addicts, and while this has a certain degree of uniformity from coast to coast and from Canada to Mexico, there is also a high degree of variability from city to city. This argot seems to move rather rapidly in a general East-West and West-East direction. That is, terms originating on the East Coast tend to move westward, and terms originating on the West Coast tend to move toward the East. Terms emanating from the drug subcultures in inland cities are usually caught up in this movement, though many of them remain localisms for a long time. Thus, terms which are very popular on the West Coast may be either unknown in the East or just coming into use there, while new terms or new meanings for old ones popular on the East Coast may be unknown or little known in the West. This is the most unstable of all the criminal argots I have studied, and I have observed three or four phases in its growth and development. First, there was the rather limited special language of the opium smokers which was the only argot up to the passage of the Harrison Narcotic Act. Then the morphine and cocaine addicts flocked to the opium centers, adapted some of this language, and invented some new terms. Scarcity and high prices forced smokers and morphine addicts alike to go to the needle (a hard choice for many a dignified Chinese-American smoker) and further adaptation of the argot occurred. These addicts looked askance at marihuana users and did not accept them into the subculture, nor did they take cognizance of their special language. Then the Marihuana Tax Act of 1937 made pot just as illegal as opium or morphine or heroin, and the marihuana users joined the criminal addict subculture in large numbers. Then came *speed,* the barbiturates, and the hallucinogens, and a new breed of user joined the subculture, with new terms and new adaptations of older ones as well.

There is much leakage of this argot into the dominant culture in the form of slang. Teen-agers especially affect it, though often without a full understanding of the meanings of the terms they are using; however, all levels of the dominant culture borrow it, and a term like *uptight* is suddenly common throughout all levels of the dominant culture. Whenever this diffusion of argot takes place in other subcultures, I have observed that the subculture itself is weakening and may be on the way to oblivion. The widespread diffusion of the argot of the criminal narcotic addict—so different from the secrecy surrounding it only thirty-five years ago—may indicate that the waves of squares from the dominant culture have softened the rather tight though limited organizations of the original group. As a permissive attitude grows in the dominant culture toward drug use of all kinds, and especially that of marihuana, it is remotely possible that eventually the dominant culture may absorb the subculture of the addict, and he may be a criminal no more. But that possibility is indeed remote.

The *hangout* is a significant guide to territoriality, since various types of user and various types of criminal tend to congregate in certain places well suited to their needs and tastes. For instance, in any large drug center we might observe very different concepts of territoriality if we contrasted the congregation areas and locations of, say, hippies, professional thieves of various kinds, and prostitutes.

Temporality

A sense of time is a valuable cultural index, and we of the dominant culture are rather securely locked in a time concept which is inflexible to say the least. Everything is geared to an eight-hour day and a five-day week. Time is money, and is so regarded by both employee and employer. In the criminal subcultures, there are few employers, and there is in each sub-culture a differing time sense based on needs, opportunities, and pure chance. Some professionals grind away at a racket endlessly, depending on the law of averages to give them a living. Others plan with impressive forethought for each big job, then execute it with split-second timing. Big-time confidence men, for instance, may travel internationally in the most casual fashion until they meet the wealthy *mark* they can trim for, say, $100,000.

A single *roper* or a *roper* and his partner then move in on him, and there follows a period of several days to several weeks of very intense and concentrated work until the *score* comes off. The score is *cut up* according to an established pattern after expenses are deducted, and there often follows a short period of big-timing it in order to enjoy the fruits of work well done, after which the *ropers* go back on the road looking for another *mark*, secure in the knowledge that the *inside man* with his highly organized staff is ready and waiting back at the *store*, meanwhile trimming the *marks* brought in by other *ropers*. This rather casual sense of time in the larger sense is balanced by a very different and highly acute sense of time involved in the *play* itself, which we cannot go into here. A big-con man who *ropes* and *trims* two or even three good *marks* a year is in a very good financial situation. Safecrackers and big-time stick-up *mobs* observe parallel but different time patterns in their work. Pickpockets may have their working hours rather rigidly set by certain events in the dominant culture, such as the hours when detectives in a certain city are known to be present during the *show-up* at police headquarters, or the hours when the *slave grift* goes to and from work, or the days on which crowds with money attend sporting events, conventions, or religious festivals. The *stall* for a good *mob* has the responsibility for knowing all these things and setting the time pattern for a given *mob*.

In the subculture of the criminal addict, there is no established time pattern, except insofar as some members of criminal sub-cultures apply the time pattern of their own subculture. The addict who is a refugee from the dominant culture usually abandons the time sense of that culture, but does not develop another. He works his *hustle* whenever he can, or when the need for drugs drives him to get money. So, in a sense, the nature of the drug he takes and the way he uses it determines his time sense. Eventually the hard-drug user is acutely aware of only two time periods—that when he is *fixed* and comfortable and time disappears, in contrast to that when he feels his habit coming on, and must fight time frantically to raise the money for the next *fix*. After a while he is living from *fix* to *fix* and eventually he loses most of his feeling for the past and the future and lives only in the present, all of which helps to explain why hard-drug addicts may have trouble holding a regular job in the dominant culture.

Users of *speed*, the barbiturates, and LSD experience different impressions of time, with *speed* users, for example, having the illusion that time is passing rather rapidly; convicts like to use amphetamines in prison for this reason. Users of marihuana, on the other hand, experience an agreeable slowing down of time, which, along with the illusion of prolonged sensation, may be one reason why jazz musicians originally used it, and why so many jazz fans like to smoke it while listening to jazz. Opium smokers report a monumental detachment from time (and place also), which gives them delusions of grandeur which no other drug seems to produce. However, we know that different individuals react somewhat differently to different drugs under varying conditions, and pat generalizations are often misleading.

Probably the only situation in which a well-established criminal addict (whatever his drug) reverts to a realistic measurement of time by the watch is while he is making a *buy* from a connection. He has learned the hard way that he had better be on time to the minute; he has also learned that the *connection*, in the interests of self-preservation, is always equally careful to make the contact a little late.

Education

While addicts carry into the drug culture the education they have received in the dominant culture—or in another criminal subculture—there is little evidence of the development of a working pattern of education like that existing in other criminal subcultures. In other words, there is no generation-to-generation indoctrination in technology, social philosophy, language, moral values, and so forth. Addicts teach each other about drugs (including a good deal of folklore and misinformation) and addicts *turn on* nonaddicts when there is a good reason for so doing. One addict may teach another something about his *hustle*, and there is some cooperation among addicts in the commission of crimes to raise money or to steal drugs. There is also some exchange of information about law enforcement, strategy to avoid arrest, behavior in prison, and so forth. However, this is usually on an individual basis, with each man learning by experience, then passing on his experience to another individual for what it may be worth. And its worth may be questionable. For example, every heroin addict fears death from an overdose, either taken accidentally or given to him deliberately as a *hot shot*. In the eastern part of the United States, there is a widespread word-of-mouth remedy for an overdose in the form of an injection of a teaspoon of salt into the vein; in the West, the injection of instant coffee is favored. But the word has not gotten around that 5 mg of N-allylnormorphine (Nalline®) injected intravenously or intramuscularly every fifteen minutes is a very effective antidote if the addict is not already in either coma or shock, or both. This ignorance is surprising, since many addicts are familiar with Nalline, which is widely used as a test drug to determine whether or not addicts are using heroin or any other opiate.

Probably the subculture of the criminal addict is too new and too rapidly populated with fresh recruits from the dominant culture to have developed the crude though effective education systems found in other criminal subcultures. Furthermore, there is a dog-eat-dog philosophy, a general belief that every man should take care of himself and little sense of the common good. After all, practically the only factor held in common by all members is the use of drugs together with the need to obtain them. And this need often sparks competitive rather than cooperative behavior. Notable also is the widespread lack of what professionals call *grift sense* (an acculturated aspect of criminal potential) among addicts who have not grown up in another criminal subculture.

Recreation or Play

Within this subculture the situation with regard to what the dominant culture considers recreation is so spotty that it is difficult to make reasonably sound generalizations. That is, we can say that skiing is very popular in South Germany, or that chess is almost universally played in Russia, but we would be hard put to it to find any sport or recreation pursued consistently in the subculture. Quite apparent is the lack of interest in participating sports. That is, the thought of an organization such as The Mainliners Bowling League or The Skinpoppers Soccer Team is only ludicrous. Nevertheless, many addicts do have some knowledge of or some skill at some participating sport or some recreation carried over from the dominant culture. Also, since recreation is an important part of any rehabilitation program, many addicts who have been institutionalized have acquired some knowledge of or skill at some form of sport or recreation, though they are little inclined to participate in it while on drugs. In addition, one finds in the addict culture some skilled or even former professional athletes who have gone downhill, and others skilled to some degree in the performing arts. Their knowledge is there even if they are not at the time functioning. Furthermore, there is a good deal of desultory reading, and a rather strong interest in some forms of music, especially jazz, rock, and folksinging. Music is especially attractive to many marihuana users, and is always an integral part of the group consumption of LSD. Many addicts pass the time with television and follow the spectator sports available. There is also a good deal of gregarious activity in bars and joints, which is recreation of a limited kind.

However, most forms of recreation pale before the pleasures which an addict experiences in the earlier stages of addiction, and in the later stages he is likely to lose interest in most of what goes on around him except insofar as it affects his obtaining drugs. Many users, especially those on the opiates, eventually lose interest even in the basic pleasures which may be derived from food, drink, and sex. The addict refers to the enjoyment of anything as *getting his kicks*, or *getting a high*, and usually each addict selects his own poison. However, when Dr. Vogel and I were working on the last edition of *Narcotics and Narcotic Addiction* in 1967,[1] Mr. Martin Ortiz of Los Angeles brought to our attention an interesting example of supervised *kicks* along with controlled criminal activity. In East Los Angeles the Varrio Nuevo gang maintained four levels of "apprentices" below true Varrio Nuevo status. This started at the bottom with the Pee Wee Winos (age 6-9) who were allowed to beg money and buy cheap wine at a grocery store. They *got their kicks* from simple intoxication. Then initiates progressed to The Midgets (10-11), The Little Dukes (12-13) and The Cut Downs (14-15). With each progression they learned different types of crime and were initiated into various levels of *kicks*, which included marihuana, speed, barbiturates, hard liquor, sex, and heroin. Once initiated into the Varrio Nuevo gang at age sixteen, they were rather accomplished criminal addicts. The rate of attrition was high, however, and at that time the oldest gang member was twenty, the rest having graduated into state and Federal penitentiaries. How widespread this type of organization may be is at present unknown, but I believe it to be rare.

Defense

Few members of the addict culture ever participate in *defense* as conceived by the dominant culture, but there are some addicts who are veterans of past wars, and more than a few who acquired the habit on army bases or while in service abroad. The criminal addict sees defense as an effort to protect himself against enemies both in the dominant culture and in the underworld.

In the dominant culture the chief enemies are representatives of law enforcement, who, because of the general disapproval of addiction in the dominant culture, pursue the addict relentlessly and sometimes sadistically. The only defense which addicts in general have against the law is secrecy in operation, the protection of the *connection*, and the uncertain protection afforded stool pigeons by the law. However, this last is a temporary security, for all detectives use a stool pigeon until he is known or highly suspect, then abandon him either to the penalties of the subculture, or to a prosecutor who sends him up to do time. This is relatively easy since most laws, local, state, and Federal, are written with the point of view that the peddler is somehow the root of all evil. Because every criminal addict is sooner or later a peddler by the very nature of the drug traffic, it is easy to prosecute him on the basis of possession of drugs or the sale of drugs to another addict or an undercover purchaser. The general public, and indeed the men who write the laws, conceive of addict and peddler as separate operators and provide heavier penalties for the peddler. Some legislators play with the idea of a death penalty for peddlers who sell to minors—overlooking the fact that these very minors whom they hope to protect often turn peddler themselves.

Those addicts who already have membership in the subcultures of the professional criminal sometimes use *the fix* as established for that racket, but these are in a minority. However, the addict as such has no well-organized machinery for *the fix*, and so tries to avoid arrest at all costs. On the other hand, the upper-echelon operators of the drug traffic have a highly developed system of protection from the law, and demonstrate increasing immunity from the law as one goes up in the hierarchy. Those at the top are practically untouchable. It is true that addicts tend to congregate in areas where the top men in the racket seem to enjoy protection, partly because they believe that this to some extent protects the source of supply, and partly because they believe, erroneously I think, that they may enjoy some degree of protection reflected from the men higher up. However, these top men are not of the type inclined to intervene to protect addicts; they are rarely addicted themselves and regard the addict with complete contempt.

By and large, addicts live under a considerable fear complex. The first factor, and perhaps strongest, is fear of deprivation of drugs. Few addicts make any provision for their future drug needs—even so much as a week in advance—and live in constant fear that they will not be able to raise the money for the next *fix*. Concomitant to this is the fear that they cannot make a *connection*, or that they will lose contact with the *connection*, or that they may be locked up in jail or otherwise detained where they cannot get drugs. Second, they fear the *hot shots*, which may be administered in retribution for some grievance; they all know someone or know of someone who has been thus summarily disposed of, and the fear is always present, especially if it is abetted by a guilty conscience. Third, there are the frame-ups engineered either by the law or by other addicts, or even by other types of criminal who are not addicts. These *bum raps* are unpredictable and very hard to fight in court, especially if one is an addict. Last, the addict may be exploited by other rackets in ways which they would not dare to apply to a nonaddict criminal, and against which he has little defense.

To a limited degree the argot may serve as a sort of protective device, especially in that a knowledge of it identifies him pretty definitely as a member of the drug culture and may facilitate his making a *connection;* certainly, a lack of knowledge of the argot would identify him immediately as an outsider and open to suspicion. Even more so than in other criminal subcultures, the addict circulates freely in his subculture on the basis of a knowledge of various customs and manners, plus a knowledge of the argot; in the absence of anyone to vouch for him personally, familiarity with the argot would enable him to get drugs and to establish friendly contacts. On the other hand, regardless of who might vouch for an outsider with no knowledge of the argot, he would be received with suspicion if at all.

Incidentally, we see in the addict subculture an aspect of argot usage which occurs in no other criminal subculture familiar to me. This is the reversal of the relation of age to youth so far as usage is concerned. In all other subcultures, the language is passed down from the older generation to the younger generation. However, because of the swift and heavy influx of young people into the subculture, older addicts have been forced to acquire the usage of the younger newcomers in order to maintain their identity and to be accepted in the subculture. Therefore, the old-timers in the culture all know the newer argot, even though most of them deplore the "corruption" of the older argot, both in form and meaning, as they formerly knew it. Here, I think, is a unique application of the argot as a protective device for older addicts, who are now very heavily outnumbered.

Several other means of identification are encountered in different areas. Perhaps the most widespread of these is the use of tattoo marks, especially on the hands, but also on other parts of the body. Those relating to addiction are usually small, unobtrusive, and not readily noticeable to the uninitiate. They differ from the tattoos found on seamen and other rough types of worker, which are in color and in the form of recognizable pictures, designs, or mottoes. Often they consist of a single black or blue dot in the crease on the back of the hand, between the thumb and forefinger. Sometimes crosses or other simple designs are used, usually in black or blue. Both men and women tend to wear these marks; in one correctional institution for women on the West Coast I found that more than half the inmates wore tattoos associated with drug use. I am inclined to believe that this phenomenon may be motivated partly by narcissism, but nevertheless, tattoos do serve as identification and give a certain security, both psychological and physical, within the subculture.

On the whole, however, the subculture of the criminal drug

addict lacks most of the powerful protective devices which other criminal subcultures have developed through the centuries.

Exploitation of Resources

Every human culture, or subdivision thereof, has developed means for converting the products of nature to its own use. This is done by the application of some technology, however primitive, through physical or mental activity, or both. In all cultures the net result may be considered beneficial (in terms of cultural needs) to the group as well as to the individuals involved. Even the other criminal subcultures, though parasitic on the dominant culture, practice their craft largely for the purpose of financial gain. Some of these subcultures have become quite well off as a result of their parasitic activity, and today we see some of them investing money in the dominant culture in legitimate or semilegitimate business because they cannot spend all their revenue otherwise. Hotels, banks, restaurants, bars and nightclubs are among some of the ventures owned wholly or partially by professional criminals.

In the subculture of the criminal addict, however, we see little effort made to acquire money beyond that for immediate personal needs. And the most pressing of these needs is drugs. More than that, addicts exploit their own bodies as the last of their personal resources in the pursuit of pleasure. They are not addicted long before pleasure is largely absent, and they become slaves to the habit which eventually literally consumes them as persons.

REFERENCE

1. MAURER, DAVID, AND VOGEL, VICTOR: *Narcotics and Narcotic Addiction.* Springfield, Charles C Thomas, 1967.

Chapter Three

DEVELOPMENT OF A SUCCESSFUL TREATMENT PROGRAM FOR NARCOTIC ADDICTS IN ILLINOIS*

JEROME H. JAFFE

I APPRECIATE THE opportunity to present my views on the present state of research and treatment in the field of narcotics addiction. These views evolve out of my past experiences with programs in several parts of the United States and out of my more recent work over the past three years in planning, developing, and directing a treatment program for the State of Illinois. Two years ago today there were virtually no public treatment facilities for narcotics users in the entire State of Illinois. In order to withdraw from drugs, narcotics users were required to plead guilty to a misdemeanor and to petition the court to avail themselves of a bed in the hospital unit of the city jail. The Legislature had acted upon a treatment and research program proposed to it by the Illinois Narcotic Advisory Council, but the legislation had not been signed.

Today, in Illinois there is a coordinated network of treatment services that is rapidly expanding. More than 1100 drug users have sought treatment voluntarily without any attempt to publicize the program. More than 500 individuals have been offered some form of treatment, and more than 325 are currently in active treatment. Of outpatients able to work more than 60 percent hold legitimate paying jobs. The arrest rate has dropped dramatically. More than ten new patients are entering treatment each week. The multimodality program now in operation includes some of the best features of programs operative in other parts

* Statement to the United States Senate Special Subcommittee on Alcoholism and Narcotics of the Committee on Labor and Public Welfare, August 8, 1969.

of the country (methadone maintenance, withdrawal, aftercare, and therapeutic communities), but it was designed specifically as a response to the problem of narcotics use in the Chicago area. Built into the program is a system of continuous evaluation that will permit it to continually modify its operations with changing conditions and to maximize its effectiveness in reaching clearly defined goals for specific subgroups within the narcotics using population.

We feel that we have demonstrated that it is possible to develop a multimodality treatment system within a single administrative structure, and that such a system can reduce or eliminate much of the inefficiency and destructive rivalry that often characterizes the operations of single-modality treatment programs in other communities.

Given so intense an involvement with one program, it is difficult for me to claim total objectivity when evaluating other approaches to the problem. Therefore, I would like to describe the evolution and present status of that program and point out those features which may have special relevance for other communities.

BACKGROUND

Two years ago, there were virtually no public treatment facilities for narcotics users in the entire State of Illinois. Therefore, in planning it was necessary to consider not only what kinds of treatment programs would be best suited to the needs of a given community, but what kinds of programs could be made operational with the financial, physical, and human resources that could be made available in the foreseeable future. It was immediately apparent that any attempt to develop within a single two-year funding period a program that could deal with all of Illinois' estimated six thousand known narcotics users and its unknown numbers of barbiturate and amphetamine users would necessitate the kind of crash effort that is usually wasteful and often merely shifts already scarce personnel from one activity to another. The history of such crash programs is usually characterized by large-scale activity long before the value of *any* activity is demonstrated, and, just as disheartening, an inability to reduce the level of activity if and when careful evaluation indicates that some aspects of the program are of doubtful value.

After considering the conflicting claims and counterclaims about the effectiveness of treatment programs in operation in other places throughout the country, the Illinois Narcotic Advisory Council (INAC, a commission created by the Illinois Legislature in 1965) proposed a program based on an explicit set of premises and principles. I was fortunate enough to be asked to serve as chief consultant to the council.

PRINCIPLES AND PREMISES

First the problem of narcotics abuse is only one band in the spectrum of drug abuse, and perhaps, from a social viewpoint, not the most significant band. However, because of the social conditions surrounding the use of narcotics and the high morbidity, mortality and criminality associated with the compulsive narcotics user, it seems appropriate for Illinois to begin with treatment programs focusing on the treatment of narcotics users.

Second, the narcotics-using population is a heterogenous one. Those who make up this population have different reasons for initiating drug use, exhibit different patterns of drug use, relapse for different reasons, and have widely differing experiences as a result of their narcotics-using behavior. Such a heterogenous group may require a number of distinct treatment, rehabilitative, and resocialization approaches. Treatment cannot be considered the exclusive domain of any profession or philosophical persuasion.

Third, at present there is no reliable way to determine in advance what types of narcotics users will respond best to what kinds of treatment, and it is necessary to develop a method for predicting treatment response.

Fourth, the *goals of treatment* must be clearly defined before any meaningful inferences can be made concerning the *outcome* of treatment approaches. In defining the goals of treatment, the INAC rejected the concept that abstinence from narcotics must be the sole or even the most important criterion of successful treatment. Instead it adopted the concept of a hierarchy of goals, applicable to any treatment approach.

Ideally, a treatment program should attempt to help all compulsive narcotics users become emotionally mature, law abiding, productive, non-drug-using members of society, who require no additional medical or social support to maintain this ideal status. But, this is *an ideal* set of goals, a set which society does not expect any other group with medical or psychiatric disabilities to meet. For example, we do not expect middle-aged people with mild congestive heart failure to become marathon runners, we do not even insist that, after some arbitrary period of treatment they abstain from digitalis, diuretics, and visits to the doctor. The INAC took the position that compulsive drug use should also be thought of as a chronic disorder, in many cases requiring continued or intermittent treatment over a period of years. It followed, then, that while all treatment programs should attempt to help every individual reach all the components of the ideal set of goals, any evaluation of the overall effectiveness of any specific treatment must take into consideration that different programs tend to place their emphasis on different goals.

Fifth, these goals can be arranged into a hierarchy, with some goals considered more important than others. However, any such hierarchical arrangement will be somewhat arbitrary. Nevertheless, the INAC felt that as a public agency operating in a large Midwestern state, it should at least make its own arbitrary hierarchy explicit.

Thus, in the program which evolved, the minimum expectation is that all patients who are treated will become law abiding citizens—even if they do not become productive, mature, or even drug free. At the next level patients would be law abiding and also gainfully employed, even though they may require continued psychological and medical support and may even use illicit drugs from time to time. Close to the ideal is the state where patients are law abiding and productive, and do not use illicit drugs, even though they may require either continued medical or psychosocial treatment.

The INAC was aware, even while arranging these behaviors

hierarchically, that they are actually often quite independent, and that some individuals may show behavior at the "upper" levels. For example, some patients may stop using illegal drugs and work at legitimate jobs and require no medical treatment, but continue nevertheless to engage in illegal activities. Others may not use drugs nor engage in illegal activity, but may require prolonged or semipermanent residence in a therapeutic community. In addition, some treatment approaches may be more effective in helping patients achieve one goal than another.

Sixth, programs receiving public support must be prepared to demonstrate objectively just how much the public (including the drug using population) is getting for its money. Closely related to this last proposition is the view that large programs for any given community should be built on the basis of objective data from smaller programs specifically designed to permit extrapolation to large populations *within that community*. Programs which, after adequate trials, do not achieve any substantial movement toward any of the goals described should be abandoned no matter how attractive they may appear to be in theory. The more costly the program in terms of the cost per person achieving particular goals, the more rapidly it should be evaluated, since each day of operation of an ineffective program drains resources from those treatment approaches which are potentially more effective.

A MULTIMODALITY PILOT PROGRAM

Much of what the INAC could rationally recommend was directly derived from the foregoing premises and principles and their corollaries. For example, given the principle of population heterogeneity, the likelihood that different types of drug users would require different kinds of treatment, and the absence of detailed knowledge of the typology and demography of the narcotics using population of the state, it would have been irrational to propose large scale programs using any one specific kind of treatment approach even if money and human resources had not been limiting factors. Therefore, the INAC recommended the development of a "multimodality pilot program" designed to focus on a *limited geographic area* in Chicago with a relatively high prevalence of narcotics use (based on police arrest records). The word "pilot" implied that the structure should be *flexible* enough to *disassemble entirely* should none of the specific treatment approaches prove helpful, yet *sturdy enough* to provide a framework on which a full state-wide program could be built if any of all of the components proved to be valuable. Since it was not possible to know in advance which of the several treatment modalities used elsewhere in the country would be most effective with this as yet unstudied Chicago population, the INAC recommended that the pilot program develop and carefully evaluate several distinct modalities, i.e. a multimodality approach. As a minimum, the specific modalities or treatments to be developed, evaluated and compared to each other were the following:

1. Standard periods of hospitalization for withdrawal followed by group therapy in the community—narcotic antagonists such as cyclazocine were to be evaluated in this context.
2. The use of oral methadone in the context of a rehabilitative program.
3. Residence in therapeutic communities such as Synanon or Daytop Village.

Descriptions of these methods and concepts are summarized and appended.

It was recognized that proposing the simultaneous development of several major treatment programs was a formidable undertaking, but after considering the difficulties experienced by other states where competition between autonomous single modality programs has often led to inefficient reduplication of effort, barriers to the movement of patients from one program to another, and vituperous public attack by the proponents of one program on the motives of the proponents of another, Illinois elected at least to attempt to develop the multimodality approach. It was hoped to demonstrate that placing all modalities within a single administrative structure would eliminate duplication, facilitate patient movement, and permit a uniform and objective evaluation.

THE STATE-UNIVERSITY COLLABORATION

Although these were rational recommendations, there was a major risk that even if the INAC's recommendations were accepted by the state legislature, the program might still prove impossible to implement, particularly if it were funded on the usual two-year basis. Since there were no programs operating in the state, the most difficult obstacle was the absence of experienced personnel. Furthermore, even the recruitment of personnel could not be initiated until legislation and appropriations were passed and signed. The problem of recruiting appropriately trained personnel was even more perplexing. It could not be done under the existing personnel codes, and the state was reluctant to change its personnel codes without proof that the changes were required. Yet without the personnel, no programs, and therefore no proof, could be developed.

The INAC turned, therefore, to the academic community for help. If the universities could recruit and house key personnel on the basis of an anticipated passage of the new legislation, the state, once the legislation was passed, could enter into a collaboration which would (1) advance our knowledge in the field (a traditional interest of the academic community) and (2) establish a desperately needed medical-social service to the community (a newer interest of academic communities located in urban areas).

The formula for this collaboration has been used successfully in other mental health areas and involves the vesting of responsibility and operational authority for both the university and state segments of the collaborative enterprise in one or more people chosen jointly by both groups. That is, these individuals would simultaneously hold university and state positions. Such arrangements pose risks to both university and state and repeatedly place the program directors in conflict of interest situations. Nevertheless, its inherent advantages for both parties outweigh its disadvantages. The university can participate in a large scale research and evaluation project on the efficacy of treatment without incurring a long-range commitment for continuing direct services to the community. The state can obtain a well-designed and executed research project without making long-term commitments to highly specialized researchers. The most important benefits accrue to the state which, because of the peculiarities of the funding procedures, is often required to develop its own programs on an unrealistically short time base. New and potentially valuable programs are often cut off in their infancy because they cannot become demonstrably effective within a two- or three-year period. By offering a modest (but long-term) grant to the university, it can enable the university to enlist the full-time efforts of experienced people. By working at first within the university, they can initiate the first stages of the collaboration in a structure that is usually more flexible and more easily moved than the civil service structures of most large cities and states.

The involvement of the academic community yields one other major benefit. Having its major interest in evaluation rather than in the perpetuation of any given program, the university-based evaluation group can afford to be brutally objective. In the State of Illinois program, this notion of independent evaluation has been carried to a logical extreme. Through a grant from the Federal Government to the University of Chicago, we have made the jobs of the evaluators independent of any single treatment approach supported by the state.

Early in the course of the INAC deliberations, its chairman, Dr. Harold Visotsky (who was the director of the Department of Mental Health), had sought the advice and consultation of Dr. Daniel X. Freedman, the newly appointed chairman of the Department of Psychiatry at the University of Chicago. Dr. Freedman, in turn, was responsible for interesting the author in joining the Department of Psychiatry at the University of Chicago and for providing the financial (as well as the moral) support for the overall planning of the program which eventually evolved. Since the architects of the program were already part of the University of Chicago's Department of Psychiatry, it was not illogical for this Department to join with the Department of Mental Health in trying to implement the program.

SPECIFIC PROGRAM COMPONENTS

Even after the participants, the premises, and the situational demands were defined, the INAC and its University of Chicago collaborators still faced the problem of formulating specific plans and a timetable for the development of facilities, personnel, and treatment procedures. At this point another set of goals and principles evolved. This time, goals for the program rather than for the patients were established.

For example, as a general principle the INAC felt that wherever possible clinical facilities should be located for the convenience of patients rather than staff. Most narcotics users are unlikely to be able to own cars if they give up illicit sources of income. They must be able to reach the clinical facilities by walking or by public transportation. This is particularly important when treating those types of narcotics users who engage in few conventional activities. When such users give up illegal drugs they will have large blocks of unstructured time. If they are to make significant long-term changes, they will have to acquire a new set of associates and learn new patterns of speech and behavior. Facilities should be designed to provide a structure for filling empty time with new and constructive behavior patterns. Not only must the clinical facilities be accessible but also comfortable and "possessable." The notion of "possessability" is particularly important. To be optimally effective, the clinical programs must generate *involvement* in the treatment process. A new and imposing structure not only costs five times as much as a renovated old house, but unlike such an old house, a new structure cannot "belong" believably to a group of urban heroin users with police records and therefore is probably not as useful. Similarly, the size of the patient population at any given location should be small enough to permit a sense of group identity and individual participation. Superficially, such small units may appear to be less efficient economically. However, if efficiency is based on patients successfully treated per dollar rather than merely the total number of patients served per dollar, smaller units yielding greater involvement may actually be more efficient.

Other general operating principles include the employment of patients in the program wherever possible, and maximum articulation with other community agencies. But what this program emphasizes as the most critical considerations for establishing pilot programs for the treatment of drug abuse are the continual monitoring of the efficacy of treatment and the feedback of this information into the clinical process so that as a result the clinical process can be continuously modified.

CURRENT STATUS

The State of Illinois-University of Chicago collaborative program became operational in January of 1968 when a single patient began to receive methadone on an ambulatory basis. At that time there were about six staff members and its total operating space was a six-room apartment lent to it by the Department of Psychiatry of the University of Chicago. As each of the projected units became operational (the hospital withdrawal unit in June, 1968, the first short-term methadone unit in May, the first Gateway House unit in July, research and administrative offices in September, and the first halfway house unit in December) it became progressively more feasible to implement the research design previously described. Obviously, random assignment could not be initiated until all treatments were operative and would not be meaningful until all were operating at optimal effectiveness. A three-way random assignment became fully operational in December of 1968. Currently (August, 1969), the treatment program consists of a number of cooperating and coordinated clinical units.

1. Three methadone outpatient facilities.
2. Therapeutic communities operated by Gateway Houses Foundation, Inc. (as an Illinois not-for-profit corporation).
3. A halfway house—crisis center in the community for detoxified patients—some of whom are taking the narcotic antagonist, cyclazocine.
4. A multimodality training and residential facility at the Tinley Park Mental Health Center.

At present, all voluntary patients seeking treatment from the program and actively using narcotics are randomly assigned to one of the four units described above.

Patients are not required to accept the treatment program to which they are assigned, but they must at least make the effort to participate in a face-to-face interview with the staff of the assigned treatment unit. If, after such a personal interview, the patient still elects not to accept the treatment offered, he may return to the intake unit and after an arbitrary waiting period (currently four weeks) seek entry into any of the treatment units.

This system permits the program to obtain some measure of the acceptability of the various treatment approaches and to attempt to correlate treatment acceptance with a number of characteristics of the patients seeking treatment. Such estimates of treatment acceptability are important in planning new facilities in other parts of the community. Programs in which 90 percent of the patients in a given community refuse to participate may have markedly limited value even if they are relatively effective in rehabilitating the 10 percent who accept the treatment.

Since the procedures in this program's methadone unit differ in some significant ways from the procedures described by Dole and co-workers (1966), a summary of the differences is in order. The outpatient methadone programs now operating in Chicago are *entirely ambulatory* (patients are transferred from heroin to methadone while still living in their own homes). The *dosage is lower* (the mean dosage of oral methadone is under 40 mg per day in contrast to the 100 mg per day used in the Dole-Nyswander program). There is *no preselection of patients* (the methadone treatment units accept patients regardless of past histories of barbiturate or amphetamine use, alcoholism or psychosis). Lastly, some patients enter a short-term methadone unit where they are offered methadone treatment for a maximum period of six months, after which they are expected to enter one of the other treatment units (therapeutic community, hospital withdrawal-aftercare, or long-term methadone maintenance).

PROGRAM EVALUATION

Each week after entering a treatment unit, every patient fills out a standardized questionnaire covering the following areas: housing, living arrangements, employment, earnings, antisocial activity, arrests, drug and alcohol use, and types of program activities utilized. In addition, the treatment units obtain from each patient a urine specimen at least twice a week. Using thin-layer chromatography, the urines are examined for opiates, quinine, amphetamines, and barbiturates. Some units are now using breathometers to check on excessive use of alcohol. Reports from each patient's counselor, the medical unit, and the legal unit are also fed into a central location. Computer programs are now under development which will merge, store, and print out this information with a short enough "turn around time" (e.g. three days) for maximum utilization in the care of patients and in the modification of the clinical procedures. Systematic organization of computer printouts permit program and clinical directors to review the entire patient population weekly. Such "online feedback" helps us to spot small troubles in our decentralized network before they become big ones.

RESULTS TO DATE

Through today, more than 1100 narcotics users have made contact with the program on a voluntary basis. Over 500 individuals have received some form of treatment, more than 320 are still actively engaged in treatment in one of the units, and about 10 narcotics users are entering treatment each week.

The program takes the position that there can be no single statement about the success of any particular approach. There can only be a statement about what kinds of individuals are moved more effectively toward which goals by which treatments and at what cost over a given time base.

We are not yet able to provide such a detailed analysis. Yet, our preliminary analysis does indicate that for the narcotics users we have encountered thus far, some form of methadone maintenance is the most acceptable form of treatment. It is also the form of treatment which is most effective in keeping patients in continuous treatment and in which there is the highest rate of gainful employment. Based on man-weeks of exposure, the rearrest rate is as low as for any other form of treatment, and the cost of treatment is lower than the cost of any other form of treatment we have employed.

We cannot claim that the system we are developing is appropriate for other communities where the size or the characteristics of the narcotics using population may be quite different.

Where the size of the problem is small, it may be uneconomical to create so diversified a system. On the other hand, we must assume that the narcotics problem will not simply disappear and that the systems of care designed today will be with us a decade from now. It is, therefore, appropriate to ask whether, in those areas with significant problems, this country can afford to approach the development of a system with less careful planning or less built-in evaluation than we have used in Illinois.

APPENDIX A

The methadone maintenance approach is predicated on the proposition that any medication that permits a compulsive narcotics user to become a law-abiding, productive member of society should be considered as a therapeutic technique. If the medication is a narcotic, it need not be eliminated from consideration, since the goal of treatment is socially acceptable behavior, rather than abstinence per se. It has been shown that when given daily, in high dosage, methadone produces at least two effects: it relieves the persistent "drug hunger" that often plagues the former narcotics user following withdrawal; and, it induces a marked tolerance to opiate-like drugs, including methadone itself. As a result of this tolerance, the patient treated with methadone cannot feel the effects of other narcotics such as heroin, nor does he feel any significant effects of the methadone. Methadone maintenance has been criticized as the "substitution of one habit for another," implying that all habits are equally deleterious. This implication is supported neither by common sense nor by the observation that more than two thirds of the 750 former heroin users treated in the Dole-Nyswander methadone maintenance research program are now either working or going to school; and that the amount of known antisocial behavior in this group is remarkably low. Methadone maintenance has also been called "legalized euphoria." If the criticism were accurate, it would be merely a moralistic objection to a valuable treatment technique. However, such a criticism bears no relationship to the clinical state of the patients, who cannot be distinguished from normal controls with any of the standard techniques employed to detect euphoria in other clinical situations.

It is important to distinguish between the use of oral methadone maintenance as a rehabilitative technique and the current British practice of prescribing narcotics to addicts. With methadone, the dose of the drug and frequency of administration is determined entirely by the physician. Intensive efforts are made to direct the patient's energies, previously given over to the problems and mystique of the "junkie" subculture, into productive channels. Almost as important, the technique of dispensing all methadone in fruit juice makes it virtually impossible to use the drug intravenously; and in terms of the effect on behavior, differences in the route of administration cannot be flippantly dismissed by the simplistic assertion that a narcotic is a narcotic no matter how it is used. By contrast, in the British situation the addict is given a prescription for a narcotic, often unaccompanied by any effort toward rehabilitation. The prescription is usually for heroin, and the addict is free to administer the drug to himself by whatever route and with whatever frequency he chooses.

In New York City, the methadone maintenance approach is now being used with almost one thousand former heroin users. In other parts of the country other investigators are studying modifications of the orginal Dole-Nyswander procedures to determine if the costs can be lowered, the flexibility of approach increased, or the risk of illicit redistribution of methadone can be reduced.

APPENDIX B

The use of narcotic antagonists, such as cyclazocine, is the most recent development in the continuing effort to find more effective treatment for narcotics addiction. Cyclazocine is not a narcotic itself, does not produce physical dependence of the morphine type, and is not "liked" by narcotics users; but it can prevent heroin, morphine, and other narcotics from reaching the sites in the nervous system where they have their actions. As a result, a patient taking cyclazocine regularly cannot feel the effects of the usual dose of narcotics. Furthermore, as long as he takes cyclazocine regularly, he can take narcotics several times a day and will not become physically dependent because the narcotic never actually gets to its site of action. Cyclazocine can be used in treatment in several ways. First, since it prevents patients from becoming physically dependent, it makes it possible for them to work or to participate in rehabilitation programs even if they never get to the point of total abstinence from narcotics. In addition, there are theoretical grounds for believing that just as conditioning may play a role in the development of compulsive drug use, patients taking cyclazocine who use narcotics and feel no effect will "decondition" themselves, so that eventually even the cyclazocine can be discontinued. Obviously, cyclazocine in and of itself cannot change an individual's well-established patterns of associating with other drug users nor his antisocial behavior, nor can it give him vocational skills or hope for a better way of life. To be effective, it must be used in the context of a broad program of social rehabilitation. Over the past three years, cyclazocine has been given clinical trials by several groups of investigators. Work now is in progress to attempt to develop narcotic antagonists that will be longer acting than cyclazocine and will also be free of its undesirable side effects. At present, we can only state that the number of patients who have been treated with narcotic antagonists in a comprehensive program is still too small to decide how much the drug adds to the effectiveness of the overall program. Nevertheless, researchers using cyclazocine and other antagonists are cautiously hopeful.

APPENDIX C

Self-help programs such as Synanon, Daytop Village, Phoenix Houses and Gateway Houses (a network of therapeutic communities established in Chicago in July of 1968) are run almost entirely by rehabilitated ex-addicts or by ex-addicts working in close collaboration with a professional staff. They usually entail several years of residence in a therapeutic community. Experience demonstrates that many former compulsive drug users are able to remain drug free and to function productively so long as they remain in residence. This is certainly a worthwhile achievement, even if it falls short of the ideal of totally independent function in the community at large. Of all the approaches now under evaluation, however, this one may be best suited to yield that elusive, ideal, long-term goal of drug free, productive behavior, without the need of continued medical or psychological treatment. It is also worth emphasizing that unlike the pharmacological approaches described for the treatment of narcotics use which are not relevant for the treatment of barbiturate or amphetamine abuse, the therapeutic community concept is equally applicable to all forms of drug abuse.

There was considerable discussion about the development of a civil commitment or a supervisory deterrent system, but Illinois finally took the position that until the community could provide treatment for all those who wanted to be treated, it would not be appropriate to spend public resources to develop treatments for those who were not seeking treatment.

Chapter Four

THE ENGLISH DRUG PROGRAM: ITS SUCCESS AND ITS PROBLEMS

RICHARD PHILLIPSON

HISTORICAL BACKGROUND

Introduction

T HE FIRST TIME abuse of drugs in England, and elsewhere in Britain, gave cause for concern to the authorities was for a period during and immediately after World War I (1916-1918). In 1916 the Commissioner of Police for Metropolitan London reported that trafficking in cocaine, chiefly by prostitutes to members of the Armed Forces in London, was "assuming huge dimensions," and special regulations for the control of transactions in this drug were strengthened in 1917, and were continued after the war under the Dangerous Drugs Act 1920 which Act extended the control to all those drugs to which the first International Opium Convention of 1912 applied.

Abuse of cocaine, however, continued to be a problem in London for years, as is shown by the fact that in 1921, the first year of operation of the Dangerous Drugs Act (1920), out of 67 prosections in respect of drugs other than opium, 58 related to cocaine; and in 1922 and 1923 the corresponding figures were 70 out of a total of 110 and 68 out of a total of 128. From 1924 onward drug abuse became a minor problem, the only consistent illicit traffic in the years between the wars being in respect of opium, which was used by a comparatively small number of Chinese, both British residents and transient seamen.

At this time (1924), as the practice of smoking opium showed no signs of spreading to the indigenous population, and was viewed with a large degree of tolerance by the authorities, offenders were usually dealt with by way of a small fine.

During World War II the volume of the opium traffic showed a very marked increase, both because of the increase in the number of Chinese seamen based in British ports following the Japanese occupation of Hong Kong and Singapore, and because of the interruption of the established opium smuggling route from the Far East across the Pacific, which led to the passage of much opium through Britain in transit to North America. This, however, proved to be a temporary phase, and after the end of the war in 1945, the opium traffic reverted to its minor prewar level. This opium problem apart, once the cocaine problem was controlled, drug abuse in Britain from 1945 until recent years was negligible, the total number of all drug addicts known to the Home Office (The Department of Home Affairs) in any one year averaging about five hundred. Moreover, of this number some 85 percent (425) were cases of "therapeutic addiction," that is, persons who had become addicted as a result of the administration of a potent addicting analgesic, usually morphine, in the course of legitimate medical treatment of some painful physical condition. Most of these "therapeutic addicts" were aged fifty years or more and were scattered throughout Great Britain in complete isolation from each other. Of the remaining 15 percent, some 10 percent at any one time were members of the medical and allied professions (dentists, pharmacists, nurses) who had become addicted through access to drugs in the course of their professional work. This left but about 5 percent (20-25 in actual number) of nontherapeutic addicts who had first become addicted to drugs obtained illicitly; they differed from the "therapeutic addicts" in being somewhat younger, mainly aged between thirty-five and fifty, and they formed a closely knit circle centered on the West End of London.

The Rolleston Committee

In Britain it has always been the custom to treat all forms of drug addiction as primarily a medical problem.

In 1924 the Minister of Health appointed a departmental committee under the chairmanship of Sir Humphrey Rolleston (an eminent physician). The task of the Rolleston Committee was to advise on a number of problems which had arisen in operating the Dangerous Drugs Act, 1920. The terms of reference of the Rolleston Committee were:

> to consider and advise as to the circumstances, if any, in which the supply of morphine and heroin to persons suffering from addiction to these drugs may be regarded as medically advisable and as to precautions which it is desirable that medical practitioners administering or prescribing morphine or heroin should adopt for the avoidance of abuse, and to suggest any administrative measures that seem expedient for securing observance of such precautions.

The Rolleston Committee reported in 1926, and on the question of the supply of drugs to addicts, expressed the view that

> morphine or heroin may properly be administered to addicts in the following circumstances, namely, a) where patients are under treatment by the gradual withdrawal method with a view to cure; b) where it has been demonstrated after a prolonged attempt at cure, that the drug cannot be safely discontinued entirely, on account of the severity of the withdrawal symptoms produced; c) where it has been similarly demonstrated that the patient, while capable of leading a useful and relatively normal life when a certain minimum dose is regularly administered, becomes incapable of this when the drug is entirely discontinued.

The Committee considered, but rejected, (1) the desirability of requiring medical practitioners to notify cases of addiction to the Home Office, and (2) the question of "providing by regulations that a practitioner should obtain a second medical opinion before consenting to administer morphine or heroin for an indefinite time to a person who does not need them otherwise than for the relief of symptoms of addiction."

The Rolleston Committee did, however, recommend that, in addition to the power which the Home Secretary already had of withdrawing from a medical practitioner (who had been convicted of an offense against the Dangerous Drug Act) the authority to possess and supply drugs to which the Act applied, provision should be made for withdrawal of that authority by the Home Secretary on the advice of a medical tribunal, without the need to obtain a conviction in the courts.

The recommendations of the Rolleston Committee were accepted by the Government, and amending regulations were introduced in 1926, giving the Home Secretary the power to withdraw a doctor's authority on the advice of a tribunal consisting of three medical members and a legal assessor.

Although this method of dealing with doctors who abused their authority was regularly used thereafter in Northern Ireland where similar regulations were introduced, the tribunal procedure was never invoked in Britain, for reasons which have never been clearly established. Cases continued to occur, from time to time, after 1926, of so-called "script doctors" who were prepared, at a price, to ignore the Rolleston Committee's warnings against too ready an acceptance of the need for continuing supplies but, in general, the freedom of the addict to obtain supplies legitimately caused no major problem for many years.

In retrospect, however, it is apparent that the so-called British System was workable only so long as there was no widespread tendency towards any abuse in Britain, and the first signs of a change in this respect began soon after the Second World War. In 1951 a large quantity of morphine, heroin, and cocaine was stolen from the dispensary of a hospital in Kent in the South of England, and it was subsequently learned that the young man responsible for the theft began to peddle these drugs around the London jazz clubs and the coffee bars frequented by jazz musicians. He was finally arrested by the Metropolitan Police some three months after the theft when it was found that while the morphine he had stolen was still virtually intact, the heroin and cocaine had been largely disposed of; and documentary evidence found on him indicated that he had some fifteen regular customers for these two drugs. All these fifteen "nontherapeutic addicts" were not only associated with jazz music, they were also under thirty-five years of age, and most sinister of all when they approached the script doctors for supplies, some of them began to ask for larger quantities than they themselves needed in order to supply the drugs to others in their group who, when they became addicted, approached doctors in their turn.

The First Brain Committee

By 1958 the number of known addicts (to all narcotic drugs) had almost doubled that known in 1947. As a result of this, The First Interdepartmental Committee on Drug Addiction was appointed on the third of June, 1958 (under the chairmanship of the then Sir Russell Brain). This came to be known as the First Brain Committee and was composed of seven members.

The terms of reference of this Committee were

> to review, in the light of more recent developments, the advice given by the Departmental Committee on Morphine and Heroin Addiction in 1926 (the Rolleston Committee); to consider whether any revised advice should also cover other drugs liable to produce addiction or to be habit-forming; to consider whether there is a medical need to provide special, including institutional, treatment ouside the resources already available, for persons addicted to drugs; and to make recommendations, including proposals for any administrative measures that seem expedient, to the Minister of Health and the Secretary of State for Scotland.

The first Brain Committee reported in November, 1960, and included among twenty separate conclusions and recommendations were (1) the committee was satisfied that the incidence of addiction to dangerous drugs *was still very small;* (2) that departmental arrangements ensured that nearly all addicts to dangerous drugs were known; (3) the Home Secretary should not establish medical tribunals to investigate the grounds for recommending him to withdraw a doctor's authority to possess and supply dangerous drugs; (4) apart from item three, the Committee underlined and supported the main conclusions of the Rolleston Committee, which were included in a memorandum on the Dangerous Drugs Act and Regulations, which was prepared by the Home Office for the information of doctors and dentists.

The Second Brain Committee

In the three years following the publication of the first Brain Report (1961), there was a further steep rise in the incidence of addiction to dangerous drugs. The number of known addicts to heroin increased fourfold, and most of these were also addicted to morphine. The Brain Committee was therefore reconvened in July, 1964, as it was by then evident that the sudden increase was due, at least in some measure, to the prescribing methods of a certain small number of doctors,

The terms of reference of the Second Brain Committee were "to consider whether in the light of recent experience the advice the Interdepartmental Committee gave in 1961 in relation to the prescribing of addictive drugs by doctors needs revising and, if so, to make recommendations."

The Second Brain Committee reported in July, 1965, and a summary of the twelve main conclusions and recommendations made by them included the following:

1. There has been a disturbing rise in the incidence of addiction to heroin and cocaine, especially among young people. (Through the years 1959-1964 the total number of addicts to dangerous drugs rose from 454-753, and this included a rise in addicts to heroin from 68-342; of the 342 known addicts, 328 were of nontherapeutic origin.)

2. The main source of supply is the overprescribing of these drugs by a small number of doctors. (The Second Brain Committee was informed that in 1962 one doctor alone prescribed 600,000 tablets of heroin (i.e. 6 kg) for addicts, the same doctor on one single occasion prescribed 900 tablets (9 gm) to one addict, and three days later prescribed for the same patient another 600 tablets (6 gm) "to replace pills lost in an accident." The Second Brain Committee also noted "the evidence further shows that not more than six doctors have prescribed these very large amounts of dangerous drugs for individual patients and these doctors have acted within the law and according to their professional judgment."

3. There is now a need for further measures to restrict the prescription of heroin and cocaine. "We remain convinced that the doctor's right to prescribe dangerous drugs without restriction, for the ordinary patient's needs, should be maintained. We have also borne in mind the dilemma which faces the authorities responsible for the control of dangerous drugs in this country.

To prevent this abuse without sacrificing the basic advantages of the present arrangements we suggest:
a. A system of notification of addicts.
b. The provision of advice where addiction is in doubt.
c. The provision of treatment centers.
d. The restriction of supplies to addicts."

4. The Committee defined an addict, for the purposes of their report, as follows: "A person who, as a result of repeated administration, has become dependent upon a drug controlled under the Dangerous Drug Act and has an overpowering desire for its continuance, but who does not require it for the relief of organic disease."

5. There should be a power for compulsory detention of addicts at treatment centers.

6. The prescribing of heroin and cocaine to addicts should be limited to doctors on the staff of treatment centers.

7. It should be a statutory offense for other doctors to prescribe heroin and cocaine to addicts.

8. Disciplinary procedures against doctors alleged to have prescribed heroin or cocaine, irregularly, to addicts should be the responsibility of the general Medical Council.

9. An advisory committee should be set up to keep under review the whole problem of drug addiction.

The Implementation of the Second Brain Report

Following the publication of the Second Brain Report in July, 1965, the following events are worthy of note:

1. On April 28, 1966, the Minister of Health, replying to a question in the House of Commons "To ask the Minister of Health what action he had taken to implement the recommendations of the Brain Committee on drugs" said "The treatment facilities are under review and the Government has decided to accept the recommendation to set up an advisory committee on the whole problem of drug addiction. Consideration is still being given to the Committee's other main recommendations which require legislation."

2. On August 2, 1966, in a written answer, the Minister of

Health, replying to a question in the House of Commons "To ask the Minister of Health whether following his announcement about the Standing Advisory Committee he would now make a statement about the other recommendations in the Brain Committee Report," stated "There are already centers for the treatment of addicts and more beds could be made available if the demand increases. A conference of doctors experienced in the treatment of drug addicts is being convened in order to have the medical knowledge of the subject. Steps are being taken to set up a unit in which research into the problem of drug dependency can be undertaken. The Government is preparing legislation to implement the Committee's recommendation for the compulsory notification of addicts by doctors and for limiting the authority of doctors (other than those at treatment centers) to prescribe or supply heroin and cocaine to addicts, except where it is required for the relief of pain due to organic disease or following injury or operation. The details will be discussed with the medical profession. The Government has, however, decided not to provide initially for the detention of addicts at treatment centers, but would reconsider the position if experience showed that such powers were essential."

Memorandum on Treatment

On the seventh of March 1967 the Minister of Health issued a hospital memorandum on "The Treatment and Supervision of Heroin Addiction." Paragraph three of the memorandum, on the question of power to detain at treatment centers patients who wish to break off a course of treatment they entered into voluntarily, stated: "The question of compulsory treatment raises wide and difficult issues and the Minister is not satisfied that the case for this recommendation has been fully established."

Paragraph eight of the memorandum under the heading, "Out-patient Services" stated:

> Some addicts will not accept withdrawal treatment, at any rate to start with, and complete refusal of supplies will not cure their addiction—it will merely throw them on the black market and

encourage the development of an organized illicit traffic on a scale
hitherto unknown in this country. The aim is to *contain the spread
of heroin addiction* by continuing to supply this drug *in minimum
quantities* where this is necessary in the opinion of the doctor, and
where feasible to persuade addicts to accept withdrawal treatment.

Paragraph ten of the memorandum, on the question of the supply
of drugs, stated: "The decision to supply an addict with drugs
and whether to seek to substitute other drugs, the assessment of
dosage, and the method of supply rest with the clinician."

In assembling material for this presentation I came across
the following paragraph in an address given by Sir Derek Dunlop
to the Royal Society of Medicine in May last year. His address
was entitled "The Control of Drugs and Therapeutic Freedom."
The closing paragraph reads as follows:

> I sometimes envy those people with strong principles and con-
> victions who, confronted by any controversial problem, immediately
> seem to know what is right and what is wrong. They are the people
> who do most good in the world and the most harm. I am not one
> of them, for, as I get older, I seem to find the answer to most contro-
> versial questions more and more difficult. There always seems to be
> so much to be said on both sides. Nevertheless, a proper *under-
> standing* of the problems involved is the first stage to their intelligent
> solution.

In the same address, Sir Derek had the following to say on
the specific question which concerns us today, the English
Drug Program:

> Reforms and revolutions, no matter how salutary, are bound to be
> hurtful to some and may sometimes create further problems more
> formidable than the abuses they have sought to remedy. Thus, the
> drunken motor car driver had become such a menace that additional
> measures were required to deal with him but their imposition has
> interfered with our freedom to enjoy, with any peace of mind, a
> bottle of wine with a friend at dinner before driving soberly home.
> In the same way, largely due to a very few doctors who have
> prescribed potent narcotics and hallucinogenic agents so injudiciously
> (I do not use a stronger term), addiction to them in Britain—at one
> time so minimal as to be a matter of almost incredulous envy in
> other countries—has suddenly assumed serious proportions. In con-
> sequence, under the 1968 Dangerous Drugs Regulations, the legal
> right to prescribe heroin and cocain to addicts—though not, curiously
> enough, morphine—has been taken away from us ordinary doctors

and confined to those working in special clinics. Further, the Safety of Drugs Committee has restricted the supply of L.S.D. to the very few psychiatrists who continue to regard that rather sinister drug as a valuable agent in diagnosis and therapeutics. These are perhaps necessary measures but are possibly the thin edge of the bureaucratic wedge to professional medical freedom. The trouble is that although we nearly all maintain that freedom is good and restriction bad, when someone else's freedom of action becomes inconvenient, we usually clamour for its restriction—a restriction which then seems essential in the public interest and based on the purest of motives. "The Government must do something about it," we say. Such restrictions may be particularly undesirable when proposed hysterically to meet some crisis.

And this brings me to the first of what I consider are the successes of the new English Drug Program, and that is the fact that less than three years after the second Interdepartmental Committee on Drug Addiction had reported, of some twelve main conclusions and recommendations made by them, it has been possible to implement all but two. I will deal with these conclusions and recommenadtions more fully, but may I say now that although many people thought the British Government were very slow to act on the recommendations of the Second Brain Committee, it should be remembered that when the Rolleston Committee, which was formed in 1924, reported in 1926 the very few restrictive measures they recommended were still "under discussion" with the medical profession some thirty years later when the First Brain Committee was convened. Many of you may remember also the feeling that was aroused among many doctors in Britain some twelve years ago when measures were proposed in Parliament to control and possibly eliminate the use of heroin as a therapeutic substance, yet there were few if any dissenters when the Second Brain Committee recommended that heroin and cocaine should be restricted in their availability (to all but therapeutic addicts) and that nontherapeutic addicts should only be able to obtain these two drugs from licensed doctors in recognized treatment centers.

Before I deal in detail with the twelve recommendations and conclusions of the Second Brain Committee, I would also like to refer in brief to the findings and recommendations of the First Brain Committee, as these two committees were, of course, complementary and, indeed, the second committee was formed of exactly the same members (with but two exceptions), and comprised but seven members in all. The first Brain Committee convened on June the third, 1958, and reported some two and one-half years later in November, 1960. Included in twenty separate conclusions and recommendations were three that did not really stand up to critical evaluation less than four years later when it was necessary to reconvene the Committee. These were as follows:

Firstly, "The Committee was satisfied that the incidence of addiction to dangerous drugs was still very small," but within three years there was a steep rise in this incidence, and the numbers of known addicts to heroin had increased fourhold. To me, it seems, either the First Brain Committee did not have access to all relevant information or it did not pay due attention to some of the evidence presented to it.

Secondly, "Departmental arrangements ensured that nearly all addicts to dangerous drugs were known." This was possibly true, in some measure, with regard to therapeutic addicts but undoubtedly not so for nontherapeutic addicts, as it subsequently became clear that many such addicts maintained themselves, without working, by selling their surplus drugs to other addicts who wished to avoid going on the Home Office Index as long as they possibly could. The Home Office Index was a method of recording, centrally, the names of doctors who were prescribing narcotic drugs for patients either regularly or in unduly large amounts at any one time. The records of retail pharmacists throughout Britain were scrutinized at irregular intervals by policemen of the local constabulary. The names of doctors so prescribing were notified to the Ministry of Health by the Home Office, and regional medical officers of this Ministry would visit these doctors and encourage them to reduce such prescribing and also ask them to endeavor to persuade the patients to enter hospitals for treatment. No action was ever taken against the addicts themselves in this exercise, but nevertheless many addicts often refused to go to doctors for their drugs, as they did not wish their names to be recorded at the Home Office.

Thirdly, "The Home Secretary should not establish medical tribunals to investigate the grounds for recommending him to withdraw a doctor's authority to possess and supply dangerous drugs." Yet within a few years it became necessary to introduce severe restrictions on the right to prescribe. Could it be that the storm in Parliament in 1957 was still felt in 1959-1960, but that it had died down sufficiently by 1965 for restrictive measures to be recommended?

Now to return to the conclusions and recommendations of the Second Brain Committee. The first three conclusions of this Committee dealt with the disturbing rise in the incidence of addiction to heroin and cocaine, especially among young people. It also dealt with the fact that the main source of supply was the gross over prescribing of these drugs by a very small number of doctors (not more than six the report said), and do remember there are some 3,500 general practitioners in metropolitan London. The report also concluded that there was now a need for further measures to restrict the prescription of heroin and cocaine but the Committee decided not "to grasp the nettle" of severe restriction, much less elimination of the drugs heroin and cocaine to nontherapeutic addicts. In explanation of this, the Committee had the following to say: "We have also borne in mind the dilemma which faces the authorities responsible for the control of dangerous drugs in this country," and it continued, "If there is insufficient control, it may lead to the spread of addiction—as is happening at present. If, on the other hand, the restrictions are so severe as to prevent or seriously discourage the addict from obtaining supplies from legitimate sources, it may lead to the development of an organized illicit traffic." Even at this point in time, those of us who were involved with the foreseen problems of setting up treatment facilities did not envisage a situation where it was entirely up to the addict to decide whether he or she should come in for such treatment or whether they should continue to obtain their heroin and cocaine as outpatients, albeit on a day-to-day basis. In a further effort to explain this very liberal approach, a hospital memorandum on the treatment and supervision of heroin addiction published in 1967 had the following to say: "The decision to supply an addict with drugs and whether to seek to substitute other drugs, the assessment of dosage and the method of supply rests with the clinician," yet no advice was offered to the unfortunate clinician as to how he was to assess the required dosage in an addict, who, you must remember, could only be seen in an outpatient department, often only once a week, for a period of time that seldom, exceeded ten to fifteen minutes.

Returning to the second Brain Committee's recommendations, in dealing with the need for further measures, to restrict the prescribing of heroin and cocaine to addicts, it was suggested that the following measures be introduced:

1. A system of notification and identification.
2. The provision of advice where addiction was in doubt.
3. The provision of treatment centers.
4. The restriction of supplies to addicts.

It should, I consider, be recorded on the success side that by April sixteenth, 1968, when the majority of doctors practicing in Great Britain were no longer permitted to prescribe heroin and cocaine for nontherapeutic addicts, the notification and identification system had been introduced, although some would say that the exclusion of fingerprints and photographs made it anything but a foolproof system. Advice was also available by this date from panels of specialists throughout the country to doctors who were uncertain whether a patient was an addict or not. Although here again, few of the members of these panels were specialists in psychiatry and therefore had no day-to-day clinical acquaintance with nontherapeutic addicts. Treatment centers, although slow to start, had by this date expanded to a total of seventeen in the London metropolitan area and by the end of May, 1968, they had a total of 895 addicts (808 males and 87 females) on their books. Of these, some 722 (659 males and 63 females) were receiving treatment as outpatients and only 87 (63 males and 24 females), as inpatients,

On the question of restriction of supplies to addicts, again there is little doubt that the exclusion of certain general practitioners, well known for their generosity in prescribing heroin and cocaine, made substantial reductions on the amount of heroin circulating on the black market, and the price in London rose rapidly from 2.4 dollars to 3.6 dollars per grain; but as this heroin was pure unadulterated British Pharmacopoeia heroin, albeit in tablet form, it was still very much cheaper than a bag of "what have you" bought illegally in this country.

The Brain Committee also suggested a definition of an addict which reads, "a person who, as a result of repeated administration, has become dependent upon a drug controlled under the Dangerous Drugs Act and has an overpowering desire for its continuance but who does not require it for the relief of organic disease." There are some who consider that it would not be too difficult to get around this definition and prescribe for a nontherapeutic addict with safety, but I have yet to know of any doctor so challenging it.

The seventh of the twelve recommendations and conclusions of the Second Brain Committee reads, "there should be power for compulsory detention of addicts at treatment centers." On the second of August, 1966, the Minister of Health said in the House of Commons "The Government has, however, decided not to provide initially for the detention of addicts at treatment centers but would reconsider the position if experience showed that such powers were essential." Also, in the hospital memorandum on the Treatment and Supervision of Heroin Addiction, one reads, "The question of compulsory treatment raises wide and difficult issues and the Minister is not satisfied that the case for this recommendation has been fully established." He has decided to proceed initially without any new power of compulsory treatment and he will reconsider the position if experience suggests that a new power is necessary. One never heard details of the "wide and difficult issues" that would be raised, but it is quite certain that the inability to compel any addict over twenty-one years of age to remain in a hospital raised wide and difficult issues for the doctors and their ancillary staff who volunteered to take on the work at treatment centers.

Recommendations nine and ten were concerned with the questions of what to do with doctors who offended against the new law. The Committee was of the opinion that disciplinary procedures should be the responsibility of the General Medical Council and that such doctors "should come before a tribunal of their professional colleagues to justify their actions." It was subsequently decided that such doctors should come before the civil courts of law, and there are some of us who consider that this measure was somewhat weaker than that proposed by the Second Brain Committee.

The eleventh recommendation of the second Brain Committee dealt with precautions in prescribing heroin and other dangerous drugs and the necessity to use words as well as figures to specify quantities.

The final recommendation concerned the setting up of an advisory committee on drug dependence. This was done and the committee met for the first time in the home office on Thursday, January twelfth, 1967. It was comprised of a chairman and twenty-four members. Its terms of reference were "to keep under review the misuse of narcotic and other drugs which are likely to produce dependence and to advise on remedial measures that might be taken or on any other related matters which the ministers may refer to it."

It soon subdivided into three subcommittees:

1. Cannabis and *LSD.*
2. Rehabilitation.
3. Health education and publicity.

The reports of these subcommittees are awaited.

Before I close I would like to refer briefly to the opinions of one or two senior consultant psychiatrists in London, working full time in this field of hard drug addiction.

When Dr. Yolles first asked me to prepare this paper, I wrote to these doctors and asked them for any comments they might like to make that I could include.

Dr. Thomas Bewley, a member of the Advisory Committee on Drug Dependence and one of the most experienced doctors in Britain in the field of narcotic drug addiction replied to me in August last year, as follows:

> I think, myself, it is still early to say how successful or otherwise the Clinics will be, but I think the main successes are due to cooperation between the Clinics and to all the consultants agreeing to behave in a fairly similar way from the point of view of how much should be prescribed and so forth. I think that also the fact that it is now possible to monitor the amount of drugs being prescribed is a great advantage so that if there is a steady increase we can change over to

oral methadone maintenance or, generally cut down all round. I think the main problems arise from the use of intravenous methedrine and other drugs that are not scheduled under the DDS at present, in that the clinics can deal with heroin and cocain but can't deal very sensibly with methylamphetamine while other doctors prescribe unlimited amounts of it. I suspect that this may be changed and this may make more sense of the situation. I would say also that the Clinics have been successful in insisting that people turn up regularly for appointments, attend at a specific chemist and, in general, lead more ordered lives. I am afraid I can only give one or two rather vague impressions at the moment. If I were to sum up my views in a sentence about the clinics, I would say that I think that they are successful provided we continue to keep a close watch on what we are doing and provided all the Clinics continue to coordinate their policies."

Dr. John Willis, consultant in charge of a treatment center run jointly by Kings Hospital and Guys Hospital (2 of Londons 12 teaching hospitals) told me when I visited his clinic last August that in his opinion one of the main successes of the English Drug Program was the general "tidying up" of the addicts approach to life; some addicts now possibly felt that working for one's living was not after all so awful. Another good thing, he considered, was the rationalization of methods of prescribing heroin and cocaine.

One problem he referred to was the difficulty addicts had in collecting their drugs daily from retail chemists often some distance from their residence, and although he readily admitted that this was a factor of some importance in controlling illicit trafficking, he felt that it allowed heroin to continue to dominate their lives.

Dr. John Willis also referred to the difficulties presented by many voluntary organizations who were clamoring to take part in the drug program. In his opinion one of the biggest problems here was that whereas professional workers knew their jobs and kept to regular hours of work, nonprofessionals were not so knowledgeable and often were irregular in their attendance at clinics and other facilities. Other successes, in Dr. Willis opinion, included the fact that we were now, in Britain, in a better position to study the natural history of hard-drug addiction and to get to know more clearly what actually happened to addicts. He saw little future for halfway houses for addicts, run by local government authorities and considered that such facilities must be provided from central funds.

Finally, he mentioned his liking for what he referred to as the Freedman Philosophy that "total abstention from narcotic drug abuse is not a practical goal for all addicts."

A third consultant in charge of a treatment center, Dr. N. Rathod, of Horsham Surrey, writes as follows:

> As for the general scene I cannot help feeling that dependence on heroin may be achieving far more clinical importance than it deserves and the medical profession is somehow or other getting into a situation where fear of the black market is forcing them to be blackmailed into dishing out heroin as distinct from prescribing heroin. To illustrate the point—people have claimed that some surplus heroin has been prescribed and this has prevented the black market, stressing that clinically we have been worried over the black market.
>
> Secondly, although there has been a good deal of provision to maintain patients on heroin, strangely enough very little has been done to ensure an accurate assessment prior to deciding whether a) the patient needs to be kept on heroin, and b) whether there is a case for pressure reduction in dosage. Thirdly, very little seems to have been done to promote active rehabilitation programs, as opposed to giving lip service as to how important rehabilitation is.

In conclusion, may I refer to a letter I received recently from Mr. C. G. Jeffrey, Chief Inspector of the Dangerous Drugs Department of the Home Office. I wrote to him when I heard that the British Government had banned the ability to prescribe methylamphetamine even by licensed doctors at drug treatment centers last October.

He replied as follows:

> On the question of the effects of the restriction on supplies of injectable methylamphetamine it is really too early to reach any firm conclusions. I should point out, however, that it is not available even through the treatment centers, so that all the users have had either to give up entirely or find a substitute. According to Steve Abrams (for what his statements are worth), all his acquaintances who were using it have simply stopped, and everything in the garden is lovely. However, other sources suggest that most are trying a variety of substitutes; there is some evidence of injection of crushed oral tablets on the Swedish model, but on what scale we don't yet

know. What seems pretty certain, despite Abrams, is that the great majority of confirmed users of intravenous methylamphetamine will continue to inject something, even if it's whiskey or scent, as in two cases we know of.

SUMMARY

To sum up, the successes of the English Drug Program could be said to include the fact that in less than three years after the Second Brain Committee had reported (in July 1965) the Government had introduced measures to implement ten of its twelve major recommendations.

It is also already evident that cooperation between the major treatment centers in metropolitan London and meetings, arranged by the Department of Health, of the consultant psychiatrists in charge of these faciliies, has ensured a substantial degree of uniformity of prescribing of heroin, cocaine, and other hard drugs to addicts in the community.

Methylamphetamine is no longer available for prescription, but it is being replaced by the numerous other amphetamines available in tablet form, and we know already the complications that can arise when the addict in the street becomes his own dispenser.

Other good points include the fact that regular attendance at clinics, at least once a week, encourages a more orderly life for the average addict; although I must say that some of those I prescribed for as recently as last September were in very poor physical shape; underweight, toxic, and obviously suffering from severe malnutrition.

Dr. Willis has drawn attention to the necessity for a more disciplined approach from some of the members of voluntary bodies who were clamoring to help in the Drug Program. It was my opinion that a number of these people, including ordained members of churches, were basically unstable and indeed more than one of the most vociferous who received major press publicity later were successfully prosecuted for drug abuse.

Dr. Rathod has drawn attention to the lack of facilities for active rehabilitation programs, and it could be that this failure early on in the scheme might eventually be the Achilles Heel of the whole program.

Chapter Five

CONTRIBUTIONS OF LABORATORY WORK TO THE ANALYSIS AND CONTROL OF DRUG DEPENDENCE

JULIAN E. VILLARREAL

IT IS NOT LIKELY that too many observers of the skies living before the time of Galileo and Newton would have guessed that experiments with freely falling objects and with balls rolling on inclined planes would provide the key to the behavior of the noble bodies residing in the celestial spheres. Nowadays the accumulated accomplishments of experimental science have taught us to be more respectful of the possible implications of seemingly trivial findings in the laboratory. Yet, when dealing with a problem as complex as drug dependence, it might appear at first thought that experiments with mice, rats, and monkeys are unlikely to contribute in a major way to our understanding and our ability to control the bizarre lives of human drug addicts.

Laboratory work in medicinal chemistry and pharmacology has a long history of valuable contributions in this field. Experience with a vast number of compounds of many chemical classes has established profiles of similarities and differences in the responses of animals and of man to many drugs of dependence. With some of the best known classes of drugs, prediction from one species to another can be made with a degree of probability close to certainty. In the area of narcotic analgesics, for instance, nobody should find cause for surprise in learning that a new drug which has been found to be morphine-like in mice is also found to be morphine-like in humans.

A more recent approach in laboratory work on drug dependence has been the application of techniques for the experimental analysis of behavior to the rigorous study of drug-seeking behavior in animals. There is already strong evidence indicating a very promising correspondence between animals and man with respect to the self-administration of drugs. Just as one of the tasks of research in the area of physiological pharmacology has been to search for those elements of drug action which have generality across animal species, studies of self-administration of drugs in animals are likewise defining general properties of drug-seeking behavior which may indicate what kinds of findings may be more confidently extrapolated to man.

Furthermore, as has been pointed out elsewhere[34] the use of infrahuman organisms for the study of drug-seeking behavior has the special advantage of forcing the investigator to ask empirical questions and of making him less prone to bring up personality or character disorders to account for his findings. Confidence in the significance of these animal studies for man is based not only on the proposition that man shares many of the mechanisms of his behavior with animals but also on the likely hypothesis that the causes of much of the behavior of addicts may be totally inaccessible to verbal probes of the preconscious and unconscious memories of these subjects and, consequently, must be investigated through empirical work.

The material for the present discussion will be primarily the work on dependence to drugs of the morphine type. Narcotic analgesics have generated a vast amount of research, beginning with the isolation of morphine from opium more than a century and a half ago. This research has led not only to the formation of a large body of knowledge and to the production of compounds which have served as excellent instruments of investigation and therapy, but also to the development of techniques which have found general use in the study of other forms of drug dependence. This brief review deals only with selected aspects of the subject which were chosen according to the author's own interests, acknowledging that numerous important contributions and entire areas of valuable research must of necessity go unmentioned.

THE CHEMOPHARMACOLOGICAL APPROACH TO OPIATE DEPENDENCE

Early in this century, the use of the local anesthetic cocaine as a drug of dependence declined rapidly following the introduction of the synthetic local anesthetics procaine and pontocaine.

Encouraged by this precedent, a group of investigators directed by Small and Eddy set up a large scale program aiming at the synthesis of new analgesics which could replace morphine in human medicine.[38] Over the last forty years the number of workers responding to this same challenge has multiplied many times. They are now scattered all over the world in private industry laboratories, universities, and in government agencies.

The synthesis of morphine substitutes was hoped to contribute to the solution of the problem of narcotic dependence in two ways. First, it could facilitate the worldwide control of opium production through the achievement of independence from this source of indispensable drugs for medical use. Second, it could lead to the development of compounds as effective as analgesics as morphine, yet free from its capacity to induce dependence.

Ever since the League of Nations first tried to achieve control of the world's production of narcotics for illicit purposes, efforts of this kind have been frustrated by national and international entrepreneurs. As a consequence of this, synthetic dependence-free analgesics should not be expected to contribute to the solution of the "street" type of dependence to opiates. Nevertheless, there has been much need for strong analgesics which could be prescribed, dispensed, and stored without setting up occasions for the development of dependence in patients, nurses, pharmacists, or the physicians themselves. It should also be pointed out that the search for morphine substitutes has made available, as an unexpected side benefit, compounds such as the morphine antagonists and the long-acting analgesics which are currently being employed in the treatment of "street" addicts to opiates.

Nathan B. Eddy, who shared with Small the direction of the first serious program for the synthesis of morphine substitutes forty years ago, has reviewed the highlights in the history of this "chemopharmacological approach" to the problem of narcotic dependence.[6]

COMPOUNDS WITH MORPHINE-LIKE ACTION

Because of historical precedence, vast use, and pharmacological specificity, morphine is the prototype narcotic analgesic.

Heroin is a semisynthetic drug which, ironically, seems to have been the first analgesic to be introduced into medical use with the claim of freedom from dependence liability (1889). Meperidine (pethidine) was the first totally synthetic potent analgesic, likewise initially thought to be dependence-free be-

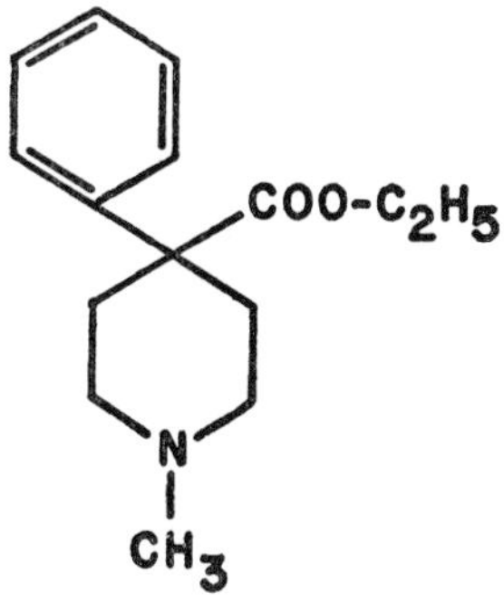

PETHIDINE

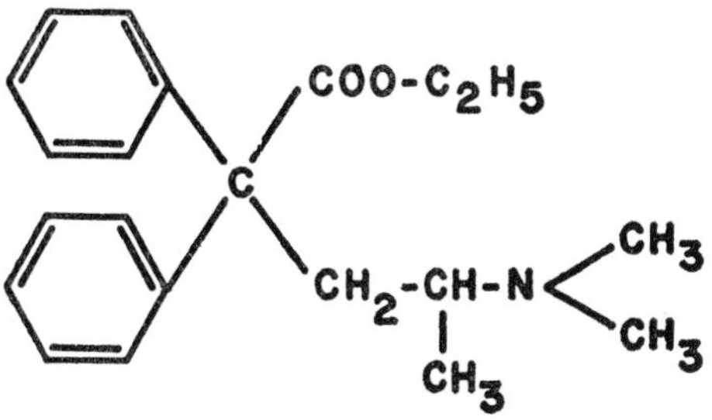

METHADONE

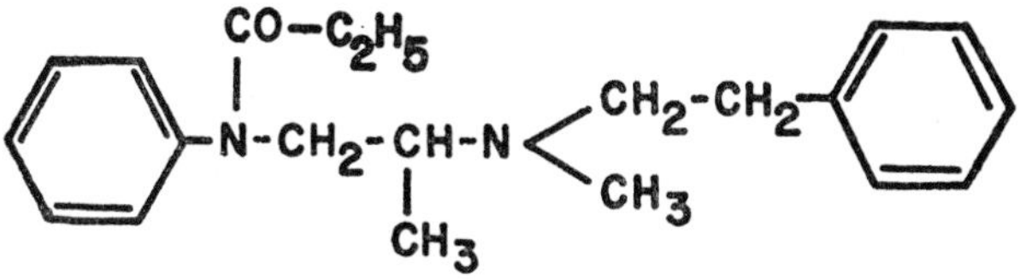

DIAMPROMIDE

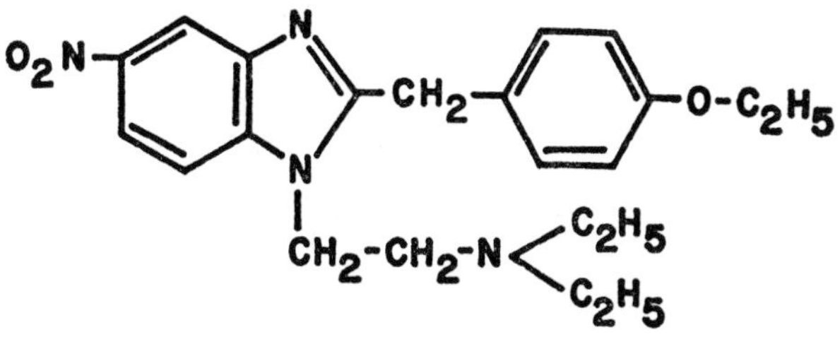

ETONITAZINE

FIGURE 5-1.

cause of its structural disimilarities with morphine. The discovery
of meperidine was reported in 1939.

Since then, large numbers of analgesics of many different
chemical families have been synthesized and studied pharmacologically. Figure 5-1 shows representatives of some of the best
known families of totally synthetic morphine-like analgesics.
Morphine and these synthetic compounds have served as models
for chemical modification in attempts to separate their analgesic
from their dependence-producing properties. Chemical modification in the case of morphine has been highly elaborate, leading
to the synthesis of compounds which consist of simplified or more
complex versions of the structural skeleton of the parent alkaloid.
Representatives of three classes of these morphine analogues
are shown in Figure 5-2.

In spite of the wide chemical diversity and the large number
of these compounds, their analgesic and dependence-producing
properties have been found to covary with a remarkable

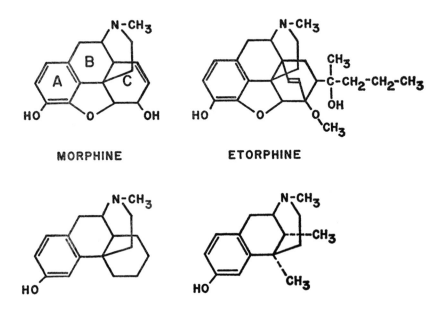

FIGURE 5-2.

parallelism. Very potent analgesics, up to 15,000 times more active than morphine, and very weak drugs have been developed, but the order of their potencies for dependence-production has corresponded to the order of their analgesic activity.[7, 8, 29, 37] The very few notable exceptions to this general parallelism will be discussed further on.

The close correspondence between analgesia and dependence-production in compounds of so many different chemical classes is very compelling evidence that the receptors mediating these two actions are either one and the same or else that they are chemically nearly identical. Attesting to the widespread tacit acceptance of this proposition is the fact that most of the current attempts to develop analgesics with low dependence potential have the explicit objective of producing compounds with low overall morphine-like instrinsic activity. The number and variety of drugs which have been tested for analgesia and physical dependence has been large enough (nearly 800 compounds have been tested for physical dependence capacity in monkeys) to expect a significant separation of these properties if there were singular biological receptor sites for morphine which alone had the role of mediating physical dependence production.

It must be noted here that it is no longer thought desirable to look for drugs which might show only a quantitative separation of analgesia and dependence potential, requiring higher doses to produce dependence than those necessary for the achievement of effective analgesia. In spite of a quantitative separation, it should be expected that prescribing physicians or more likely self-administering subjects would let themselves be drawn into increasing dosage. One of the advantages of the recently marketed analgesic, pentazocine, consists in its low ceiling of physical dependence production which apparently cannot be surpassed regardless of increments in dosage.[10, 18, 32]

Pharmacological Characterization of Morphine-Like Drugs

Drugs of the morphine type produce quite different behavioral effects in different animal species.[21] Mice, for instance, show an increase in locomotor activity under the influence of morphine, which can be about twice as intense as the peak stimulation of activity obtainable with dextroamphetamine.[31] Cats are thrown into a "sham rage" syndrome by relatively high doses of morphine. On the other hand, dogs and monkeys respond like man to a large fraction of the morphine-like agents in that they show primarily stupor, coma, and death in respiratory depression with these drugs. Still, it is known from wide experience that even the monkey tends to show much less depression than is shown by man with compounds that have mixed depressant and stimulant properties.

Notwithstanding the differences between species in the overt behavioral changes produced by morphine-like agents, pharmacological analysis permits highly reliable predictions from animal studies to man. Regardless of the kind of overt behavioral effect produced in any given species, if a drug is shown to be morphine-like in its actions, there is a strong probability that it will also be morphine-like in man. The characterization of a compound as a morphine-like agent is based on the establishment of the pattern of properties outlined in Table 5-I. First, these drugs

TABLE 5-I

PHARMACOLOGICAL PROPERTIES OF NARCOTIC ANALGESICS

1. Morphine-like CNS depression
2. CNS depression antagonized by nalorphine
3. Tolerance and cross-tolerance
4. Capacity to initiate and sustain morphine-like physical dependence. Cross-substitution
5. Reinforcement of self-administration behavior

all induce behavioral and subjective effects which closely resemble those obtained with morphine. Second, their central depressant effects are blocked or reversed by nalorphine and other specific antagonists such as levallorphan and naloxone. Figures 5-3 and 5-4 illustrate the reversal of morphine's effects by these narcotic antagonists in experiments carried out in monkeys, using spontaneous blinking rate to monitor the level of central nervous system depression. Third, all the morphine-like analgesics induce tolerance to their effects after repeated administrations at short intervals; remarkably, there is a high degree of cross-tolerance between these drugs, which is present

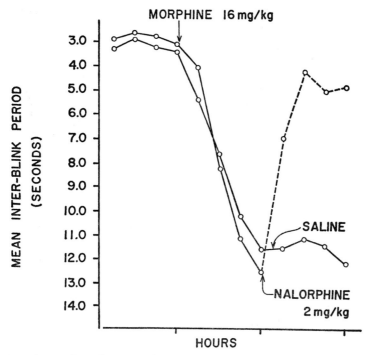

FIGURE 5-3. The effect of morphine and its reversal by nalorphine on the spontaneous blinking rate of one monkey. The two records included were obtained in experiments performed one week apart.

independently of their chemical type. Fourth, these compounds are also pharmacologically equivalent with respect to physical dependence; they not only can produce very similar forms of physiological dependence, but also they can effectively substitute for one another in dependent organisms. Finally, all these drugs seem to have the capacity to induce psychological dependence, defined as strong self-administration behavior, which can be generated independently of physical dependence production.

NARCOTIC ANTAGONISTS

The discovery and development of specific antagonists of narcotic analgesics has been an invaluable contribution to the scientific and practical aspects of narcotic drug action and

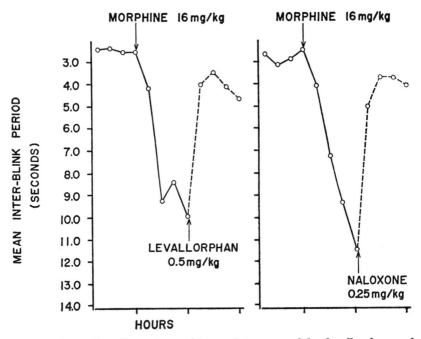

FIGURE 5-4. The effect of morphine and its reversal by levallorphan and naloxone on the spontaneous blinking rate of two monkeys.

narcotic dependence. They have furnished us with effective antidotes against narcotic overdosage and with the first group of strong analgesics with low dependence potential. They also hold some promise as pharmacological adjuncts for the prevention of relapse in human dependence on narcotics.[27] The pharmacology of narcotic antagonists has been reviewed by Woods[48], Wikler[46], Archer and Harris[1], Martin[24], and Villarreal.[43]

Besides their ability to block the effects of morphine-like drugs, the large majority of narcotic antagonists exert direct effects of their own. Some of these resemble the actions of the classical narcotic analgesics, but they also have certain distinct properties which characterize them as a group (Table 5-II).

A few of these compounds are "pure" antagonists, having practically no direct effects of their own in either man[16] or animals.[2, 20] The best known of these pure antagonists is naloxone, the N-allyl derivative of the potent narcotic oxymor-

TABLE 5-II

PHARMACOLOGICAL PROPERTIES OF CYCLAZOCINE
AND RELATED DRUGS

1. CNS depression unlike that produced by morphine
2. CNS depression antagonized by naloxone, not by nalorphine
3. Antagonism of the CNS depressant actions of narcotics
4. Failure to substitute for narcotics in narcotic-dependent animals
5. Capacity to initiate and sustain a mild type of physical dependence distinct from that developing to narcotics
6. Weak or no reinforcement of self-administration behavior

phone.[2] It is ten to thirty times more potent than nalorphine as a morphine antagonist.

Chemically, narcotic antagonists are close analogues of morphine and other narcotics. The nature of the substituent group on the nitrogen atom is the most decisive factor in conferring antagonistic activity. Studies with derivates of morphine and the other chemical families represented in Figure 5-2 have shown that increasing the length of the side chain on the nitrogen atom from one carbon (as in morphine) up to three carbons markedly reduces morphine-like properties, but it brings forth strong antagonistic activity. Further increases in chain length, however, restore morphine-like actions with a corresponding loss of antagonistic properties. The cyclopropylmethyl group of drugs such as cyclazocine is chemically very similar to the 3-carbon allyl side chain of nalorphine and can also confer strong antagonistic action.

Mixed properties are shown by compounds with N-substituents of intermediate length between the optimals for either morphine-like action or antagonism. Reversals in pharmacological activity and the structural changes that accompany the transition from strong antagonistic properties to strong morphine-like actions are of great interest because it seems that the borderline compounds or those with mixed properties are the most promising as strong analgesics with low dependence potential. Pentazocine is a case in point. This benzomorphan is a weak narcotic antagonist, is an effective analgesic in man but weak or inactive in animal tests, and has a low physical dependence capacity. Its nitrogen substituent, 3,3-dimethylallyl, can be considered as a large fragment of the N-phenethyl substituent of phenazocine, one of its analogues with high dependence capacity.[9] Moreover, the counterpart of pentazocine in the morphinan series [1-3-hydroxy-N-(3,3-dimethylallyl)-morphinan] is not a narcotic antagonist[41] and has a morphine-like spectrum of action which includes the capacity to partially suppress morphine abstinence in monkeys.[5]

The power of synthetic chemistry to manipulate drug molecules in order to achieve almost any shade of morphine agonist and antagonist actions is very promising with regard to the medical use of tailor-made drugs of this type. The following case illustrates this point. The potent narcotic antagonist cyclazocine has been under clinical trial in the treatment of narcotic dependent subjects to prevent their tendency to relapse to drug self-administration. Cyclazocine has the advantage of its long duration of antagonistic action which will protect from the effects of opiates even if it is administered only once a day. However, the dysphoric nature of the direct effects of this drug make it sometimes objectionable. Another drug, the pure antagonist naloxone, has no direct effects of its own, but it has a short duration of action even in high doses.[49] Recently, the present writer has had the opportunity of testing in monkeys the N-cyclopropylmethyl analogue of naloxone. This compound is a potent, long-acting antagonist nearly devoid of direct effects. These properties may render it superior to cyclazocine for the prevention of relapse to opiate self-administration.

Even though nalorphine is the best known of the antagonist analgesics, Table 5-II represents cyclazocine as the pharmacological prototype for this class of drugs because its actions in both animals and man exhibit a more marked contrast with the actions of the classical morphine-like narcotics. The direct effects of nalorphine in several animal species were reported by Unna.[42] Compared with morphine, nalorphine produced only mild sedative effects in rabbits and dogs. Unlike morphine, nalorphine did not increase locomotor activity in mice and also failed to produce excitement in cats. In the rhesus monkey[14] nalorphine produced only mild sedation and ataxia and, like morphine, pupillary dilation; high doses produced signs of central nervous system stimulation.

Cyclazocine and other N-cyclopropylmethyl derivatives produce a very marked central nervous system depression which is of great interest because it probably represents a new type of action by drugs which share the structural skeleton of potent narcotic analgesics. The picture of depression induced by these compounds includes prominent motor effects of the type found with central muscle relaxants.[11, 12] In the monkey, this type of depression differs in several important respects from that caused by morphine and other classical narcotics. An almost complete flaccid paralysis can be produced in these animals without, however, producing respiratory arrest and without preventing the semiparalyzed monkey from following the movements of observers with movements of his eyes.

In man, the direct effects of nalorphine were first studied in former opiate addicts by Wikler et al.[47] The subjective effects of this drug were described as being comparable to those of whiskey, barbiturates, and small doses of morphine. Nalorphine failed to give these former addicts the subjective feeling of "drive" which they experience with morphine-like drugs. Other effects of nalorphine included pupillary constriction, giddiness, dizziness, increased perspiration, and occasionally copious diuresis. Dysphoric and psychotomimetic effects were sometimes obtained after low doses (5-15 mg), increasing in incidence and severity with larger doses (30-75 mg). The direct effects in man of cyclazocine[26] and other antagonists[19, 22, 41] reproduce with more or less intensity the effects of nalorphine outlined above.

Table 5-II also points out that the morphine antagonist nalorphine is not an antagonist of cyclazocine. The results of an experiment studying this drug interaction in monkeys are shown in Figure 5-5. Blumberg et al.[4] have reported that the analgesic effects of cyclazocine cannot be reversed in mice with the morphine antagonist levallorphan. In man, Keats and Telford[19] found that nalorphine does not reverse respiratory depression produced by pentazocine.

On the other hand, the potent pure antagonist naloxone can effectively prevent or reverse the direct actions of cyclazocine-like drugs in animals.[3, 20] and in man.[17]

In spite of the strong central depressant properties exhibited by cyclazocine and certain other narcotic antagonists, none of these drugs substitutes for narcotics in monkeys or human

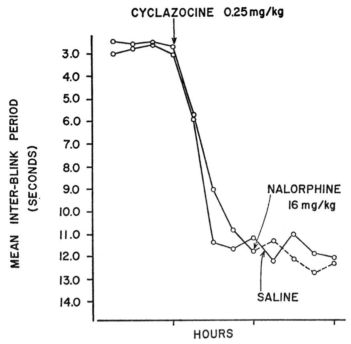

FIGURE 5-5. The effect of cyclazocine followed by nalorphine on the spontaneous blinking rate of one monkey. The two records included were obtained in experiments performed one week apart.

subjects in a state of physical dependence to morphine-like drugs. In fact, the administration of any narcotic antagonist in this situation precipitates an "acute abstinence syndrome." Wikler first described this effect in man with nalorphine.[47]

PHYSICAL DEPENDENCE

Notwithstanding the long history of the use of opium and morphine, recognition of the problem of physical dependence is a rather recent phenomenon. Sonnedecker[39] has published an excellent brief review of the emergence of the concept of dependence to opiates. As early as 1701, an English physician (John Jones) could write a book section entitled "The Effects of Sudden Leaving Off the Use of Opium After a Long and Lavish Use thereof." Yet, as late as 1929, clinical investigators of the problem could not decide whether the signs and symptoms of abstinence were physical, psychological, or were due to malingering.[23] Laboratory studies in infrahuman organisms began building evidence of the physiological aspects of opiate dependence as early as 1883.[37] The clearest proof was obtained by Wikler,[45] who showed abstinence signs in decorticate and spinal dogs, thus demonstrating that neurons from all parts of the central nervous system become dependent on morphine. Isbell and Fraser[15] and Seevers and Deneau[5] have published extensive reviews of research work on dependence to drugs of the morphine type.

Interestingly, there are large differences in susceptibility to the production of physical dependence by narcotic analgesics between animal species, man being the most sensitive by far. Rats withdrawn from chronic treatment with 320 mg/kg/day of morphine[25] develop an abstinence syndrome which appears mild compared to the abstinence syndromes shown by dogs, monkeys and man. The morphine abstinence syndrome of rhesus monkeys is very similar to that seen in man, but dosage schedules of the order of 12 mg/kg/day are necessary to achieve levels of dependence comparable to those obtained in man with 3-4 mg/kg/day.

The condition of chronic intoxication with narcotic analgesics has the peculiarity that the organism is subject to the influence of the drug both in its presence as well as when it is removed. On the one hand, when drug administration is maintained, the organism exhibits those effects to which complete tolerance does not develop. On the other hand, when the drug is removed, a number of severe behavioral and physiological disturbances ensue, the abstinence syndrome, reaching a peak intensity when blood concentrations of the drug have decreased to minimal levels (2 days in the case of morphine), followed by a return to near normality in about a fortnight.

Studies by Martin et al.[25, 28] have revived interest in certain long-term physiological changes which follow a cycle of chronic morphine intoxication. Minor deviations from predependence baselines in blood pressure, heart rate, body temperature, and sensitivity of the respiratory center to CO^2 have been shown to persist for as long as four months of observation. These authors have suggested the term "secondary abstinence syndrome" to designate such long-term changes.

It is generally assumed that chronic treatment with narcotic analgesics does not impose major physiological hazards as long as infections and injections of toxic contaminants are avoided. However, recent experiments in morphine-dependent monkeys have demonstrated that stressing stimuli which cause only minor disturbances in normal animals can cause profound derangements in the state of morphine physical dependence.[13] These studies resulted from the discovery that physical restraint produced very large falls in body temperature (as large as 8° C, 14° F) in dependent monkeys even during a schedule of regularly spaced doses of morphine. This increased physiological vulnerability starts only three to four hours after a regular dose of morphine, long before frank manifestations of an abstinence syndrome become evident. Morphine and other narcotic analgesics were shown to reverse the hypothermia produced by restraint. It is not known whether human subjects physically dependent on morphine-like drugs may also respond abnormally to physiological stress, but this possibility should be considered seriously in view of the close similarity between man and the monkey with regard to physical dependence to narcotic analgesics.

SELF-ADMINISTRATION OF MORPHINE-LIKE DRUGS

The stories of drug addicts, alcoholics, gamblers, and others who compulsively engage in behavior which predictably brings about life tragedy have always been a source of great puzzlement for more fortunate mortals. Drug dependence has been more enigmatic than gambling, since the nature of the occasional winnings of the gambler have an attraction which is more or less universal. In contrast, the effects of opiates, which induce a most tenacious form of dependence, are either dull or unpleasant in the experience of a great many people. Not surprisingly, many have agreed with John Jones, who, at the turn of the eighteenth century, concluded that the source of mischief in opium dependence is not in the drug but in the people.[39] However, attempts to define the nature of this "mischief" through studies of the personality or character of drug addicts have been far from revealing factors which are either necessary or sufficient conditions for the compulsive tendency to self-administer certain drugs.

Against a background in which self-administration of drugs appeared to be unaccountable except by the postulation of a psychological disorder in the addict, the emergence of the concept of physical dependence had a profound impact. Physical dependence was made the defining characteristic of "addiction."[40] Physical dependence was established as a strong biological "need" satisfied only with further drug administration, and which could be represented as a physiological "hunger" to a large extent responsible for the strong drug craving of the addict.

From the beginning of serious study of the problem, however, it was acknowledged that factors other than physical dependence play a very important role in drug dependence. It was found that cocaine does not produce physical dependence.[40] Human addicts to opiates continued to crave for these drugs even after prolonged drug-free periods, when they were no longer physically dependent.[23] Furthermore, stabilizing schedules of drug administration which met the physical requirements of opiate addicts did not always satisfy their "emotional" needs for drug.[38]

The findings of laboratory studies have now made it clear that physical dependence is neither a necessary nor a sufficient condition for the initiation or the maintenance of self-administration of morphine-like drugs. There is ample evidence that narcotic analgesics share with cocaine, amphetamine, and other stimulants the capacity to generate self-administration behavior independently of physical dependence production.

Figure 5-6 illustrates the results of an experiment on self-administration with profadol, an analgesic with a low physical dependence capacity in the rhesus monkey. A previous study[44] has shown that chronic administration of this compound in very high doses (64 mg/kg/day) produced only physical dependence of low-to-intermediate severity. Yet, when the monkey whose behavior is shown in Figure 5-6 was given the opportunity to take intravenous injections of very low doses of profadol (0.1

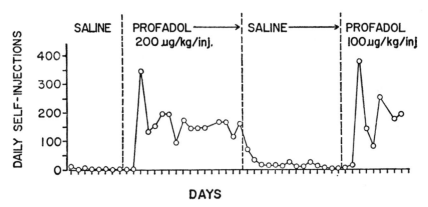

FIGURE 5-6. Self-administration of profadol by one monkey. Saline or profadol solutions were available for self-injection around the clock for the periods indicated. (Villarreal and Schuster, unpublished.)

and 0.2 mg per kg per injection), he quickly started self-administering the drug, stabilizing at about 160 injections per day. (For intravenous self-administration experiments, animals are surgically prepared with chronic indwelling catheters which are connected to an automatic injector containing the drug solution. The animals have access to a microswitch level which energizes the injector).

Schuster and Woods[35] have shown that monkeys will self-administer morphine in doses which do not produce detectable physical dependence (0.01 mg per kg per injection). It must be pointed out, however, that physical dependence can markedly enhance the strength of self-administration behavior. Large increases in lever pressing for opiates are seen during the abstinence syndrome.[34]

Many other drugs have been shown capable of generating self-administration behavior in animal species such as the rat and the monkey, with a very good correspondence to man in regard to patterns of drug taking and to the type of drug which is self-administered. Schuster and Thompson[33] have recently published a comprehensive review of this field.

In the opinion of the present writer, there have been three major contributions of this work to our understanding of human drug dependence. First, the fact that "simpleminded" organisms behave like man when they are given access to drugs of dependence indicates that compulsive self-administration is a relatively simple form of reflex action (operant reflex), eliminating the necessity to postulate needs or disorders peculiar to the mind of man. Second, the fact that for practical purposes all animals that are given the opportunity to take the major drugs of dependence will develop steady self-administration behavior indicates that any individual differences in susceptibility which may exist in this regard are of secondary import when drugs are freely available to subjects who do not have other strong competing behaviors. Third, that animals who have passively received dependence-producing drugs[30] show no more of a tendency to take drugs than naive animals indicates that it is the act of self-administration and not the simple experience of a drug effect which is the critical factor in the generation of drug-seeking behavior.

Analysis of the mechanism through which the major drugs of dependence induce self-administration behavior has barely begun. A reasonable working hypothesis is that all these compounds may have in common the ability to stimulate the subcortical structures mediating the effects of other reinforcers such as food and water, perhaps through the release of specific neurotransmitters. Recently, it has been shown that a number of narcotic analgesics of different chemical families all produce a partial depletion of brain norepinephrine and that this effect shows the pattern of pharmacological properties of the specific actions of morphine-like drugs.[31]

There is reason to conclude at this point that the possibilities of laboratory analysis of self-administration behavior in infra-human organisms and its underlying physiology offer good promise for our further understanding of human drug dependence and for our ability to achieve its effective control.

REFERENCES

1. ARCHER, S., AND HARRIS, L. S.: Narcotic antagonists. In Jucker, E. (Ed.): *Progress in Drug Research.* Basel, Birkhäuser Verlag, 1965, pp. 261-320.
2. BLUMBERG, H.; DAYTON, H. B.; GEORGE, M., AND RAPAPORT, D. N.:

N-allyl-noroxymorphone: a potent narcotic antagonist. *Fed Proc,* 20:311, 1961.

3. BLUMBERG, H.; DAYTON, H. B., AND WOLF, P. S.: Counteraction of narcotic antagonist analgesics by the narcotic antagonist naloxone. *Proc Soc Exp Biol Med, 123*:755-758, 1966.

4. BLUMBERG, H.; WOLF, P. S., AND DAYTON, H. B.: Comparison of narcotic antagonists naloxone and levallorphan in counteraction of narcotic antagonist analgesics. *Pharmacologist, 9*:231, 1967.

5. DENEAU, G. A., AND SEEVERS, M. H.: Addendum, Minutes of the Committee on Drug Addiction and Narcotics, NAS-NRC, Washington, D. C., 1959.

6. EDDY, N. B.: The chemopharmacological approach to the addiction problem. *Public Health Rep, 78*:673-680, 1963.

7. EDDY, N. B.; HALBACH, H., AND BRAENDEN, O. J.: Synthetic substances with morphine-like effect. Relationship between analgesic action and addiction liability, with a discussion of the chemical structure of addiction-producing substances. *Bull WHO, 14*:353-402, 1956.

8. EDDY, N. B.; HALBACH, H., AND BRAENDEN, O. J.: Synthetic substances with morphine-like effect. Clinical experience: potency, side-effects, addiction liability. *Bull WHO, 17*:569-863, 1957.

9. FRASER, H. F., AND ISBELL, H.: Human pharmacology and addiction liabilities of phenazocine and Levophenacylmorphinan. *Bull Narcot, 12*:15-23, 1960.

10. FRASER, H. F., AND ROSENBERG, D. E.: Studies on the human addiction liability of 2'-hydroxy-5,9-dimethyl-2-(3,3-dimethylallyl)-6,7-benzomorphan (Win 20,228): a weak narcotic antagonist. *J Pharmacol Exp Ther, 143*:149-156, 1964.

11. HARRIS, L. S.: Narcotic antagonists in the benzomorphan series. Respiratory, cardiovascular and behavioral effects in dogs. *Arch Exp Pathol Pharm, 248*:426-436, 1964.

12. HARRIS, L. S., AND PIERSON, A. K.: Some narcotic antagonists in the benzomorphan series. *J Pharmacol Exp Ther, 143*:141-148, 1964.

13. HOLTZMAN, S. G., AND VILLARREAL, J. E.: Morphine dependence and body temperature in rhesus monkeys. *J Pharmacol Exp Ther, 166*:125-133, 1969.

14. IRWIN, S., AND SEEVERS, M. H.: Acute and antagonistic effects of nalorphine in the monkey. *Fed Proc, 13*:369, 1954.

15. ISBELL, H., AND FRASER, H. F.: Addiction to analgesics and barbiturates. *Pharmacol Rev, 2*:355-397, 1950.

16. JASINSKI, D. R.; MARTIN, W. R., AND HAERTZEN, C. A.: The human pharmacology and abuse potential of N-allylnoroxymorphone (naloxone). *J Pharmacol Exp Ther, 157*:420-426, 1967.

17. JASINSKI, D. R.; MARTIN, W. R., AND SAPIRA, J. D.: Antagonism of the subjective, behavioral, pupillary, and respiratory depressant effects of cyclazocine by naloxone. *Clin Pharmacol Ther, 9*:215-222, 1968.

18. JASINSKI, D. R.; MARTIN, W. R., AND HOEDTKE, R.: Reported to the Committee on Problems of Drug Dependence, NAS-NRC, Washington, D. C., 1969.

19. KEATS, A. S., AND TELFORD, J.: Studies of analgesic drugs. VIII. A narcotic antagonist analgesic without psychotomimetic effects. *J Pharmacol Exp Ther*, 143:157-164, 1964.

20. KOSTERLITZ, H. W., AND WATT, A. J.: Kinetic parameters of narcotic antagonists, with particular reference to N-allylnoroxymorphone (naloxone). *Brit J Pharmacol*, 33:266-276, 1968.

21. KRUEGER, H.; EDDY, N. B., AND SUMWALT, M.: The pharmacology of the opium alkaloids. *Public Health Rep* (Suppl. 165), Parts I and II, 1941 and 1943.

22. LASAGNA, L.; DEKORNFELD, T. J., AND PEARSON, J. W.: The analgesic efficacy and respiratory effects in man of a benzomorphan "narcotic antagonist." *J Pharmacol Exp Ther*, 144:12-16, 1964.

23. LIGHT, A. B., AND TORRANCE, E. G.: Opium addiction. VIII. The effects of intramuscular and intravenous administration of large doses of morphine to human addicts. *Arch Intern Med* (*Chicago*), 44:376-394, 1929.

24. MARTIN, W. R.: Opioid antagonists. *Pharmacol Rev*, 19:463-521, 1967.

25. MARTIN, W. R.; WIKLER, A.; EADES, C. G., AND PESCOR, F. T.: Tolerance to and physical dependence on morphine in rats. *Psychopharmacologia* (*Berlin*), 4:247-260, 1963.

26. MARTIN, W. R.; FRASER, H. F.; GORODETZKY, C. W., AND ROSENBERG, D. E.: Studies of the dependence producing potential of the narcotic antagonist 2-cyclopropylmethyl-2'-hydroxy-5,9-dimethyl-6,7-benzomorphan (cyclazocine, Win 20, 740. ARC II-C-3). *J Pharmacol Exp Ther*, 150:426-436, 1965.

27. MARTIN, W. R.; GORODETZKY, C. W., AND McCLANE, T. K.: An experimental study in the treatment of narcotic addicts with cyclazocine. *Clin Pharmacol Ther*, 7:455-465, 1966.

28. MARTIN, W. R.; JASINSKI, D. R.; SAPIRA, J. D.; FLANARY, H. G.; VAN HORN, G. D.; THOMPSON, A. K.; LOGAN, C. R., AND KELLY, D. A.: Reported to the Committee on Problems of Drug Dependence, NAS-NRC, Washington, D. C., 1967.

29. MELLET, L. B., AND WOODS, L. A.: Analgesia and Addiction. In Jucker, E. (Ed.): *Progress in Drug Research*. Basel, Birkhäuser Verlag, 1965, p. 155-267.

30. NICHOLS, J. R.: How opiates change behavior. *Sci Amer*, 212:80-88, 1965.

31. RETHY, C. R.; SMITH, C. B., AND VILLARREAL, J. E.: Effects of narcotic analgesics upon the locomotor activity and brain catecholamine content of the mouse (Abstract). *Fed Proc*, 29, 685, 1970.

32. SANDOVAL, R. G., AND WANG, R. I. H.: Tolerance and dependence on pentazocine. *New Eng J Med*, 280:1391-1392, 1969.

33. SCHUSTER, C. R., AND THOMPSON, T.: Self administration and behavioral dependence on drugs. *Ann Rev Pharmacol,* 9:483-502, 1969.
34. SCHUSTER, C. R., AND VILLARREAL, J. E.: Experimental analysis of opioid dependence. In Efron, D. H. (Ed.): *Psychopharmacology— A Review of Progress 1957-1967.* Washington, U. S. Government Printing Office, 1968, pp. 811-828.
35. SCHUSTER, C. R., AND WOODS, J. H.: The reinforcing properties of morphine, cocaine and SPA as functions of unit dose. *Int J Addict,* 3:223-230, 1968.
36. SEEVERS, M. H.: Laboratory approach to the problem of addiction. In Livingston, R. B. (Ed.): *Narcotic Drug Addiction Problems.* Washington, U. S. Government Printing Office, 1963, pp. 101-114.
37. SEEVERS, M. H., AND DENEAU, G. A.: Physiological aspects of tolerance and physical dependence. In Root, W. S., and Hofmann, F. G. (Ed.): *Physiological Pharmacology,* vol. 1. New York, Academic Press, 1963, pp. 565-640.
38. SMALL, L. F.; EDDY, N. B.; MOSETTIG, E., AND HIMMELSBACH, C. K.: Studies on drug addiction. With special reference to chemical structure of opium derivatives and allied synthetic substances and their physiological action. *Public Health Rep* (Suppl. 138), 1938.
39. SONNEDECKER, G.: Emergence and concept of the addiction problem. In Livingston, R. B. (Ed.): *Narcotic Drug Addiction Problems.* Washington, U. S. Government Printing Office, 1963, pp. 14-22.
40. TATUM, A. L., AND SEEVERS, M. H.: Theories of drug addiction. *Physiol Rev,* 11:107-121, 1931.
41. TELFORD, J.; PAPADOPOULOS, C. N., AND KEATS, A. S.: Studies of analgesic drugs. VII. Morphine antagonists as analgesics. *J Pharmacol Exp Ther,* 133:106-116, 1961.
42. UNNA, K.: Antagonistic effect of N-allyl-normorphine upon morphine. *J Pharmacol Exp Ther,* 79:27-31, 1943.
43. VILLARREAL, J. E.: Recent advances in the pharmacology of morphine-like drugs. In *Advances in Mental Science. vol. 2 Drug Dependence.* Houston, University of Texas Press, 1969.
44. VILLARREAL, J. E., AND SEEVERS, M. H.: Addendum, Minutes of the Committee on Problems of Drug Dependence, NAS-NRC, Washington, D. C., 1969.
45. WIKLER, A.: Recent progress in research on the neurophysiological basis for morphine addiction. *Amer J Psychiat,* 105:329-338, 1948.
46. WIKLER, A.: Opiates and opiate antagonists. A review of their mechanism of action in relation to clinical problems. *Public Health Monograph No. 52.* Washington, U. S. Government Printing Office, 1958.
47. WIKLER, A.; FRASER, H. F., AND ISBELL, H.: N-Allylnormorphine: effects of single doses and precipitation of acute "abstinence

syndromes" during addiction to morphine, methadone, or heroin in man (postaddicts). *J Pharmacol Exp Ther, 109*:8-20, 1953.

48. WOODS, L. A.: The pharmacology of nalorphine (N-allylnormorphine). *Pharmacol Rev, 8*:175-198, 1956.

49. ZAKS, A.; FINK, M., AND FREEDMAN, A. M.: Reported to the Committee on Problems of Drug Dependence, NAS-NRC, Washington, D. C., 1969.

Chapter Six

SOME IMPLICATIONS OF CONDITIONING THEORY FOR PROBLEMS OF DRUG ABUSE

ABRAHAM WIKLER

T HOUGH FORTUNATELY SOME members of the human race are, at times, more than "creatures of habit," it would be a serious mistake to underestimate the role of conditioning factors in shaping our responses to particular events and much of our so-called voluntary behavior, including the rationailzations we offer to prove that our "choices" are the result of cognitive deliberation. Indeed, the power of what we call "conditioning" today has been recognized from antiquity—witness the old adage, "Whose bread I eat, his song I sing," or its variants in other languages. Were infrahuman species able to speak, it might be most embarrassing to hear them "explain" the odd behaviors which we, the experimenters, have induced by conditioning. No doubt, we would find that they, too, have ideologies, cults, emotionally-laden slogans and, perhaps, political parties. Were we to argue that their behavior had been shaped, as in man, by specifiable conditioning factors, they might very well reply, "Animals are not men," just as some men have argued, in reverse, that "Man is not an animal."

Among the oddities of human behavior that may be explained, in part, by conditioning theory is the recurrent emergence of drug using subcultures. The qualification, "may," is used here advisedly because experimental proof that what are essentially social phenomena have come about through conditioning is very difficult to adduce, and indeed, this has not yet been attempted in connection with drug abuse. Nevertheless, scientific theories are of value, not only in making new, objectively demonstrable discoveries, but also in understanding and dealing with problems that cannot be analyzed experimentally.

Perhaps the most obvious way in which conditioning plays a role in drug abuse is through "primary reinforcement." In the animal laboratory, or in the circus, the trainer induces "needs" which permit him to reward specific behaviors selectively, so that the animal 'emits" a behavior under the desired conditions with a high degree of probability. Thus, he may deprive an animal of food, water, or sex, and then provide a bit of food, water, or sex whenever the animal, spontaneously or through the trainer's manipulations, happens to do the "right" thing. Or the trainer may deliver electric shocks to the animal, withholding them only when the animal performs "correctly." In these ways, animals can acquire habits that distinguish them from their confrères under "natural" conditions. Getting an animal to abuse drugs is ordinarily more difficult, though some monkeys will intoxicate themselves with amphetamine, cocaine, or morphine repeatedly when they are merely provided with a lever-pressing or panel-pushing device which, if activated, injects these drugs through a previously inserted intravenous catheter; also, some monkeys will drink alcohol to the point of unconsciousness if only offered the opportunity.[1] Even in animals that reject morphine initially, "voluntary" acceptance of this drug can be induced by first making the animal physically dependent by repeated injections of morphine and then training the animal to suppress the abstinence distress that ensues when the drug is withheld by forced drinking of morphine solutions.[2] Such an acquired habit may outlast any objectively demonstrable "need" for the drug following complete and permanent withdrawal.

In our affluent society, means other than drugs are usually available for satisfying such biological "needs" as hunger and thirst and, to a lesser extent, relief from pain. Sex is still a problem, though I understand the youth of today are making a concerted effort to solve it. Peculiar to man, however, are "needs," perhaps biological in orgin, but strongly influenced by social conditions, such as the "needs" for identity, status in society, curbing or facilitating aggression, avoidance of boredom and, I have come to suspect, relief from the intellectual strain of maintaining "objectivity" despite frustration. Because of their specific pharmacological properties, various drugs are able to satisfy or appear to the user to satisfy one or another of these special human "needs." The oldest drug of all, alcohol, and the more recently developed barbiturates and some of the so-called "minor tranquilizers" can produce states of intoxication characterized by release of inhibitions on aggression. Morphine and other opiates rather reduce aggression (unless the habitual user is driven by abstinence distress) as well as hunger, pain, fatigue, sexual desire, and fantasy (De Quincey and Coleridge to the contrary notwithstanding). Amphetamine and its congeners, and cocaine reduce hunger and fatigue, and can produce a state of elation. Tetrahydrocannabinol (the presumed active principle in manihuana), mescaline, LSD, and many other hallucinogenic drugs[3, 4, 5, 6] can distort perception, intensify fantasy, and at least in the case of LSD, restore orienting responses to stimuli that had been extinguished in consequence of the failure of these stimuli to signify anything of importance to the organism[7, 8, 9]— all of which can certainly relieve boredom and provide a respite from logical thinking, if nothing else. Depending on his particular "needs" of the moment, a given individual may find the pharmacological effects of one or another of these drugs highly rewarding and report that he feels "unusually well," though he may not be able to explain why in any scientific sense. In contrast, the observer usually applies the term, "euphoric," to describe the subject's drug-altered state, implying thereby that the subject's report of unusual well-being is not justified by his actual condition—in other words, that the subject's judgment has been impaired by the drug. Indeed, accompanying the state of "euphoria," are changes that should give rise to "dysphoria," at least in the opinion of the observer. Thus, alcohol or barbiturate intoxication can produce incoordination, ataxia, slurred speech and profound impairment of mental functioning, as well as a degree of emotional lability that is inconducive to "law and order." Opiates can produce nausea, vomiting, hypotension, "nodding," inattentiveness, and at least slowing, if not gross impairment, of performance on a variety of mental and psychomotor tasks.[10, 11, 12] Amphetamines and cocaine can produce "jitteriness," insomnia, anorexia, cardiovascular dysfunction, paranoid delusions and frightening hallucinations.[13, 14] Marihuana can produce impairment of immediate recall,[15] distortion of time sense, and, depending on dosage and individual predisposition, delusions and hallucinations.[16] Mescaline, LSD, psilocybin, "STP" (DOM) and a number of other drugs can produce changes that, were they to occur spontaneously without benefit of drug or other means of self-induction, would probably alarm the user himself as well as the psychiatrist to whom he would certainly be taken: perceptual distortions, distortion of body image, abnormally low auditory and visual thresholds, synesthesias, visual and auditory hallucinations, paranoid delusions, catalepsy, feelings of disembodiment, depersonalization and derealization.[17] The "psychedelist," however, hails these psychotic reactions as manifestations of "mind, or consciousness expansion," or of a "transcendental experience." How do such seemingly magical semantic transformations come about?

Here, I believe, conditioning factors only indirectly related to the pharmacological properties of the drug in question come into play. Surrounding the use of intoxicants in human society are elaborate rituals and argots that defy pharmacology. Except in the case of the solitary drinker, the consumption of alcohol in our society is highly ritualized, the particular ritual involved being that most appropriate to the tavern, the cocktail party, the dinner party, or the morning airplane flight. Participation in these rituals with appropriate comments on the "smoothness," "body," "bouquet," and other intangibles of the booze, identifies the drinker as "belonging" to the social set in question. "Mainlining" dope, according to the prescribed rules of "addict society" and affirming the "high," "pep," "kick," or "drive" thereby produced, confers membership in that exclusive group to which many of the "big shots" of the ghetto slums also belong. Smoking pot or taking trips on acid in "psychedelic" surrounding opens the "doors of perception," and reveals the universe in its pristine splendor, the way "Adam must have perceived it on the first day of creation,"[18] to the initiates alone, of course.

To belong to any of these drug-using subcultures, it is not enough to use the drug in question, but also to affirm perception of its effects, in the indefinable terms supplied by those who already are members and dispense the drug. That such affirmation will be made by those who have a strong "need to belong" is not difficult to understand, but it would seem that a bona fide "member" actually believes he perceives these effects, whatever they may be. Conceivably, such "brainwashing" could come about through the operation of secondary reinforcement. For example, if a hungry rat is rewarded with a pellet of food for pressing a lever, and the food-dispensing mechanism happens to make a noise whenever it dispenses a pellet, the rat will, eventually, continue to press the lever for the noise alone, without food pellet rewards. Were the rat able to talk, I believe it would "explain" its newly acquired fascination for the noise in language worthy of Aldous Huxley rather than in the prosaic terms of its former association with food pellet rewards. To be sure, the rat would cease to press the lever after some time if food pellet rewards were permanently withheld—that species is certainly a materialistic one. But such is the power of words for man, that their very absurdity reinforces his belief in their truth. "Certum est quia impossibile est" ("It is certain *because* it is impossible") proclaimed Tertullian[19] in the third century AD, and this dictum seems to have become the watchword of those who reject "scientism" to this very day. Viewed from the standpoint of secondary reinforcement, the eternal verities perceived by the drug cultists become understandable ethologically if not pharmacologically.

This essay has been concerned mainly with that variety of conditioning known as "operant" or "instrumental" or ("Type II," in which the behavior to be reinforced by an immediate "rewarding" stimulus is "emitted" by the subject. Another variety is that of "classical" or "Type I" conditioning, in which the behavior to be reinforced is "elicited" by the rewarding stimulus. I believe a single neural model can be constructed to account for both varieties of conditioning, taking into account the functions of the limbic system of the brain; but this is as yet an undecided matter, and need not detain us now. Suffice it to say that there is considerable evidence, principally from animal studies, that some drug effects can be conditioned to previously "neutral" stimuli by repeatedly pairing them. Thus, not only certain direct effects of morphine[20, 21] but also a morphine abstinence sign[22, 23] can be elicited in the dog and rat, respectively, by the physical environment in which these phenomena regularly occurred in the past. Also, "relapse" can be facilitated by such environmental stimuli acting as "secondary reinforcers" in monkeys previously addicted to morphine after withdrawal signs can no longer be detected.[24, 25] It is conceivable, therefore, that in addition to serving as "secondary reinforcers," the rituals and argots constantly associated with use of particular drugs may come, in time, to elicit effects similar to those produced by the drug itself which, if "rewarding" for any of the reasons mentioned earlier, would be "primarily reinforcing" too, and thus facilitate renewed participation in the cult, including drug use. Thus the user would become entangled in an interlocking web of self-pepetuating reinforcers, which perhaps explains the persistence of drug abuse, despite disastrous consequences for the user, and his imperviousness to psychotherapy which does not take such conditioning factors into account because neither the subject nor the therapist is aware of their existence.

In our speculations about the role of conditioning factors in drug abuse, we have been concerned so far with the mutual interactions between the pharmacological effects of drugs and events external to the drug user, of which he obtains information through his "exteroceptors"—the sensory apparatus of his skin, eyes, ears, nose and tongue. Theoretically, it is possible that mutual interactions can also occur between the pharmacological effects of drugs and events internal to the drug user, of which he obtains information, often without awareness, through his "interoceptors"—the sensory apparatus of his viscera, vestibular organs, and in the central nervous system itself. It should be remembered that drugs act on neural structures designed by nature to respond to "physiological" stimuli, and although the patterns of neural activation evoked by drugs usually differ from those evoked by stimuli arising physiologically, one or more elements of these patterns may be shared. It is not inconceivable that frequent pairing of drug-induced and physiological patterns of neural activation may result in conditioning of the former to the latter. That is to say, after a sufficient frequency of drug use, certain physiological stimuli may come to evoke patterns of neural activation that resemble those produced by the drug, or by drug withdrawal in those types of drug abuse in which physical dependence is generated. Such "interoceptive conditioning"[26] could have behavioral consequences similar to those of "exteroceptive conditioning," with the even greater likelihood that neither the drug user nor his therapist would have the faintest notion of what was going on. Probably, both would ascribe the drug user's behavior under these circumstances to "anxiety," and possibly this is as good a term as any to conceal our ignorance about the murky goings-on in the "unconscious" in the absence of any visible reason for seemingly irrational behavior.

While these ideas are admittedly speculative, they can be reduced to "models" that may be tested experimentally in animals, and should they be validated for infrahuman species, they would gain more plausibility for man. Though difficult to carry out, more research on the interactions between the pharmacological effects of drugs and conditioning factors, both "exteroceptive" and "interoceptive," could lead not only to better undersanding of the genesis of drug abuse, but also to more rational methods of coping with the problem. For example, it is not beyond the realm of possibility that new drugs could be synthesized that block the "primary" reinforcing effects of drugs of abuse and, as such, could be employed, together with appropriate conditioning procedures, to hasten extinction of drug-seeking behavior. Indeed, for the opiates, such specific "antagonists" are already available (though they have some drawbacks), and one of them, cyclazocine, is currently being tried on a small scale in the postwithdrawal treatment of narcotic addicts.[27] Perhaps some day we will have antagonists for alcohol (disulfiram, or Antabuse®, is *not* a specific antagonist for alcohol in the sense used here!), barbiturates, amphetamines, cocaine, marihuana, LSD, and other hallucinogens. While, because of the "power of words," pharmacological intervention coupled with extinction procedures will probably not be sufficient to solve the problem of drug abuse, their application could help make educational and social measures more effective. It is to be hoped that although efforts in the directions of education and social ameliora- tion can and should be expanded, the need for expansion of basic laboratory research on problems of drug abuse will not be neglected because of the admittedly urgent need for "doing something now" in the ghettos, on the campuses, and wherever else drug-abusing subsocieties forgather.

SUMMARY

Viewed from the standpoint of conidtioning theory, the development of drug cults appears to be based initially on "primary reinforcement" attributable to interactions between specific human needs and specific pharmacological effects of certain psychoactive agents, and later on the process of "secondary reinforcement" through temporal contiguity between "primary reinforcement" and sets of rituals and mystical beliefs about drug effects that are supplied by those who already are cult- members and dispense the drugs. The observable effects of drugs of abuse in man are reviewed, and illustrations of the processes of "primary" and "secondary" reinforcement in animal experimentation are given. The possible role of "interoceptive" conditioning in maintaining drug-using behavior is also discussed. Some therapeutic applications of conditioning theory are in- dicated, with special reference to the possible use of drug-specific antagonists to facilitate extinction of drug-seeking behavior. Expansion of basic psychopharmacological research, as well as of educational and social ameliorative efforts are stressed as desiderata for eventual control of the problem of drug abuse.

REFERENCES

1. YANAGITA, T.; DENEAU, G. A., AND SEEVERS, M. H.: Evaluation of pharmacological agents in the monkey by long term intravenous self or programmed administration. In *Proc Union Physiol Sci (23rd International Congress, Tokyo, Japan)*, 4:453-457, 1965.

2. NICHOLS, J. R.; HEADLEE, C. P., AND COPPOCK, H. W.: Drug addiction. 1. Addiction by escape training. *J Amer Pharm Ass*, 45:788-791, 1956.

3. ISBELL, H., AND JASINSKI, D. R.: A comparison of LSD-25 with (-) $\triangle^9$-

trans-tetrahydrocannabinol (THC) and attempted cross-tolerance between LSD and THC. *Psychopharamacologia (Berlin)*, *14*:115-123, 1969.

4. HOLLISTER, L. E.; RICHARDS, R. K., AND GILLESPIE, H. K.: Comparison of tetrahydrocannabinol and synhexyl in man. *Clin Pharmacol Ther*, *9*:783-791, 1968.

5. WIKLER, A.: Clinical and electroencephalographic studies on the effects of mescaline, N-allylnormorphine and morphine in man. *J New Ment Dis*, *120*:157-175, 1954.

6. SNYDER, S. H.; FAILLACE, L., AND HOLLISTER, L.: 2-5-dimethoxy-4-methyl amphetamine (STP): a new hallucinogenic drug. *Science*, *158*:669-670, 1967.

7. KEY, B. J., AND BRADLEY, P. B.: The effects of drugs on conditioning and habituation to arousal stimuli in animals. *Psychopharmacologia (Berlin)*, *1*:450-462, 1960.

8. KEY, B. J.: The effect of LSD on the interaction between conditioned and non-conditioned stimuli in a simple avoidance situation. *Psychopharmacologia (Berlin)*, *6*:319-326, 1964.

9. KEY, B. J.: Alterations in the generalization of visual stimuli induced by lysergic acid diethylamide in cats. *Psychopharmacologia (Berlin)*, *6*:327-337, 1964.

10. BAUER, R. D., AND PEARSON, R. G.: The effects of morphine-nalorphine mixtures on psychomotor performance. *J Pharmacol Exp Ther*, *117*:258-264, 1956.

11. SMITH, G. M., AND BEECHER, H. K.: Measurement of "mental clouding" and other subjective effects of morphine. *J Pharmacol Exp Ther*, *126*:50-62, 1959.

12. SMITH, G. M.; SEMKE, C. W., AND BEECHER, H. K.: Objective evidence of mental effects of heroin, morphine and placebo in normal subjects. *J Pharmacol Exp Ther*, *136*:53-58, 1962.

13. CONNELL, P. H.: *Amphetamine Psychosis*. London, Chapman and Hall, Ltd., 1958.

14. WIKLER, A.: Drug addiction. In Baker, A. B. (Ed.): *Clinical Neurology*, 2nd ed. *2*:1054-1083, 1962.

15. WEIL, A. T., AND ZINBERG, N. E.: Acute effects of marihuana on speech. *Nature*, *222*:434-437 (May 3) 1969.

16. WILLIAMS, E. G.; HIMMELSBACH, C. K.; WILKER, A.; RUBLE, D. C., AND LLOYD, B. J.: Studies on marihuana and pymbexyl compound. *Public Health Rep*, *61*:1059-1083, 1946.

17. WIKLER, A.: *The Relation of Psychiatry to Pharmacology*. Baltimore, Williams & Wilkins, 1957.

18. HUXLEY, A.: *The Doors of Perception*. New York, Harper Brothers, 1954.

19. *The Oxford Dictionary of Quotations*, 2nd ed. New York, Oxford University Press, 1955, p. 542:4.

20. COLLINS, K. H., AND TATUM, A. L.: A conditioned reflex established by chronic morphine poisoning. *Amer J Physiol,* 74:14-15, 1925.

21. KLEITMAN, N., AND CRISLER, G.: A quantitative study of a salivary conditioned reflex. *Amer J Physiol,* 79:571-614, 1927.

22. WIKLER, A., AND PESCOR, F. T.: Classical conditioning of a morphine-abstinence phenomenon, reinforcement of opioid-drinking behavior and "relapse" in morphine-addicted rats. *Psychopharmacologia (Berlin),* 10:255-284, 1967.

23. GOLDBERG, S. R., AND SCHUSTER, C. R.: Conditioned suppression by a stimulus associated with nalorphine in morphine-dependent monkeys. *J Exp Anal Behav,* 10:235-242, 1967.

24. THOMPSON, T., AND OSTIUND, W.: Susceptibility to readdiction as a function of the addiction and withdrawal environments. *J Comp Physiol Psychol,* 60:388-392, 1965.

25. SCHUSTER, C. R., AND VILLARREAL, J. E.: The experimental analysis of opioid dependence. In: Psychopharmacology. In Efron, D. H. (Ed.): *A Review of Progress 1957-1968. Proceedings of the Sixth Annual Meeting of the American College of Neuropsychopharmacology. Public Health Service Publication No. 1836.* Washington, U. S. Government Printing Office, 1968, pp. 811-828.

26. BYKOV, K. M., AND GANTT, W. H.: *The Cerebral Cortex and the Internal Organs.* New York, Chemical Publishing Co., 1957.

27. MARTIN, W. R.; GORODETZKY, C. W., AND McCLANE, T. K.: An experimental study in the treatment of narcotic addicts with cyclazocine. *Clin Pharmacol Ther,* 7:455-465, 1966.

Chapter Seven

THE SEDUCTION THRESHOLD AS A CONCEPT FOR PROPHYLAXIS OF DRUG ABUSE

PAUL H. BLACHLY

T HE PURPOSE OF THIS presentation is to enable you to (1) identify persons and situations vulnerable to drug abuse (and other self-destructive activities), and (2) to intervene so as to decrease this vulnerability. The emphasis will be on prevention rather than treatment after the damage has occurred.

We have found it useful to consider drug abuse as one of the seductive behaviors. Seductive behaviors have the following four qualities:

1. The victim actively participates in his own victimization.
2. Negativism. (He knows the danger, but does it anyway.)
3. Short-term gain.
4. Long-term penalty.

Seduction is not persuasion. For our purposes, seduction is something you do to yourself. Within this framework, seductions may be diagrammed in the following three-hump graph (Fig. 7-1): The first hump is the hustle hump. It is the investment necessary to achieve the reward. Though a form of punishment, the hustle is coupled with anticipatory pleasure of the reward to follow. The specific reward depends on the kind of seduction; it may be the euphoria or relief of abstinence pain of the heroin addict, the increased buying power of the embezzler, or the relief of anxiety by the person paying off the blackmailer. The punishment may be the reappearance at an augmented level of all the symptoms that the hustle was intended to eliminate, be they hunger for drugs, financial need, or anxiety. The punishment is

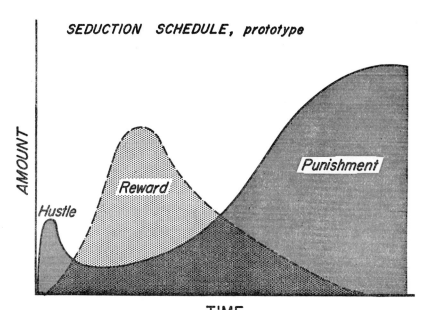

FIGURE 7-1.

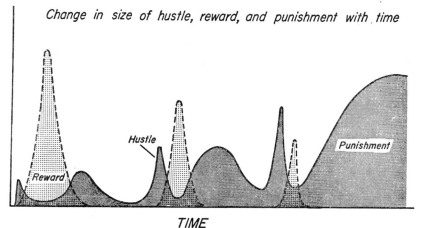

FIGURE 7-2.

intensified by the memory of the previous reward and what rewards might happen again, thus setting the stage for the next cycle of seduction. Aesop's fable of the boy who called wolf illustrates the recurring cycles of seduction, as seen in Figure 7-2.

The following types of behavior are included in the seductions: drug abuse, sex deviations, truancy, rape, robbery, smoking, rioting, gambling, alcoholism, and divorce. Criminal law was developed by society to deal with persons engaging in the seductive behaviors. Common knowledge reveals that persons engaged in one seduction are likely to be involved in others.

Some illustrations may help solidify the general concept of seduction. Cigarette smoking with a relatively low intensity hustle and reward and a very delayed punishment may be considered at one end of the spectrum (Fig. 7-3). At the other end of the spectrum, we have seductions of high intensity reward and punishment occurring over a short span of time, such as methedrine use, armed robbery, or rape (Fig. 7-4). And there are special forms such as suicide (Fig. 7-5).

The implications of the fact that these behaviors are episodic like robbery, rather than continuous like poverty, have not been sufficiently appreciated. The significance of the episodic phenomenon lies in the fact that we can identify high-risk periods

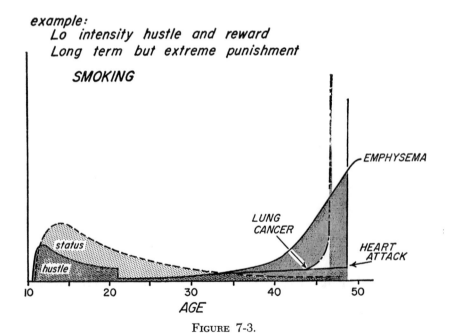

FIGURE 7-3.

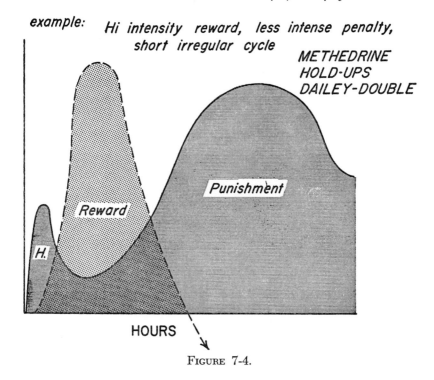

example: Hi intensity reward, less intense penalty, short irregular cycle

METHEDRINE
HOLD-UPS
DAILEY-DOUBLE

Punishment

Reward

H.

HOURS

FIGURE 7-4.

and high-risk people and take appropriate action. The fact that we have all engaged in seductive behavior suggests that it is a universal experience, yet we see that most adults engage in such activities rarely; a few seem unable to avoid them, getting in trouble repeatedly, seemingly unable to benefit from their experience.

Let us consider a concept I will call the *seduction threshold.* The common phrase, "every man has his price," refers to the universality of the seduction threshold, which implicitly recognizes that the "price" varies between people and in the same person at different times. The seduction threshold is the likelihood at any specified time that a person will pursue seductive behaviors. Like a seawall, if the threshold is very high, only the spray from storm waves will get over; but if low, waves will be avoided only at low tide and fair weather. Figure 7-6 diagrams the concept of the seduction threshold for a well-motivated heroin addict during a single day.

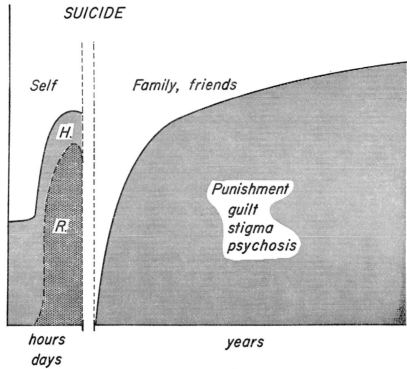

FIGURE 7-5.

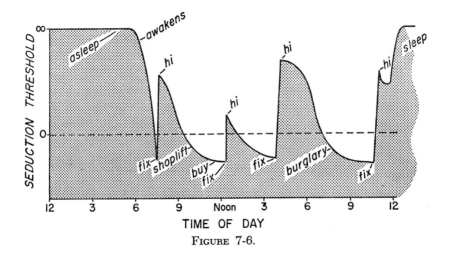

TIME OF DAY

FIGURE 7-6.

HIGH RISK PERSONS AND PERIODS

We now have sufficient data regarding human development to predict both high- and low-risk persons and periods as efficiently as we can predict the weather. And our ability to change behavior may be even more advanced than our ability to change weather. But important now is the fact that if we would but use our presently existing behavioral forecasting ability, we could weather behavioral storms with far less damage than presently exists. Such methodical detailed studies as those of Robins[1] and of Sheldon and Eleanor Glueck[2] at the Harvard Law School conducted over the past four decades convincingly indicate that the pattern for juvenile delinquency* is set very firmly by age six, almost as firmly by age three. The Gluecks even found they could derive a numerical formula for predicting juvenile delinquency using the following five factors:

1. Discipline of boy by father.
2. Supervision of boy by mother.
3. Affection of father for boy.
4. Affection of mother for boy.
5. Cohesiveness of family.

This predictability may be dramatized by considering how we might maliciously and deliberately set about in childhood to grow a person to be a high risk for seductive behaviors. The fundamental rule is to structure the environment so that the child is unable to make any long-range allegiances or predictions; particularly, make it impossible for him to predict the consequences of his own behavior. Operationally, this can be done by first breeding the child to have sufficient energy and drive to react with the environment rather than withdrawing into himself.[3,4] Then raise him (her) by multiple caretakers in a variety of "homes," seeing to it that he remains with no one home or caretaker more than six months. At ages three to five see that the father is frequently drunk, away from home, or capricious. We must emphasize the capriciousness, for if the parent is always unreliable, brutal, drunk, or psychotic, the child

---

* A term which includes multiple repeated seductive behaviors.

will learn to predictably discount him. Greater damage seems to occur when the parent is unpredictably "normal." Meals and bedtime should be at irregular periods and amounts. As he grows older, move two months to a year after he has established friends in the neighborhood. In this way he will have indelibly learned to live for the moment, make no intense or long-term investments in people or course of action. Because his commitments are neither sustained nor intense, he will not experience the intensity of depression felt by persons who develop predictable sustained behavior habits. But, assuming average intelligence, he will have learned the proper verbal responses such as "Yes" or "I'm sorry" to such questions as "You know you shouldn't have done it," for such responses usually result in short-term gain.

In adolescence he should be placed with adults whose predictions are frequently wrong, who say, "You'll be punished if you do that," or "If you're good or work hard you'll be rewarded," but who can predictably deliver neither punishment nor reward.

Consultants

Because of inability to trust persons, the high-risk person has less capacity to benefit from the experience of others. The child who frequently moves must associate with children who are in the same dilemma or those rejected by more stable elements. Thus, advice from seduction prone peers is little better than his own. And "identity," that feeling of comfort stemming from predictable human reference points, may have to be obtained by forcing excessive stimulation or predictable "punishment." Punishment is preferable to nothingness. And rather than no consultation, he will use that of peers. With this background it should come as no surprise that such a person will repeatedly be involved in a variety of the seductions. Proclivity for a single seduction such as burglary or drugs is rare. But the choice of seduction, that which is most commonly practiced, may be in part an accident depending on the fashions of his times and peer consultants.

High-Risk Periods

"He was such a good boy (girl), came from a fine family; no one would have thought he (she) would have got in that kind of trouble." "He (she) used to be such a hell-raiser, in one scrape after another, father was a lush, but he sure turned out well." Such common expressions reflect the everyday observation that a high-risk or low-risk person may drastically change his behavior. Although often attributed to miraculous or idiosyncratic events, careful observation usually reveals that definable changes occurred in the person's environment or internal physiology.

Physiological Influences

Changes in the body's functioning influence both the specific vulnerability and the energy brought to bear on the vulnerability. Normal thirst may whet the pathological appetite of the alcoholic. Normal hunger may increase the chance of theft. Periodic fluctuations of sexual drive alter the probability of rape. Calls by women to a suicide prevention center have been shown to fluctuate markedly, depending on the stage of the menstrual cycle.[5] Unusual vitality increases the chance that one may undertake sports which quickly become dangerous at the onset of fatigue (skiing, mountain climbing, scuba diving). Only persons who have cancer are susceptible to cancer cure hoaxes. The soldier far from home may make a marriage due to high sex drive and environmental deprivation that he would otherwise avoid. Drug dependence becomes a major problem in adolescence in part because narcotic drugs are so efficient in their ability to suppress the primary biological drives.[6] On the other hand, the person coming down with a bad cold is relatively safe from most seductions because of low energy level and unconcern about solving conflict situations; they simply do not matter when he feels so bad.

Environmental Influences

The environment acting upon a background of heightened physiological drive sets the stage for seduction. It is probably impossible to separate the geographic environment from the interpersonal environment, for a change in one usually assures at least some degree of change of the other. But it is common knowledge that a person may take many more (or occasionally many fewer) risks if he is away from his home town. Reno and Las Vegas could not exist were it not for this apparently powerful tendency for some people to seek a change of environment for the excitement of testing their seduction threshold. The greater the hustle required to change the environment, and the harder it is to get there, the lower becomes the seductive threshold. *Whenever the environment becomes unpredictable, the seduction threshold falls.* A country whose national policy seems senseless or unpredictable will experience a predictable increase in all the seductive behaviors. A family experiencing multiple uncertainties, marital, financial, geographic, will produce seduction prone persons.

We may use the concept of seduction threshold by considering in detail a specific person or population over time. We predict the periods of lowered threshold and bring to bear counter measures designed to change the internal physiological factors and the environment so as to raise the seduction threshold. On a broad scale, we know that the seduction threshold is lowered during adolescence, mating, loss of job, menopause, and at retirement, as in Figure 7-7.

We can plot it more specifically, as for the adolescent years shown in Figure 7-8. That children are vulnerable at the points shown is universally acknowledged, but rarely do we take definitive, aggressive, constructive action to minimize the predictable consequences. I submit that the teacher, the physician, the minister, and the police must do more than pick up the predictable casualties. They must take active steps to intervene at the peaks shown in Figure 7-8, which will insure that life becomes meaningful and predictable. You see, drugs, even more than being able to relieve anxiety and depression, are exceedingly predictable.

For seductions already started, we simultaneously attempt to lower all the three humps on the seduction schedule, e.g. providing the teenager with a jalopy so he does not need to

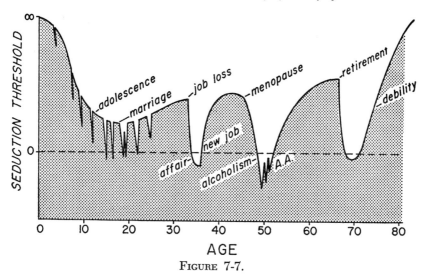

FIGURE 7-7.

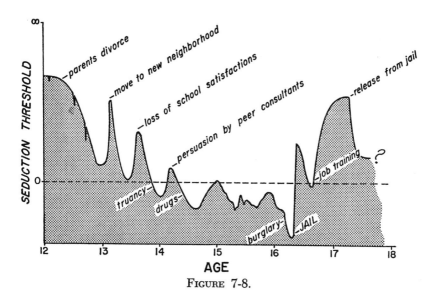

FIGURE 7-8.

steal one, letting the truant get a job, or providing methadone to heroin addicts.

It is no accident that the major turning points in the seduction threshold involve changed interpersonal relationships. Because of their predictable effects, drug pleasures can substitute for people pleasures. But so can the other seductions. Effective intervention, then, involves not only eliminating the humps on the seduction schedule, but initiating predictably satisfying people pleasures that can be sustained.

Prophylaxis of drug abuse will become a reality when society as reflected in the mass media recognizes that seductive behaviors are learned ways of solving problems, used when the seduction threshold is low, and uses its collective influence to maintain a high threshold. It will do this by deemphasizing impulsive problem-solving techniques as seen on television, discourage unnecessary geographic mobility, emphasize personal allegiances, and recognize the social advantage of personal intervention at crisis points.[7]

REFERENCES

1. Robins, L. N.: *Deviant Children Grown Up.* Baltimore, Williams & Wilkins, 1966.
2. Glueck, S., and Glueck, E.: *Ventures in Criminology.* Cambridge, Harvard University Press, 1967.
3. Glueck, S., and Glueck, E.: *Physique and Delinquency.* New York, Harper, 1956.
4. Sheldon, W. H.; Hartel, E., and McDermott, E.: *Varieties of Delinquent Youth.* New York, Harper and Bros., 1949.
5. Mandell, Arnold J., and Mandell, Mary P.: Suicide and the menstrual cycle. *JAMA, 200*:132-133 (May 29), 1967.
6. Wikler, A.: *Opiate Addiction.* Springfield, C. C Thomas, 1953.
7. Blachly, P. H.: *Seduction.* A conceptual model in the drug dependencies and other contagious social ills. Springfield, C. C Thomas, 1970.

Chapter Eight

TODAY'S DRUG ABUSE LAWS AT WORK

SIDNEY I. LEZAK

Over the years I have expressed concern about overreliance on the criminal law in the solution of our drug dependency problems. In looking at the title that was assigned to me, I almost decided to change it to "The Abuse of Today's Unworkable Drug Laws." I have been one of those who talked about putting our emphasis on the commercial trafficker and exercising restraint by police and prosecutors, both as to enforcement efforts and as to sentencing with respect to the user. I am not so sure that the world is going this way. I think that public concern over this problem, and the old American attempt to solve our problems by legislation in the criminal area, are certainly not being abandoned.

We are faced now with one of the great national debates of our times by virtue of changes which are coming in our narcotics laws. I think the best thing that I can do to aid your deliberations here is to give you a brief overview of our present narcotics laws at the Federal level, and then talk with you about the proposed changes which have just been sent to the Congress by President Nixon and the Attorney General. I think those changes are important because they set the framework for the debate which is about to ensue. I am not saying that major legislation will pass at this session, but it will be the subject of discussion for passage at the next session. I think whatever lead the Federal Government takes in this very important area is probably going to set the tone for that which is done at the state level as well, because, in connection with President Nixon's proposals, draft legislation for uniform state laws have also been presented.

Prior to 1968 there were two Federal bureaus which handled

narcotics and dangerous drugs. The Bureau of Narcotics was in the Treasury Department. I think all of you here have read about the historical reasons why the original narcotics laws were passed as taxing statutes—to bring them under the constitutional interpretations then in existence. Next, we had the Food and Drug Administration under the Department of Health, Education, and Welfare, handling legislation with respect to dangerous drugs. In 1968, the Bureau of Narcotics and Dangerous Drugs was established. This Bureau grew from the merger of the two agencies about which I have just talked, and the experience and manjower of both these agencies were welded into a tightly knit unit under the Justice Department. You will recall that the Justice Department is the department for which I work and which also includes the Federal Bureau of Investigation, the primary Federal investigative agency in the criminal area, although there are others. The Bureau of Narcotics and Dangerous Drugs was established to more effectively combat the abuse of narcotics and dangerous drugs. Emphasis has been placed, not only upon enforcement in cooperation with local, state, and other Federal agencies, but also upon education and research. The organization has been tailored to markedly reduce and, hopefully, eventually to eliminate the menace of narcotic addiction and drug abuse as a major social, economic, and medical problem in America.

Primary responsibility of the Bureau of Narcotics and Dangerous Drugs is to enforce the laws and statutes relating to narcotic drugs, marihuana, depressants, stimulants, and hallucinogenic drugs. To achieve this goal the bureau has stationed highly trained agents along the traditional routes of illicit traffic, both in the United States and in foreign countries. Their objectives are to reach the highest possible source of supply and to apprehend the greatest quantity of illicit drugs before they reach the abuser.

Besides enforcing the laws, the bureau also regulates the legal trade in narcotic drugs. This entails establishing import, export, and manufacturing quotas for various controlled drugs. Physicians, pharmacists, and other persons responsible for handling, dispensing, or prescribing narcotics and dangerous drugs may be subject to periodic inspections by bureau representatives.

Such surveillance of legitimate trade insures an adequate supply of drugs for medicine and research, but at the same time helps preclude diversion of drugs into illicit channels.

In an attempt to accumulate up-to-date information regarding the drugs under its jurisdiction, the bureau encourages and sponsors controlled scientific research in the field of drug abuse. This is an extremely important program in that field and encompasses clinical, social, psychological, physical, and biological research. The bureau also calls upon its scientific advisory committee for opinions regarding whether or not certain new drugs should be brought under its control.

The most important type of cooperation between the Bureau of Narcotics and Dangerous Drugs and state and local law enforcement agencies is the free exchange of information and mutual assistance in investigative and enforcement activities— all aimed at stamping out illicit trafficking in narcotics and dangerous drugs. The bureau also provides specialized training in narcotic and dangerous drug control to local, state, Federal, and foreign law enforcement officers at bureau headquarters and by seminars in the field in regions where drug abuse is a major problem. Special training is also provided to college deans and security officers, industrial plant security personnel, pharmacists, and forensic chemists.

Now I want to talk about the present laws because I think that in order to understand what is coming you must know what we have at the present time. The term "narcotic drug" included opium and its derivatives, such as heroin and morphine; coca leaves and its derivatives, principally cocaine; and the opiates, which are specially defined synthetic narcotic drugs.

We have four principal statutes which are enforced by the Federal authorities: the Narcotics Drug Import and Export Act, the Harrison Narcotic Act, the Narcotics Manufacturing Act of 1960, and the Marihuana Tax Act. These laws control narcotic drugs and marihuana. They are designed to insure an adequate supply of narcotics for medical and scientific needs. At the same time, these laws are planned to curb, if not prevent, the abuse of narcotic drugs and marihuana. I want to talk about each of these laws briefly.

First, the Narcotics Drug Import and Export Act. This act

authorizes the import of crude opium and coca leaves for medical and scientific needs in the United States. Import of other narcotic drugs is prohibited. Manufactured drugs and preparations may be exported under a rigid system of control to assure that the drugs are used only for medical needs in the country of destination.

The Harrison Narcotic Act sets up the machinery for distribution of narcotic drugs within the country. Under this law, all persons who import, manufacture, produce, compound, sell, deal in, dispense, or transfer narcotic drugs must be registered and pay a graduated occupational tax. The law also imposes a commodity tax upon narcotic drugs produced in or imported into the United States and sold or removed for consumption or sale. Under the Harrison Narcotic Act, sales or transfers of narcotic drugs must be recorded on an official order form. However, the transfer of narcotic drugs from a qualified practitioner to his patient, and sale of these drugs from a pharmacist to a patient with a lawfully written doctor's prescription, are, of course, exceptions to this requirement.

The Narcotics Manufacturing Act of 1960 develops a system of licensing manufacturers to produce narcotic drugs. It also provides a method to set manufacturing quotas for the basic classes of narcotic drugs, both natural and synthetic, insuring that an adequate supply of each drug will be available for medicine and science.

The Marihuana Tax Act requires all persons who import, manufacture, and otherwise are involved with marihuana to register and pay a graduated occupational tax. No commodity tax is imposed on this drug. However, a tax is imposed upon all transfers of marihuana at the rate of one dollar per ounce, or fraction of an ounce, if the transfer is made to a taxpayer registered under this act. Many of you, no doubt, have read about the case involving Timothy Leary, in which the Supreme Court set aside the major thrust of this act because the persons who were required to register would also be in violation of state law, thus violating their right under the Fifth Amendment to be free from self-incrimination. Accordingly, this law is largely not in use, and emergency legislation has been proposed to put the marihuana law in the same posture as the heroin act, where you are not required to register unless you are within the state law, so that there is no Fifth Amendment question. There are also some rather complex legal questions about the presumptions involved when somebody is in possession of marihuana, as to his knowledge of its being imported, which the Supreme Court felt were inappropriate and which also caused other portions of the act to come into question. Suffice it to say that, under new legislation which is presently proposed, these objections with respect to marihuana are expected to be taken care of.

I will cover the subject of penalties briefly, so that those among you who are not familiar with it can be impressed with just how heavy the penalties are under the Federal laws in this area. Illegal sale or importation of all narcotic drugs and marihuana can mean a penalty of five to twenty years in prison and the possibility of a twenty-thousand-dollar fine, in addition. A second or subsequent conviction carries a penalty of ten to forty years in prison, with a possible twenty-thousand-dollar fine. No probation or suspension is allowed for these offenses. The penalty for all so-called possession type offenses (persons in possession of these drugs illegally) range between two and ten years in prison for the first offense and between five and twenty years for the second offense. For a third or subsequent conviction, the penalty can be from ten to forty years in prison. There can be no probation or suspension of sentence for second or subsequent offenses, although there can be for a first offender. Because of the serious nature of narcotic addiction among young persons, the law establishes special penalties for the sale of narcotic drugs to a minor. I will not go into these matters.

In 1966 special legislation was enacted to allow those violators who are narcotic addicts to return to useful, productive lives. Briefly, the Narcotic Addict Rehabilitation Act provides first for civil commitment of certain addicts in lieu of prosecution for Federal offenses. This means that we can start the case as a civil commitment rather than prosecuting in cases where we have an addict whose Federal crime is caused through his addiction. Second, in the sentencing of an addict who has committed a Federal crime and who has been convicted, the court may sentence him to treatment for a period not to exceed ten years. That would be a pretty serious Federal offense, but one in which the man was nonetheless an addict and in which the court wanted to maintain control over him for a lengthy period of time. Third, is civil commitment of persons not charged with any criminal offense. This is the most common of the commitments under the Narcotic Addict Rehabilitation Act of 1966, although it is somewhat misleading in that many of the people involved are, in fact, persons who have been charged with a state crime but released by state court on condition that they come into our program and accept treatment and rehabilitation. We have made rather substantial use of, and with excellent cooperation from, the Alcohol and Drug Section of the Mental Health Division, who have handled the aftercare program in cooperation with the Federal Narcotic Addict Rehabilitation Act administrators. I have been told that in terms of the number of persons whom our office, which is the screening agency, has sent to the hospitals in Texas and Kentucky for civil commitment, Oregon is second in the country—which is most remarkable for a small state. This activity may decrease because of the establishment by the state of a methadone maintenance treatment program, under which some of the people whom we have been sending to Federal hospitals can better be handled. Nevertheless, the existence of this act creates possibilities for rehabilitation of the offender, rather than just having some of these people serve a life sentence on the installment plan, going in and out and in and out of Federal prisons. We appreciate the discretion with which we have to deal with some of these people under the act. We do not expect miracles, and obviously we are not getting them; but in terms of the percentage of rehabilitation prior to the act, it does appear that the aftercare program and the attention being paid to these people may effect a significant reduction in the number of recidivists.

I want to talk briefly about the present Federal dangerous drug laws, which cover three groups: the depressants, the stimulants, and the hallucinogens. These drugs are controlled under laws known as the Drug Abuse Control Amendments to the Federal Food, Drug, and Cosmetic Act of 1965 and 1968.

They control drug abuse in two ways. First, they provide stronger regulations in the manufacture, distribution, delivery, and possession of these drugs; and, second, they provide strong criminal penalties against persons who deal in these drugs illegally. Thus, all registered manufacturers, processors, suppliers, and others must keep accurate records and inventories and must make their records available to the Bureau of Narcotics and Dangerous Drugs for examination. No prescription for a controlled drug older than six months can be filled, nor can refills be made more than five times in the six-month period. When the Drug Abuse Control Act of 1965 was first enacted, it provided for penalties only for those who were sellers or manufacturers. In 1968, the law was toughened up considerably by providing penalty provisions for illegal possession of dangerous drugs, although it was made a misdemeanor rather than a felony, which is the case for marihuana and the narcotics. In the Federal system, any offense for which the law provides a penalty of more than one year is a felony, even though the judge may impose a lesser sentence. Any offense for which the law provides a penalty of one year or less is, of course, a misdemeanor. The law does provide that an offender who is in "possession" of dangerous drugs can be placed on probation for a first offense and, if he meets the conditions of his probation, the court may set aside his conviction. However, a second offense does not permit the conviction to be set aside, and the increasing offenses provide for increasing penalties. The person who illegally produces, counterfeits, sells, or otherwise deals in dangerous drugs may receive a maximum penalty of not more than five years in prison or ten-thousand-dollar fine. Again, there are special penalties for persons who sell these drugs to minors.

That is the law as it presently stands. In this connection, I note that the President, in his message to the Congress, stated that it has been a common oversimplification to consider narcotics addiction or drug abuse to be a law enforcement problem alone. Effective control of illicit drugs requires the cooperation of many agencies of the Federal, local, and state governments. It is beyond the province of any one of them alone. With these things in mind, I want to quote for you some descriptive material about the new legislation, most of which is supplied by the Attorney General to the Congress, so that you will have an idea of where we stand on the debate as it shapes up in the Congress.

The President stated, after referring to the seriousness of the problem (as did the Attorney General), that the creation of an intelligent legal framework for dealing with the serious problems of drug abuse should be the first order of society's response to the problem. The bill which is presented seeks to provide such a framework for the control of all narcotics and dangerous drugs and would replace many of the present Federal drug statutes. The problem is that, historically, we have drug abuse statutes controlling amphetamines, stimulants, and hallucinogens in one area and the narcotics and marihuana in another, and an attempt is being made now to have a correlated and consistent body of law which will bring all of these together. Thus, the bill would amend very substantially, and eliminate some of, the acts about which I have been talking. However, it will not amend nor replace the Narcotic Addict Rehabilitation Act of 1966, which is the civil commitment proposal. Although the bill contains a number of innovations reflecting current levels of knowledge, it also preserves much of the structure and concept of existing drug legislation. This, of course, has been made particularly desirable as a result of the recent governmental reorganization whereby we now have just one agency, under the Department of Justice, enforcing all of these laws. The proposed legislation contains eight separate titles, and I want to talk about a few of them.

Title II is going to result in the classification of all dangerous substances. This law will be known as the Controlled Dangerous Substances Act of 1969, and under "dangerous substances" will be all of the drugs and narcotics about which we have been talking. They are going to be classified into four separate schedules. These classifications are based upon the most current knowledge regarding the relevant danger of the substance, the patterns of abuse, and the extent of legitimate medical and industrial uses which exist for it. In this fashion, both penal and regulatory controls can be applied with appropriate degrees of severity. Additional flexibility is provided by empowering the Attorney General to alter or add to the list of substances in each schedule pursuant to certain clearly defined standards. I might define those schedules for you because they are important.

Schedule 1 contains substances such as LSD, heroin, and marihuana; and, of course, much of the controversy is going to be about whether or not those are appropriate substances to be contained in the highest and most dangerous schedule. It includes substances which have no approved medical use and are dangerous drugs requiring further research to determine the nature of their effects.

Schedule 2 contains medically important but highly dangerous drugs such as the "Class A" narcotics.

Schedule 3 contains drugs which have a moderate abuse potential and widespread medical use—such as the amphetamines and barbiturates.

Schedule 4 contains medically useful preparations having a low abuse potential, such as combination drugs containing small amounts of narcotic drugs—for example, cough medicine and some of the minor combination drugs containing small amounts of amphetamines.

Title III of the bill deals with registration and record requirements. In addition, this title establishes production quotas for dangerous substances under Schedules 1 and 2, which have the greatest potential for abuse, in accordance with the nation's needs for domestic use and exportation.

Title IV incorporates the present Narcotics Drug Import and Export Act and extends the benefits of these controls to other classes of drugs—the dangerous drugs as we now know them. Special permits will be required to cover shipments overseas and incoming shipments in each instance.

Title V (and this is where the scheduling becomes important) provides the criminal penalties that will be assessed to the various drugs. This title sets forth criminal violations and sanctions which parallel, as closely as possible, penalties available under existing Federal law. Provision for lengthy sentences is retained in the penal structure as a deterrent to illicit drug trafficking.

However, the determination of the optimum sentence structure for drug offenses involves many complex and often conflicting considerations. We must discourage professional criminals from engaging in the lucrative trade in illegal drugs which is particularly victimizing so many of our youth today. On the other hand, we must retain sufficient flexibility to rehabilitate the unfortunate victims of drug abuse and addiction and to distinguish between hard-core criminals and misinformed abusers. The Congress, in considering the bill, is expected to devote special attention to the sentencing structure and to seek and receive valuable assistance from the National Commission on Reform of Federal Criminal Laws, the American Bar Association, the American Law Institute, and others. The Department of Justice stands ready to assist the Congress in every way with this complex and sensitive analysis and evaluation task.

The administrative provisions contained in Title VI of the bill provide for research and education projects under the proposed act. In addition, there are certain sections providing further authority to agents of the Bureau of Narcotics and Dangerous Drugs to carry firearms, make arrests, and serve criminal and civil process.

The new bill contains an interesting provision concerning conviction of a first offender for "possession" of drugs listed under Schedules 3 and 4—that would include amphetamines, barbiturates, depressants, and stimulants. Under the proposed law, after a guilty finding or a guilty plea, the finding would not be entered of record, and the offender could be placed on probation at the discretion of the court. This would be a misdemeanor charge, and if the offender successfully fulfills the conditions of probation, the conviction would never be entered of record. Thus, he need not have a criminal conviction, or its disabilities, hanging over his head. I want to make it clear that this provision does not apply to "possession" of Schedule 1 and Schedule 2 drugs. Of course, I am now talking particularly about the controversy which is going to rage over whether or not marihuana should be included in Schedules 1 or 2 or in Schedules 3 or 4. In other words, the primary effect of including marihuana in Schedule 1 will be (1) that "possession" of marihuana will continue to be a felony rather than a misdemeanor, and (2) that "possession" of marihuana will not have the benefit of the provisions for the conviction not being entered, which conviction for minor drugs under Schedules 3 and 4 will have.

I believe that after you have had an opportunity to study the new bill, you will find a good deal for further discussion. I hope that, in your conference here and in your discussion, you will better prepare yourselves to be able to engage in the informed judgments that, hopefully, are going to merge the national debate into a better system of legislation than presently exists. All of us, by virtue of our being here, are extremely concerned with this problem. I think that those of you who have feelings about this should not hesitate to participate in the debate over what kind of legislation we ought to have. I think those in Congress are expecting to hear from their constituents on this matter. I am delighted that this conference is being held now, at a time when great changes are about to take place in our national legislation, in order that we can do a better job than we have been doing in the control of the abuse of these drugs, in the prosecution of those persons whom we want to handle under the criminal laws, and in the treatment of those who need primarily rehabilitation and assistance.

Chapter Nine

THE GOVERNMENT'S ROLE IN AFFECTING CHANGE IN THE TREATMENT OF NARCOTIC ADDICTION

ROBERT W. CARRICK

Huge UMAN BEINGS, homo sapiens, wise and intelligent enough to dominate the world and send men to the moon sometimes belie the name they have chosen. A catalogue of man's miseries and those he imposes on others might be cause for despair if they were separated from his achievements. To review the history of drug dependency and drug addiction is to study the effects that increased knowledge and changing social values had upon legislation, policy, and treatment. Such a review calls to mind the adage that laws may cause problems greater than the ones they were made to correct.

Laws dealing with the health and welfare of man are usually the result of an expression of concern voiced by individuals and by groups. Such concern is most effective when it is the result of an increased understanding of the problem and is accompanied by a plan for solving the problem.

In the 1800's narcotic abuse as a vice was largely identified with opium smoking and "opium dens." These activities were alien to American concepts of legitimate pleasure. This is illustrated by the following quotation taken from *A True History of White Pine County, Nevada.*

> In 1912 opium smokers were thrown into court. . . . Bessie Moore, a habitat of the *demimonde,* was given a hearing on charges of using opium and having it in her possession. . . . (Officers) captured three men and one woman who were hitting the pipe at A La Heathen Chinese. They got one pound of opium, twenty dollars worth, and two opium pipes and necessary accessories.

Narcotic abuse had more sympathetic acceptance when it was viewed as "medically induced." History reveals that narcotic addiction was prevalent among Civil War veterans who were introduced to morphine when it was prescribed for the relief of pain from injuries or for the suffering of dysentery. Morphine addiction for some years was known as the "soldiers disease." Following the Civil War, patent medicines containing opiates were widely used for treating almost any ailment, including alcoholism and narcotic addiction. The Civil War veterans and the "medical addicts" produced by physicians or by self-medication are not known to have differed greatly from the general population. The few studies available, completed during the late 1800's and early 1900's, show more female addicts than male addicts. The accepted assumption is that the addicts of the ninteenth century were not necessarily antisocial or criminal and included citizens of all economic and social class.

The extent of the use of narcotics during this period remains unknown. It is safe to say, however, that the problem was large, and by the 1890's public attitude began to change. Many physicians were now becoming aware of the destructive nature of narcotic dependence and were voicing these beliefs. Sensational stories in newspapers and in periodicals were calling to public attention the fact that great numbers of people had become addicted. With new information available to laymen and to the medical profession, attitudes toward drug use began to change. However, addicts could still purchase drugs legally and could secure assistance from physicians in maintaining their drug habits. Thus, although aware of the dangers of drug use, existing laws and social practice permitted the addict to maintain his habit legally. As a result, the addict did not need to resort to illegal sources of supply. Drug addiction and criminal behavior were, at this point in time, relatively independent activities.

LEGISLATION: CONTROL OF NARCOTICS

The legislative response to the growing public concern coalesced in legislation to establish legal controls against abuse of narcotic drugs. As early as 1885 state and local police measures were tried. By 1912 every state but one had laws governing the prescribing and selling of opiates. In practice these local and state laws were not vigorously enforced, and narcotics could still be freely purchased without prescription at pharmacies.

The first Federal legislation to control opium use, enacted in 1909 was entitled, An Act to Prohibit the Importation and Use of Opium for Other than Medicinal Purposes. No definition was given to "medicinal purposes," but prohibition was placed on opium for smoking, and the importation of opium and opiates for medicinal purposes was subjected to regulations of the Secretary of Treasury.

The Hague Convention of 1912 established an international obligation to control the domestic market as well as foreign trade in opiates. The famous Harrison Act passed in 1914 was in part legislation to meet this international commitment. The intent of the law was control of the production, manufacture, and distribution of narcotic drugs. It required that drug distribution become a matter of record through a nominal excise tax. Non-registered persons transporting or in possession of drugs were liable under the law. It further specified that only physicians could dispense narcotics and that pharmacists could sell such drugs only on written prescription.

The Harrison Act did not make addiction illegal, nor did it specifically allow or forbid a doctor to give drugs to an addict on a continuing basis. Enforcement authorities tested their interpretation that medically prescribed narcotics to sustain addiction without physical cause was, in fact, illegal. A series of decisions were made by the Supreme Court. The first Supreme Court case, *Webb v. the United States*,[18] ruled against a physician who had prescribed large quantities of narcotics for an addict. The decision was that "drugs prescribed indiscriminately for an addict not in the course of a physical ill but for the purpose of providing the user with morphine sufficient to keep him comfortable by maintaining his customary use did not fall within the exemption provisions of the law." The *Jin Fuey Moy v. United States* case[14] in 1920 reinforced the previous ruling—stating that a physician could not legitimately prescribe drugs "to cater to the appetite or satisfy the craving of one addicted to the use of narcotic drugs." The *United States v.*

Behrman case[17] of 1922 presented a decision which left the interpretation that it was illegal to give prescriptions to narcotic addicts regardless of the doctors' intent. (The court did suggest that had the physician prescribed a smaller dose of narcotics he might not have been subject to conviction!) In the *Linder v. United States* case[15] of 1925 the decision was in favor of the physician. The opinion stated: (addicts) "are diseased and proper subjects for such treatment, and we cannot possibly conclude that a physician acted improperly or unwisely or for other medical purposes only because he has dispensed to one of them in the ordinary course and in good faith four small tablets of morphine or cocaine for the relief of conditions incident to addiction." However, a year later in upholding the conviction in the *Boyd v. United States* case[13] the court said: "regardless of whether the course of treatment given by the defendent is a cure, the question is was he honestly in good faith in the course of professional practice and as efforts to cure disease issuing these prescriptions?"

The Narcotic Drugs Import and Export Act of 1922 was another major step in narcotics control by the Federal Government. This provision extended the prohibition against opium imports and other narcotics including morphine, cocoa leaves and their derivatives. An amendment passed in 1924 made importation of crude opium for manufacture of heroin illegal. Going further, in 1942 Congress passed the Opium Poppy Control Act which prohibits the production of the opium poppy in the United States except under license of the Secretary of Treasury. It should be noted that no license has ever been issued.

The Marihuana Tax Act of 1937 established similar controls and punishment over marihuana to those imposed on narcotics by the Harrison Act. The Marihuana Tax Act requires registration and payment of a gradual occupation tax by all persons who import, manufacture, produce, sell or deal in marihuana. Any person, possessing marihuana without also possessing the required order form was to be detained. Possession was *prima facie* evidence of guilt.

Thus, while the Supreme Court decisions recognized that addiction was a disease and proper subject for medical treatment, they also made it nearly impossible to treat addicts medically on an outpatient basis. As a result the majority of physicians stopped treating addicts. Cut off from both legal drugs and medical assistance, addicts were unable to meet their needs for narcotics and turned to the underworld market.

A comparison could be made between the effort to control narcotics and the effort to control alcohol which resulted from the Volstead Act (Prohibition Enforcement Act). The elimination of the legitimate alcohol market resulted in many giving up alcohol. This was also true of drug abuse, However, alcohol and drugs were still available to those who wished to pay the price. Prohibition enforcement of alcohol focused on the producer, smuggler, and dealer; whereas in the case of narcotic drugs officials tended to concentrate on the consumer of the illegal drugs, the addict. Addicts caught with narcotics in their possession were the major subjects of arrest and prosecution. In 1951 legislation known as the Boggs Amendment increased the penalty for persons violating Federal narcotics and marihuana laws. The amendment precluded suspension of sentence or probation on second and subsequent offenses and made conspiracy to violate the narcotic laws a special offense. The previous ten-year maximum sentence was changed to twenty years with probation suspension excluded. In 1956 the Narcotic Control Act was passed. Penalties were increased or made more inflexible. This Act also made the possession of heroin illegal for any purpose and required persons possessing it to surrender it to the Secretary of Treasury.

The Uniform State Narcotic Act was proposed in a number of states in 1932. Since that date the model act has provided a basis for legislation for forty-seven states, Puerto Rico, and the District of Columbia. The laws of California and Pennsylvania have been called equivalent in scope and effectiveness to the Uniform State Narcotic Act.

Some praise the Federal law and state acts because of their success as control measures. The most vocal critics concede that narcotic drugs lawfully imported and cosigned to registered distributers and dispensers rarely go astray and that the control over smuggled drugs has increased as a result of these laws.

Drug addiction is still, however, a major health and social problem. Today, the need for knowledge concerning the extent, epidemiology, and treatment of drug addiction is a major concern of the public, the states and the Federal Government.

TREATMENT: PROGRAM AND LEGISLATION

The first major treatment effort was made in 1919. With the encouragement of law enforcement and health officials, outpatient clinics were developed by local health departments on an experimental basis. By 1923 approximately forty specialized clinics had been opened throughout the country to provide narcotics to addicts deprived of their drug supplies as a consequence of law enforcement. Allegations that the clinics were handing out drugs too freely, thus spreading addiction instead of curtailing it, lead to the closing of all the clinics by 1924. This action was supported by state and local authorities and by the House of Delegates of the American Medical Association.

The first major Federal program to provide treatment in response to the problem of narcotic addiction resulted from legislation passed in 1929. This legislation authorized the establishment of hospitals for the treatment of Federal prisoners who were dependent on narcotic drugs. Voluntary patients were also authorized admission to these Federal hospitals. The intent of the legislation was multifaceted in that it would provide treatment and rehabilitation of narcotic addicts who were convicted of Federal offenses, would prevent Federal narcotic offenses by treatment and rehabilitation of voluntary patients, would encourage and assist states in providing adequate facilities and treatment for the care of narcotic abusers, and would provide information concerning the cause, diagnosis, treatment, control and prevention of narcotic drug abuse. The Act authorized the construction of two institutions for the treatment of narcotic addicts. The hospital at Lexington, Kentucky, was opened in 1935, the one in Fort Worth, Texas, opened in 1938. Until about 1950 these Public Health Service Hospitals served as the principle resources for treatment of addiction in the United States. Much of the early research in addiction also was conducted at these two hospitals.

Following World War II narcotic addiction again became a major subject of public concern. This period was the beginning of the development of state and community programs. Voluntary hospitalization or self-commitment for treatment was developed in state and county hospitals. In 1952 New York City developed a civil commitment procedure for the treatment of adolescent male addicts at Riverside Hospital. The movement toward treatment was given impetus by the 1962 White House Conference on Narcotics and Drug Abuse. Federal agencies provided funds to assist in the development and evaluation of treatment programs for narcotic addicts. A few of the treatment programs funded by the National Institute of Mental Health were the special parole supervision of narcotic addicts, the use of a halfway house for parolees with a history of addiction, the experimental treatment program in a general hospital directed by a medical school, the use of urine testing to detect drug abuse as a part of compulsory supervision of drug users, and the establishment of demonstration projects in community treatment of narcotic addicts. The Social and Rehabilitation Service funded a demonstration in the use of rehabilitation techniques with drug addicts, and the use of a halfway house in the rehabilitation of drug addicts, and the use of vocational training in treating drug addicts. The Office of Economic Opportunity funded a number of treatment centers in ghetto neighborhoods. The well-known program of methadone maintenance was pioneered in New York City and is now being duplicated in various cities throughout the United States. The self-help movement of the Narcotics Anonymous has not made much headway, but the more comprehensive program of the Synanon Foundation has become established and well-known.

In 1936 the first annual report of the Lexington Hospital reported that the treatment of voluntary patients had not been very effective because most of them left before treatment was completed. This observation was still true after twenty-five years of operation of the Lexington and Fort Worth hospitals. Community posthospital treatment programs for individuals treated at the two United States Public Health Service hospitals were never developed.

Congress was naturally conservative in attempting to legislate compulsory treatment by civil commitment because of the many questions relating to constitutionality and the subsequent legal pitfalls that could come from such a law. In addition, many philosophical objects were raised concerning compulsory treatment by civil commitment. Many psychiatrists expressed doubt that treatment could be effective if the patient were forced to accept therapy. However, follow-up studies indicated that addicts whose institutional treatment was followed by compulsory supervision in the community had higher abstinence than voluntary patients with no community supervision. Examples of follow-up studies are Pescor's 1943 report[7] which concluded that involuntary patients discharged from Lexington hospital on parole or probation had a higher abstinence rate than did voluntary patients. In a twelve-year follow-up study of one hundred addicts, reported in 1966 by Vaillant, it was found that 67 percent of those who received at least nine months of imprisonment or hospitalization followed by a year of parole were abstinent for a year or more, whereas only 4 percent of the addicts hospitalized voluntarily remained abstinent a year after discharge. The study in New York by Diskind and Klonsky[2] reported that 32 percent of 344 supervised addict parolees refrained from drug use during a median period of fifty months.

In June, 1961, California initiated the civil commitment approach to addiction. The New York Arrested Narcotic Addict Commitment Act was passed in 1962. Support for civil commitment for treatment was found in the 1962 California Court's ruling on *Robertson v. California*.[16] The courts opinion in effect says that although addiction itself cannot be punished as a crime, a state can require addicts to undergo treatment for this illness.

Legislation permitting civil commitment for certain narcotic addicts charged with Federal law violations was introduced in Congress in 1964, 1965, and again in 1966. In November 1966 the Narcotic Addict Rehabilitation Act[5] was passed. With this law Congress established a national policy for the treatment of narcotic addicts. The Act represents a view that narcotic addiction is symptomatic of an illness that should be treated and is not a criminal circumstance in itself. The law provides that patients must not only receive inpatient care but that this must be followed by continued supervision, treatment, and rehabilitation in the community. The three basic provisions of the law pertaining to civil commitment are known as Titles I, II, and III. Titles I and III are administered by the Department of Health, Education and Welfare, National Institute of Mental Health. Title II is administered by the Department of Justice.

Titles I and II exclude individuals who are charged or convicted of violence, and of unlawfully importing, selling or conspiring to import narcotic drugs. Individuals who have been convicted of a felony on two or more occasions also are excluded. Individuals who are charged with felonies which have not been finally determined, or who are on probation, or whose sentence following conviction has not been fully served including time on parole or mandatory release are ineligible for commitment under any title of the Act. However, an individual on probation, parole or mandatory release may become eligible if the authority authorized to require his return to custody consents to his civil commitment.

Title I authorizes Federal courts to commit to the Secretary of Health, Education, and Welfare narcotic addicts who are charged with certain Federal offenses who desire to be committed for treatment in lieu of prosecution. Before a patient can be committed for treatment under any of the three titles, he must be examined by two physicians, one of whom is trained in psychiatry, to determine whether he is an addict and likely to be rehabilitated through treatment. Under Title I, if it is determined the person is an addict who is likely to be rehabilitated, he is committed to the Secretary of Health, Education and Welfare for a period of thirty-six months, during which time he may not voluntarily withdraw from treatment. Treatment is first provided in an inpatient facility. When the patient improves sufficiently, he may be conditionally released from inpatient status and placed under supervised outpatient care in his own community. If he resumes the use of narcotics, he may again be placed in the hospital. When the patient successfully completes the treatment program, he will be discharged, and the criminal charges against him will be dismissed. But if it is decided at any time that a patient can no longer be treated effectively, his commitment may be ended and prosecution on the criminal charge resumed.

Title II provides for a sentencing procedure to commit for treatment narcotic addicts who are convicted of a Federal crime. If, in the opinion of the court, a convicted offender is a narcotic addict, the court may place him in the custody of the Attorney General for examination to determine whether he is an addict and whether he is likely to be rehabilitated through treatment. Authority to administer the Title II program has been delegated by the Attorney General to the United States Bureau of Prisons. A special treatment program has been developed at the Federal Correctional Institute at Danbury, Connecticut, for male commitments from geographic areas east of the Mississippi River. Female commitments from the eastern portion of the country are sent to the Federal Womens Reformatory, Alderson, West Virginia. All male and female Title II commitments from geographic areas west of the Mississippi River are committed to special treatment units at the Federal Correctional Institution, Terminal Island, California. The length of time that an individual is committed to treatment under Title II may vary, but may not exceed ten years and in no event shall the period exceed the maximum sentence that could otherwise have been imposed.

After an individual committed under Title II has been treated in the institution for a minimum of six months, he may be paroled to aftercare. A full range of aftercare services are provided and, in addition, he is supervised by a United States Probation Officer. The probation officer as an agent of the United States Board of Parole is responsible for seeing that the conditions of release, as outlined by the Board of Parole are met. Effective coordination of aftercare services necessitates a close-working relationship between the institutional treatment staff, the probation officer and the aftercare agency. Considerable freedom and flexibility are encouraged in institution and aftercare program planning and implementation.

Title III provides for civil commitment of addicts not charged with a criminal offense. The commitment must be initiated by petition to the United States Attorney of the District in which the addict lives. This may be done by the addict himself or by a related individual.

After the United States Attorney has determined that there is a reasonable cause to believe that the person is an addict, he must file the petition with the United States District Court who then may place the addict in custody of the Secretary of Health, Education and Welfare for examination. If examination indicates that the patient is a narcotic addict who is likely to be rehabilitated through treatment, the court may commit him to the custody of the Secretary for a period of inpatient treatment. This initial period of inpatient treatment cannot exceed six months. Following the inpatient treatment, the individual is returned to court where he may be committed to a thirty-six-month period of supervised care within his own community. If the patient refuses to comply or if he again resorts to the use of narcotic drugs, he may be recommitted for additional inpatient treatment or he may be discharged from the program.

The administration, program and facilities to provide this nationwide treatment program have been developed. In the beginning all patients committed for examination under Titles I and III were sent to the two Public Health Service Hospitals located in Fort Worth, Texas, and Lexington, Kentucky. These hospitals have been redesignated as Clinical Research Centers of the National Institute of Mental Health. At the present time, the inpatient phase of treatment is also being provided at these facilities.

Posthospital supervision, treatment, and rehabilitation is being provided in the patient's home community through negotiated cost reimbursement contracts with existing treatment agencies. Inpatient treatment and aftercare are viewed as phases in a single treatment plan. The inpatient phase is more than mere withdrawal from the use of drugs. It is a period of physical restoration and treatment utilizing all of the resources of the hospital. These may include psychiatric treatment, group therapy, social casework, and vocational rehabilitation counseling. Vocational evaluation, work experience both in and out of the hospital and limited vocational training are employed. Patient-led self-help groups are developed. The primary focus of the inpatient phase is the preparation of the individual for his return to the community.

The aftercare agency treatment program begins while the addict is still in the hospital. During that time contact with the family is made, and if needed and accepted, treatment with the family unit is begun. Prerelease plans are worked out for living arrangements. With the patient's participation vocational training and job plans are developed in cooperation with the inpatient facility. The contract agency provides the aftercare services for the patient upon his release and plans for continued community treatment. These services may include individual and/or group counseling, psychotherapy, education and vocational training, employment placement, temporary housing, welfare assistance, and transportation. Many of the services within the aftercare program are provided through existing Federal, state and local agencies. Utilization of all community programs to assist in the rehabilitation of the addict is established policy. Urine surveillance provides for immediate confrontation should the patient revert to drug abuse.

The civil commitment of patients under Title I and III began slowly. During fiscal year 1968, 389 patients were committed under Titles I and III. As of June thirty-first, 1969, an additional 1,847 addicts had been committed. It is interesting to note that the original concept that Title I would be the primary vehicle for civil commitment has not materialized. As of July thirty-first, 1969, 107 addicts were committed under Title I while 2,351 had entered the program under Title III for a total of 2,458 civil commitments. Through July thirty-first, 1969, 665 individuals have been returned to their home communities for post-hospitalization treatment.

Of the individuals committed for examination, 49 percent have been found not suitable for treatment. A very small number of these were found not to be narcotic addicts. The large number of individuals found not suitable for treatment during the examination process is a source of concern. This reflects the fact that it is extremely difficult to motivate addicts to continue treatment after they have withdrawn from drugs. It is also a result of the examination process. Narcotic addicts sent to an institution for a period of thirty days for examination when withdrawn from drugs may quickly lose motivation and find greatly diminished, the pressure that caused him to request treatment. He then, by destructive and disruptive behavior, may truly become an individual that cannot be treated in the institution. The phasing in of contracts with agencies to complete the examination in the local community may to some degree alleviate this problem.

The Narcotic Addict Rehabilitation Branch, Division of Narcotic Addiction and Drug Abuse, National Institute of Mental Health, was organized to develop and administer the services for Titles I and III of the Act. Field offices have been established in New York, Washington, Chicago, Atlanta, San Antonio, and Los Angeles. When the need for community-based treatment arises, the field office staff completes a study of the community to evaluate the extent of the problem of narcotic addiction and to estimate the number of potential patients that will be civilly committed during a twelve-month period. State, local, and private agencies are informed of the need for a treatment agency and are invited to submit treatment proposals. Contracts are solicited on a competitive basis. Proposals received from a community are reviewed, and agencies appearing to have the greatest competency to establish or develop appropriate treatment programs are recommended for contracts. A cost reimbursement contract is then negotiated, and a community agency is assigned responsibility for providing patient care.

There are contractual agreements with one hundred agencies located in ninety-one cities in forty-two states, with a potential treatment capacity for approximately 1,500 addicts. With the growing use of civil commitment, new contracts will be developed in new communities, and existing contracts will be expanded to provide for the rapidly growing number of patients.

The intent of the Department of Health, Education, and Welfare is to provide the total civil commitment treatment process, including examination, inpatient treatment, and aftercare in the community. Efforts to carry out this change to total community have been initiated with the negotiation of contracts with community agencies to provide the examination phase in the community. Eleven community agencies are now providing this service. Several inpatient treatment programs are in the process of being developed. This phase-in to total community care will be accomplished as community agencies are developed and budget limitations allow.

The need for flexibility within the different treatment modalities is recognized. Not all of the narcotic addicts civilly committed will be able to maintain a drug-free adjustment in spite of the impressive array of treatment, vocational, educational, and welfare resources available to him. Therefore, methadone maintenance is being developed as a treatment modality. To meet the requirements of the Act, methadone maintenance will be utilized for a period during which the full play of treatment resources will be brought to bear to assist the individual in changing his life style so that he may make a drug-free adjustment.

Research and evaluation is an ongoing part of the program. Data being collected in each phase of treatment will provide objective information about the effectiveness of the total program and its various components.

The Narcotic Addict Rehabilitation Act of 1966 had an additional title—Title IV. This title originally authorized the Secretary of Health, Education, and Welfare to make grants to states and local governments and private nonprofit organizations for the development of field testing and demonstration programs for the treatment of narcotic addicts and for the training of people to work in such programs. It also authorized the Secretary to enter into jointly financed cooperative arrangements with state and local governments and with public and private organizations to help develop, construct, operate, staff and maintain treatment centers and facilities for narcotic addicts within the states. Title IV of the Act was replaced in 1968 by Public Law 90-574, The Alcoholic and Narcotic Addict Amendments to the Community Mental Health Centers Act. This law authorizes grants to public or nonprofit private agencies and organizations to assist them in meeting the cost of construction and staffing of treatment facilities to provide comprehensive treatment for narcotic addicts in conjunction with the National Community Mental Health Centers Program. The Secretary was further authorized to make grants for developing specialized training programs or materials related to the provision of public health services for the prevention and treatment of narcotic addiction, developing in-service training, short-term and refresher courses with respect to the provision of such services, training personnel to operate, supervise and administer such services, and conducting survey and field trials to evaluate the adequacy of the programs for the prevention and treatment of narcotic addiction within the states. Six grants are operational under NARA Title IV. In July, 1969, ten grants were approved under Public Law 90-574.

In addition to the programs which resulted from the implementation of the Narcotic Addict Rehabilitation Act and Public Law 90-574, the National Institute of Mental Health is expending considerable effort in the area of narcotic addiction and drug abuse research. These studies range from the examination of the basic neurophysiology of drug action to studies of the psychosocial characteristics of the drug user.

A concentrated campaign against drug abuse is being conducted across the country by the National Institute of Mental Health. This effort includes a public service announcement series presented in cooperation with mass media. Every channel of communication is being utilized to reach the widely divergent audiences. The messages which are custom tailored to specific target groups all have one thing in common; they present the facts. It is believed that only a factual campaign can bridge the credibility gap which exists in this area.

It is the task of the National Institute of Mental Health to mount the programs needed to deal sensibly with the many problems of drug abuse. Strategies designed to understand and cope with drug abuse must reflect the dynamic and complex nature of the problem.

SUMMARY

The pendulum has swung its full arc from incarceration to effective treatment. In the early nineteenth century, when narcotics were used indiscriminately in medical treatment and discovered by many as a way to avoid psychic pain and to achieve pleasure, it was looked upon sympathetically but with some concern. Increased knowledge and understanding of the addicting quality of narcotics and increased public awareness caused the pendulum's initial swing in an effort to control drugs through legislation. These laws had both a beneficial and harmful effect. There were still those who would seek chemicals to dull the senses, to find joy, or experience the flash and feeling of well-being. Enforcement reduced the availability of drugs and the illegal market came into being. The manufacturer, smuggler, and pusher found a market with high monetary return. Penalties were increased and quarantine became the order. For nearly fifty years the primary emphasis was on control and incarceration. Without question incarceration is effective to a degree, however, in a world undergoing enormous transition in communications and technology, incarceration is not enough. The availability of new chemicals to dull the senses, create illusions, and assist in the search for utopia has created a changing group of drug abusers. The need for a change in approach to the problem was recommended by the professional community, recognized by the public and effected through legislation.

The pendulum has completed its arc. Research, prevention, and innovative treatment now characterize a major portion of the government's effort to cope with the problem of drug abuse.

REFERENCES

1. CHEIN, I.; GERARD, D. L.; LEE, R. S., AND ROSENFELD, E.: *The Road to H: Narcotics, Delinquency and Social Policy.* New York, Basic Books, 1964.
2. DISKIND, M. H., AND KLONSKY, G.: *Recent Developments in the Treatment of Paroled Offenders Addicted to Narcotic Drugs.* Albany, New York, New York Division of Parole, 1964.
3. ELDRIDGE, W. B.: *Narcotics and the Law.* New York, American Bar Association, 1962.
4. LINDERSMITH, A. R.: *The Addict and the Law.* Bloomington, Indiana University Press, 1965.
5. Narcotic Addict Rehabilitation Act of 1966, Public Law 89-793, Title I, 28 USC 2901-2906; Title II, 18 USC 4251-4255; Title III, 42 USC 3411-3426.
6. O'DONNELL, J. A., AND BALL, J. C. (Eds.): *Narcotic Addiction.* New York and London, Harper and Row, 1966.
7. PESCOR, M. J.: *Follow-up Study of Treated Narcotic Drug Addicts. Public Health Rep,* Suppl. 170, 1943.

8. *Proceedings of White House Conference on Narcotic and Drug Abuse.* Washington, U. S. Government Printing Office, 1962.
9. READ, E. O.: *A True History of White Pine County, Nevada.* Denver, Big Mountain Press, 1965.
10. *Rehabilitating the Narcotic Addict, Report of Institute on new Developments in the Rehabilitation of Narcotic Addiction, Fort Worth, Texas.* Washington, U. S. Government Printing Office, 1966.
11. VAILLANT, G. E.: A twelve year follow-up of 100 New York City addicts. *Am J Psychiat, 122*:727-738 (Jan.) 1966.
12. WINN, M., Project Editor: *Drug Abuse: Escape to Nowhere,* Philadelphia, Smith Kline & French Laboratories, 1967.
13. Boyd v. United States. 271 U.S. 104 (1929).
14. Jin Fuey Moy v. United States. 254 U.S. 189 (1920).
15. Linder v. United States. 268 U.S. 5 (1925).
16. Robertson v. California, No. 55, October Term, 1961 Published, June 25, 1962.
17. United States v. Behrman. 258 U.S. 280 (1922).
18. Webb v. United States. 249 U.S. 96 (1919).

Chapter Ten

DRUG USE AMONG HIGH SCHOOL STUDENTS

REGINALD G. SMART

C URRENT PUBLIC OPINION seems agreed that the use of non-alcoholic drugs has increased rapidly over the past five or six years. Certainly, arrests for possession and trafficking in marihuana have increased greatly since 1963. In 1963 there was one arrest for marihuana possession in Toronto, but this number changed to 360 in 1967 and to 569 by 1968. Some people have wondered whether this change is really due to better police surveillance or to their resources having been freed from a concern with heroin addiction. Some of the change may be accounted for in this way, but probably very little. Aside from police records and certain unsystematic and anecdotal information from teachers and youth workers, there is no solid evidence to support these assertions of change. Until very recently, too, there was no information whatever on the *extent* of nonalcoholic drug use in Canada, so of course trends could not be described at all. My aims in this paper are to indicate what knowledge exists of the extent of drug use in high school and college populations, and to indicate briefly what educational or preventative steps are possible.

In 1968 we began an epidemiological study which attempted to describe the nature and extent of drug use in schools in Metropolitan Toronto. This survey was an effort to determine the frequency of use of all commonly available drugs such as alcohol, tobacco, marihuana, LSD, barbiturates, tranquilizers, and stimulants. This study looked at the distribution of drug use

This paper was presented at Western Institute of Drug Problems, Portland, 1969.

Addiction Research Foundation, Toronto, Canada.

in various grades and for each sex separately; it also looked at various social and behavioral variables associated with drug use. The study was concerned with drug use and not with abuse, addiction, or dependency.

The methods used in this survey were group discussions and anonymous questionnaires. We employed two methods of gathering data for several reasons. First, we wanted to have more than one method of estimating the prevalence of drug use; and second, we used the discussions to provide questions for the questionnaire. At present, no one is certain how reliable data on drug use can be obtained. Questionnaires are typically used, but one is never sure how accurate the information obtained can be. In this study we asked students in the group discussions to estimate the number of drug users among their friends, and in the questionnaires we asked people about their own drug use.

METHODS

Subjects

The subjects in this study were drawn from all areas of Metropolitan Toronto. They were students in grades seven, nine, eleven, and thirteen; both males and females were included. We left out the even-numbered grades chiefly because of the trouble and expense of including everyone. We thought that the odd-numbered grades would be sufficient to cope with.

All six boroughs of Metropolitan Toronto cooperated in this study, as did the Separate School Board and several private Roman Catholic high schools. The schools used in the survey were randomly selected from the total number of high school districts for each borough, and each borough contributed study districts in proportion to their part of the total. We used twenty districts in all. Within each school classes were selected at random from each of the grades seven, nine, eleven, and thirteen until 120 students were obtained. All students who participated did so voluntarily and with the consent of their parents. These students were asked to fill out the questionnaires; however, group discussions were held first.

Group Discussions

Before we began the collection of questionnaire data, we held group discussions, each with six to eight high school students from the same grade. In all, 147 group discussions were held. We hoped to have one group for males and one for females for each grade in each high school district in which we worked, although in a few districts we did not have time for groups. For these groups one half of the students were chosen by their own classmates and one half were chosen at random, out of class lists.

The purpose of the groups was to have students talk freely about their attiudes, feelings, and behavior related to drug use. We hoped to gain valuable information which would allow us to construct a useful questionnaire containing all of the relevant questions about drug use and its associated characteristics. We also hoped that the members of these groups would come to value the research and would convince their classmates to cooperate in completing the questionnaire as carefully as possible. Our last purpose in having group discussions was to have another method of estimating the prevalence of drug use. At the end of the group discussions, each participant was asked to say how many persons of his *own sex*, in his *own class* he knew had used various drugs. In this study, then, we asked people about other persons' drug use and about their own. We thought that this would provide a very good check on the accuracy of the data obtained from the questionnaires.

The group discussions were entirely confidential, no schools or persons were identified during the discussions, and it was made very clear that only the researchers would have access to the material. It was stressed that Addiction Research Association had no connection with school or teachers or police. No teachers attended the group discussions, and most of them were held outside of the school—in community centers for most.

The groups selected by popular vote proved to be more animated than those randomly constructed. In general, the elected groups were more active, sophisticated, and controversial. Most groups were affairs in which members involved themselves intelligently and actively in discussion about drug use among high school students.

All group discussions were taped with the permission of the group members. No individuals or schools were identified in the tape. The leader attempted to remain passive and have the members lead and maintain the discussion. A nonjudgmental approach was taken by the leaders, and anyone was allowed to say what he pleased, except that names could not be mentioned.

Questionnaires

After the group discussions were completed, questionnaires concerning all types of drug use were given out to students in each of the selected classes; of these, 6,447 were completed. These questionnaires were completed in each school on the same day so as to minimize contact between students. Questionnaires were all voluntary, and only students who had the consent of their parents participated. Almost no one who had parental consent refused a questionnaire. The questionnaire covered the following topics:

1. Demographic characteristics, such as age, sex, occupation of parents, etc.
2. Frequency of usage of drugs such as alcohol, tobacco, marihuana, LSD, barbiturates, stimulants, tranquilizers, and opiates.
3. Various attitudes toward drug use and drug users.
4. Sources of information about drugs.

The questionnaires were administered by a member of the research group. No teachers or principals were present, and students were asked not to sign their names so as to retain anonymity.

RESULTS

This study is the largest ever attempted for drug use among high school students. It is the only published study for this age group. The first result of importance is that the two methods of estimation gave almost identical results for marihuana use and, hence, one can have considerable confidence in the data.

Drug Use Rates for the Total Sample

Table 10-I shows the average frequency of drug use for the total sample. The rates are for use during the six months prior

TABLE 10-I

INCIDENCE OF DRUG USE BY GRADE

Percentage of Students Using Drug at Least Once in Last Six Months

Grade	Tobacco	Alcohol	Mari- huana	Glue	Barbi- turates	Opiates	Stimu- lants	Tranquil- lizers	LSD
7	24.6	22.9	2.6	7.2	1.3	1.1	4.3	4.8	1.1
9	44.3	41.6	10.8	9.4	3.9	3.0	9.4	11.4	3.9
11	46.6	59.7	8.9	2.6	4.4	1.8	7.8	11.6	2.1
13	39.7	70.9	7.5	0.7	3.8	1.0	5.6	14.6	3.8
Total	46.3	37.6	6.7	5.7	3.3	1.9	7.3	9.5	2.6

to the investigation. It can be seen that alcohol and tobacco are the most frequently used substances (46.3% and 37.6%), respectively, and that the use of all other drugs is less than 10 percent. Of the illicit drugs, marihuana was used by 6.7 percent of the grade seven to thirteen population and LSD by only 2.6 percent. It should be pointed out, too, that the variation in drug use across the high school districts was very large. Marihuana use varied from 3.19 percent to 11.8 percent, glue sniffing from 1.8 percent to 14.2 percent, LSD from 0.4 percent to 5.3 percent. The smallest variation by district was found for alcohol (40.1% to 60.0%) and tobacco (27.9% to 47.2%). It is clear that rates of illicit drug use vary markedly from one area to another, in a manner quite unlike that of the socially acceptable drugs.

Drug Use Rates by Grade

An expected finding was that rates of drug use would vary substantially by grade. Table 10-I also shows the distribution of drug use by grade. Smoking involves 46.6 percent in grade eleven, and drinking as many as 70.9 percent in grade thirteen. The use of illicit drugs is less frequent, but marihuana use goes as high as 10.8 percent in grade nine and glue use as high as 9.4 percent in grade nine. Opiates, barbiturates, and LSD are used by small minorities of the students.

It can be seen that all types of drug use are less frequent in grade seven than in the other grades. Only glue use is relatively high in grade seven, and even with glue grade nine is the peak. There are several patterns which can be more easily seen from Table 10-I. Use of marihuana, stimulants, opiates, glue, and other hallucinogens (other than LSD and marihuana) is relatively low in grade seven; this usage reaches a peak in grade nine and declines in grades eleven and thirteen. It can be seen, too, that tranquilizers and alcohol are least frequently used in grade seven and increase steadily over the grades to reach a peak in grade thirteen. However, tobacco and, less strikingly, barbiturates show a sort of inverted J curve with the peak at grade eleven, less frequent use in grades nine and thirteen, and very little use in grade seven.

Frequency of Drug Use Among Users

The frequency with which various drugs are used suggests that some are associated with chronic use and others primarily with experimentation. Among all drinkers (Table 10-II) more

TABLE 10-II

FREQUENCY OF ALCOHOL USE

	0	<1	~2	~3	4+	Blank	Total
			Frequency (Times per Month)				
Percent of Students (All Grades)	53.7	24.5	9.3	5.0	7.5	0.0	100.0

than twice as many (33.8%) drank only once or twice per month as drank more than three times per month (12.5%). This is also true for students in all grades, even grade thirteen, where most students drink. A similar but less striking relationship holds for smoking (Table 10-III), as only 14.5 percent smoke as many as

TABLE 10-III

FREQUENCY OF CIGARETTE SMOKING

	0	1-5	6-10	11-20	20+	Blank	Total
			Frequency (Cigarettes per Week)				
Percent of Students (All Grades)	62.2	14.9	4.1	4.1	14.5	0.2	100.0

twenty cigarettes per day and 23.1 percent smoke fewer than twenty per week.

For the drugs other than alcohol and tobacco, those who have used them only once or twice could be called "curious experimenters" and the remainder "regular users." For drugs such as opiates, LSD, other hallucinogens, and barbiturates, the curious experimenters and regular users are similar in number, although not over 2 percent for any drug (Table 10-IV). For

TABLE 10-IV

FREQUENCY OF DRUG USE

| | | Frequency (Times per 6 Months Period) | | | | | |
	0	1-2	3-4	5-6	7+	Blank	Total
Tranquilizers	90.3	6.1	1.4	0.5	1.5	0.2	100.0
Stimulants	92.6	4.4	1.1	0.5	1.3	0.1	100.0
Marihuana	93.1	2.8	1.3	0.7	1.9	0.2	100.0
Glue	94.0	3.7	0.6	0.3	1.1	0.3	100.0
Barbiturates	96.1	1.9	0.4	0.2	0.8	0.6	100.0
LSD	97.4	1.2	0.4	0.3	0.6	0.3	100.0
Other Hallucinogens	97.4	1.1	0.4	0.1	0.4	0.6	100.0
Opiates	97.9	1.2	0.3	0.1	0.3	0.2	100.0

tranquilizers, stimulants, and glue, the experimenters are considerably more numerous than the regular users (Table 10-V). It is only for marihuana that regular users (3.9%) outnumber experimenters (2.8%). This is portrayed in Figure 10-1.

Drug Use Rates by Sex

Table 10-V shows the frequencies of different types of drug use for male and female students separately. It can be readily seen that fewer girls use all types of drugs than boys, with the exception of tranquilizers, which involve slightly more girls than boys (10.4% compared to 8.1%). Also, the ratio of male to female users varies considerably for different drugs. For the more socially acceptable drugs, such as alcohol and tobacco, there are almost as many girls as boys (40.4% and 31.1% compared to 51.7% and 42.9%). The sex ratio is also close to 1 to 1 for psychoactive drugs likely to be given on a prescription basis, such as barbiturates, stimulants, and tranquilizers. However, for the

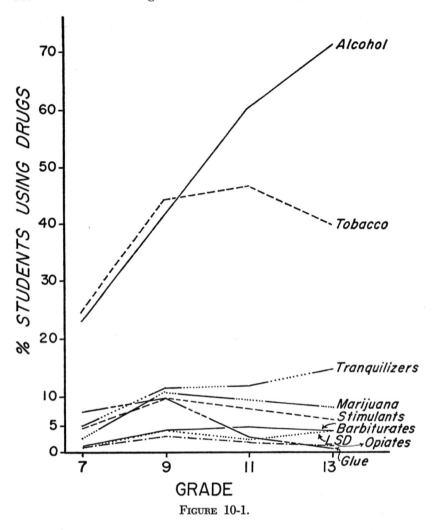

FIGURE 10-1.

newer and more dangerous drugs such as marihuana, glue, and opiates, there are about twice as many boy users as girls; for LSD there are almost three times more male than female users.

The same female caution is also reflected in the frequency of drug use among female users. It was found that female users of alcohol, tobacco, glue, other hallucinogens, and opiates use less of all these drugs than do male users. However, female users of tranquilizers, stimulants, marihuana, barbiturates, and

LSD do not show less frequent use. There is no drug for which female users show heavier consumption than do male users.

TABLE 10-V

INCIDENCE OF DRUG USE BY SEX

Percentage of Either Sex Using Drug at Least Once in Last Six Months

Sex	Tobacco	Alcohol	Mari- huana	Glue	Barbi- turates	Opiates	Stimu- lants	Tranquil- izers	LSD	Other
Boys	42.9	51.7	8.6	7.4	3.3	2.2	8.4	8.1	3.4	2.6
Girls	31.1	40.4	4.0	4.2	2.8	0.9	5.3	10.4	1.2	0.7

Group Discussions

The analysis of the group discussion tapes was done in terms of conflicts and catalysts. A conflict unit was defined as a stated perception by some person of a barrier to personal gratification. A catalyst was defined as the vehicle used to discuss the conflict. Barriers were the perceived blocks to personal gratification. The common catalysts were drugs, smoking, alcohol, sex, the future, religion, hippies, school, "what bugs you," clothes, and lastly, love, marriage, and dating. The most important barriers were self, peers, home (parents), school, the law, mass media, experts, society, and pushers. Of course, the most common topic of conversation and catalyst was drugs. The groups were structured in this way and many of the leaders' questions concerned drug use.

Most of the barriers creating conflict are internal or connected with the self, and this general statement is particularly true of drug-taking conflicts. As students move from grade seven to thirteen, discussions about drugs are less concerned with parents and more concerned with peers. That is, the locus of control over drug taking probably shifts from parents to peers, with most of this shift occurring between grades seven and nine for males and somewhat later (9 and 11) for females. This is an interesting finding, of course, when we remember that grade nine is the peak age for most types of nonalcoholic drugs.

Related Characteristics

As well as determining the basic rates of drug use, we wished to find out what social characteristics were associated with drug use. At present, analyses of these characteristics are available only for users of marihuana and LSD. We hope that further analyses will allow us to describe all types of users, e.g. solvent sniffers, drinkers, and various types of psychoactive drug users.

Age and Sex

Age and sex have been mentioned already. For most drugs other than alcohol and tobacco, the peak usage occurs at grade nine. For all drugs but tranquilizers, girls use less than boys. The sex difference is very large for marihuana, LSD, and glue; much smaller for tobacco and alcohol.

Social Class

When the rates of drug use were compared for each high school district with the social class variables for the district, there was no relationship. Also, comparisons of drug use by occupation of father showed no relationship—children of professionals and proprietors did not use more marihuana and LSD than those of semiskilled fathers.

School Activities

Several variables connected with school performance were related to drug use. More *nonusers* reported A grades than did users; users more often reported failing grades of D or E. Nonusers were also involved in significantly more extracurricular activities, but drug users were also absent in them.

Peers

Most smoking, drinking, and drug-taking activities occur in social groups, and there is little solitary drug use. Peer groups are the most important single source of drug information for users, but not for nonusers, who depend more on family and experts. Drugs and alcohol are usually obtained from friends, and drug users tend to have more friends and associates who are also drug users. Social contact, social influence and peer control are important variables in explaining drug use.

Parental and Familial Variables

Numerous factors associated with drug use are outside of the control of the drug user, and they reside entirely in the family. For example, drug users more often had parents born in the British Isles and less often in Eastern or Western Europe. Language, too, made a difference, so that if parents spoke Italian, Portuguese, or Spanish, the child was more often than expected a nonuser. Other languages, such as English, seemed to make little difference in drug use. As one would expect from the language differences, religion also made a difference; Catholics were underrepresented, but Jews and those uncommitted were over-represented among users. More than twice as many Jews and religiously uncommitted students were drug users than Catholics.

Drug use in the family is also an important variable, and the importance of modeling is obvious. More users than expected reported that parents used *both* alcohol and tobacco, although the use of tobacco or alcohol was not significant. It is clear, too, that drug use runs in families and that a drug user is likely to have siblings who are also users. Drug purchasing is probably easier for drug users as they have more money to spend. Significantly more users than nonusers have five dollars or more to spend each week.

Family structure and stability are different for drug users and nonusers. For example, more drug users were living with only one parent or less; however, the sex of the missing parent is significant. Only when the mother is missing is this variable important. Fathers are more important than mothers with regard to employment. If the father is unemployed, the student tends more often to be a drug user, but it does not seem to matter whether the mother was employed. Of course, one-parent families create more difficulties in parental control; it is more difficult for one parent, especially the father, to know what children are doing and who they are associating with.

General Conclusions

It is clear from these findings that *nonalcoholic* drug use is a frequent activity among high school students. However, alcohol and tobacco are *still* the most important drugs. Drugs such as marihuana, LSD, glue, and others, are consumed by a *minority* of the school population; they have not taken over from the older drugs, and there is little reason to see a "drug epidemic" or "drug rampage." Everybody is not doing it—yet, and those who do are rather different from those who do not. This sort of study helps to define the target population for rehabilitative or educational measures. The target population here, of course, should be Protestant males who are failing in the early grades of high school—one could further specify the population, but this could leave out many potential and actual drug users.

WHAT IS STILL UNKNOWN?

A single study, of course, cannot answer all the relevant questions about the extent of drug use; many questions remain to be answered. We now know about drug use in grades seven to thirteen, but we know little about the use before that. It seems clear that some students are initiated to drug use as early as grade five or six; this is particularly the case with solvents. Also, we know little about the way in which students stop using drugs, or about what enables so many students to refuse or avoid nonalcoholic drugs.

It should also be made clear that we know very little about college drug use in the Toronto area. So far, there has been no extensive study of drug use in Canadian colleges or universities. The studies made in the United States suggest a wide variation from college to college. For example, Eells[1] found that at California Institute of Technology 13.7 percent of the students had used marihuana, and 5.5 percent had used LSD. However, Pearlman[4] found in Brooklyn College that fewer than 6 percent had used LSD or marihuana during their college careers. Imperi, Kleber, and David[2] found that 18 percent of the students at Yale and 20 percent at Wesleyan University had tried marihuana or LSD. These results should lead us to expect considerable variation in rate of usage in universities—rates should be highest in nonsectarian colleges with large residence facilities.

To date, we have no study of nonalcoholic drug use in the adult population in Canada. But a study done in the United States by Parry[3] is suggestive for Canada. He has reported that 14 percent of all prescriptions are for psychoactive drugs and that one out of every four persons in the American adult population is currently using a sedative, tranquilizer, or stimulant.

Psychotropic drugs are more heavily used by women than men, by Jewish persons than Catholics and Protestants, and by those in managerial positions (or their wives). It is probable that more parents are using mood-modifying drugs than are their children. Of course, one can immediately see parallels with the usage patterns in the high school study, and one has to wonder whether youthful drug use is partially modeled on parental drug use. Is it really a type of ten-age protest or is it merely mimicking of an adult pattern with different drugs, i.e. marihuana and LSD rather than tranquilizers and barbiturates? Parry also found an interesting generational difference; there was a continuing decline in the use of stimulants with age. The "down" drugs (sedatives and tranquilizers) were more popular than the "up" drugs (stimulants), but not for persons aged eighteen to twenty; they were most likely to be stimulant users. Young people, then, wish to *wake up* rather than go to sleep, while the opposite is true for older people.

Educational Implications

This study of high school drug use suggests some approaches to education about drugs. The first major concern is at what age drug education should begin. This study indicates that some experimentation with drugs, especially tobacco and glue, is beginning before the student enters high school (in grade 7). It is clear, then, that drug education should start early. In Ontario it now starts at grade ten but, as mentioned previously, the peak rate for most drugs was grade nine. Students, themselves, also expressed the view that drug education was begun too late to offset drug usage.

The *type* of instruction which will be most beneficial and effective appears to be one in which the student plays an active role. Students became rapidly and easily involved in the discussion group part of this study, and there was a free exchange of valuable information. Of course, open discussion is not all that is needed; authoritative reference material and some formal instruction is very necessary. We found that students have also acquired a good deal of inaccurate and misleading information. But it was clear from the tapes of group discussions that, at present, there are communication barriers between teachers and students on the topic of drugs. Students felt that teachers were too opinionated and there was considerable distrust of information given by teachers. A basic principle, then, seems to be that teachers should steer away from a strictly didactic approach to drugs and drug use. Students should have a controlling hand in organizing and carrying out programs on this topic.

Unfortunately, there is little information, at present, on which an effective influence program can be built. Our attitudes towards drugs and even our laws regarding drugs contain much contradiction and confusion. What is needed is some sort of educational program about artificial euphoria—the need to produce euphoria out of effective living rather than out of novel drug experiences. However, the society as a whole is not agreed on this, as alcohol and tranquilizers are often used to create artificial euphorias. As long as they are so used, it will be difficult to convince all young people that they should not smoke marihuana or use other sorts of drugs.

To many adults, the use of marihuana and the use of alcohol are considered to be distinctly separate types of phenomena, the first deviant and completely unacceptable and the second normal and socially acceptable—even desirable. But some students do not feel this way, and an educational program based entirely on this rationale will not be beneficial to them. Students often feel that patterns of alcohol and marihuana use have basic similarities. For example, alcohol is often taken at social gatherings, as is marihuana. Both types of usage may stem from a desire to be part of the group or result from peer pressure. Some people say a cocktail makes them feel more relaxed and sociable, and most experienced marihuana users report the same types of feelings. It is important, then, to emphasize to students that *neither* pattern is completely normal or essential and *not* that one is normal and the other abnormal.

Attention must also be given to parents in an educational approach to drugs. In the discussion sessions some students said they felt that they could not discuss drugs at home. Their parents became disgusted at the mention of marihuana and other drugs, and they typically adopted an attitude that they did not want to hear about such things. Another student complaint was that when they mentioned drugs at home, their parents became suspicious and began "firing" questions: "Have you tried it?" followed by "Are you sure?" Many parents feel unable to answer questions about "grass," "speed," or "mary jane;" to some the words do not mean anything. Material should be made available to parents through libraries or through parent-teachers associations. If parents are unwilling or unable to adopt a "Let's discuss it" approach to drugs, then *the student* must turn to other sources, often less concerned with his well-being for his information on drugs.

The effects of drugs, both physical and psychological, their pharmacological properties and their medicinal uses, are all very important dimensions of drug education. But there is another area which is less often stressed and sometimes neglected; that is the legal aspect. Despite the publicity given to arrests for drug offences, students' knowledge of the laws governing drug possession and sale are vague, An extreme example occurred in a taped discussion with grade eleven boys; there was a general consensus reached in this discussion that the possession of marihuana was not illegal but that its sale was illegal. This is not true and, in Canada, a person convicted of marihuana possession is liable to have a criminal record for life and perhaps a jail term.

Some students are not sufficiently aware of the legal risks taken for playful or recreational drug use. In many areas drug users are expelled or suspended from schools. There are indications that forcing drug users out of school is an ineffective approach to this kind of deviance. In fact, it may make their deviance far worse and increase their drug taking. These are the individuals most in need of information and counselling and are much less likely to get it outside of school. A model of drug-taking behavior proposed by Wilkens[5] is essentially based on concepts of social deviance. This model states that certain kinds of systems and certain types of information lead to acts being defined as deviant to the extent that the individual is "cut off" from the values and control of the parent system. This definition of deviance leads to more action being taken against the deviants, and individuals so labelled begin to feel themselves as deviant. The deviant groups then develop their own values running counter to those of the parent group. This group's cohesiveness leads to more deviant acts by the alienated groups. However, the increased deviance by the deviant group results in more forceful action by the conformists. This makes the deviant groups more alienated, and the process is repeated. It seems to me that by defining high school drug users as bad, immoral, dirty, lazy or ineffectual hippies is very likely to initiate this process by which they just drop out of school, then out of society, form their own (hippie) groups, attack the larger society, be set upon by the larger society (as in hippie subcultures), then become more deviant. It is just this circular process whereby deviants are made more deviant and more alienated by definitions of deviance. Somehow, high schools and parents have to create a place for drug users, a place where they can be understood and encouraged to change, rather than arranging that they become more and more alienated. We can help to create this place by talking to drug users and understanding their problems and potentialities—not by rejecting them as beyond the pale of respectability and giving up on them.

REFERENCES

1. EELLS, K.: Marihuana and LSD: A survey of one college campus. *J Consult Psychol, 15*:459-467, 1968.
2. IMPERI, LILLIAN, L.; KLEBER, H. D., AND DAVIE, J. S.: Use of hallucinogenic drugs on campus. *JAMA, 204*:1021-1024, 1968.
3. PARRY, H. J.: Use of psychotropic drugs by United States adults. *Public Health Rep, 33*:799-810, 1968.
4. PEARLMAN, S.: Drug use and experience in an urban college population. *Amer J Orthopsychiat, 38*:503-514, 1968.
5. WILKENS, L. T.: A behavioural theory of drug taking. *Howard J Penology, XI*:264-273, 1965.

Chapter Eleven

SOCIETY AND DRUGS: A SHORT SKETCH
JEAN PAUL SMITH

MY PURPOSE IN THIS paper is to examine several of the key questions often raised about the drug abuse problem. The questions concern the nature, extent, and origin of the problem in our society. The vantage point adopted here is one of an observer attempting to sketch some of the details of this most complex and vexing social problem.

Society itself defines what we mean by "drugs" and differentiates these from "chemicals," which are called toxins, poisons, or even beverages. In times with slow rates of social change, we find rather general agreement throughout a society on what is to be called a drug, the nature of the drug abuse problem, and what society should do about it. But the period of time in which we now live is seeing very rapid social change, so that many elements of society are out of touch with each other if not in sharp conflict. The phrase, "bring us together," is popular now and for good reason. We need more consensus—reasoned, deliberate consensus —than we now have in the drug area. And if this is not possible, at least a small amount of tolerance for the foibles of our fellow-man will go a long way to getting us started in the right direction.

At this point you may feel that you are being served up a dish of platitudes when you expected to dine on something more substantial. I assure you that these are not platitudes, but recommendations for careful analysis of the problem *before* deciding on what the problem really is. This is the attitude in which I hope we may look at the problem of drugs and society.

Assuming that we have less agreement now than ever before on what a drug is—and by inference what drug abuse is—let us look at some of the core questions mentioned in the introduction.

169

EXTENT OF DRUG ABUSE

Probably the first question that arises is the extent of use of drugs—how widespread is the use of stimulants, depressants, hallucinogens, and narcotics? Our difficulty here is that we have an enormous number of studies, all providing proximate answers to this question, but for different groups of people, in different regions of the country, using different methods of study and survey, and done at different times. The best compilation of these studies that I know of was done by Mrs. Dorothy Berg of the Bureau of Narcotics and Dangerous Drugs' Division of Drug Sciences.[1] She gathered reports from fifteen colleges and universities, twenty senior high schools, and one junior high. The nationwide student study done for *Readers Digest* was included in her compilation as were studies of hippy and adult populations. In all, thirty-eight studies were surveyed. These studies were abstracted for findings as far as percent of respondents who *have ever used* the illicit-exotic drugs. It is important to note that this definition of extent is extremely strict. It would be like including in the category of smokers everyone who had ever used tobacco behind the barn at age twelve.

Several tentative conclusions may be drawn from these drug use studies. Any single percent figure given for a population will gloss over important differences that appear to exist. For example, to say that 20 percent of our young people have experimented with drugs ignores the many factors known to be associated with drug use. Some of these are age, education, social class, sex, educational institution, race, and ideological or value orientation. For each configuration of these variables and probably others, a different pattern of use and abuse of drugs emerges. Experimentation with marihuana appears to be greatest and the narcotics lowest with other drugs coming in between. Males tend to experiment more than females; and better educated and higher class members tend to "try out" drugs more frequently than persons who are less educated and from lower classes.. Young urban persons of an extreme liberal or left oriented ideology are quite likely to use drugs. It is important to note here that most populations surveyed have been college populations with far less attenion focused on the less talented and less affluent. Several illustrations of extent of use may be presented. A pilot study of hippies in New York City found 100 percent had used marihuana. Robins and Murphy (1965-1966) found that 47 percent of their sample of 221 Negro men of normal IQ in St. Louis had used marihuana. A private high school in Michigan, and males from the junior and senior class in the Castro Valley Unified School District both showed about 35 percent in the "ever used" category.

One of the most recent reports of studies done was in the *Palo Alto Times*, July sixteenth, 1969.[2] On page 1 in bold type the headline said: "DRINKERS AT 12" and just above it in slightly smaller type, "They're Smoking Less." The lead-in to the story, which was based on a survey of over two thousand students in six elementary school districts and twenty-three thousand high school students, implicated alcohol as the most serious drug of abuse—a most welcomed portrayal of the drug problem in our youth. The study, as reported, indicated that about one half of the seventh and eighth grade students have experimented with cigarettes and alcohol; and about the same number with marihuana,(amphetamines and LSD, which is quite surprising to me. Experimentation with illicit drugs is apparently not replacing the use of alcohol among young people. No evidence of substitution of one form of drug experimentation for another is found here.

What has been described so far is an increase in availability and use of drugs and a diffusion downward and outward of experimentation with them. If we tried to place a date on this phenomenon, it might be about the beginning of the 1960's. Prior to this time, the "classical drug problem" existed, by which I mean the greater agreement on what "drug abuse" meant and which drugs were included under that rubric. Previous to the 1960's, widespread experimentation with and use of stimulants, depressants, narcotics, and especially hallucinogens was a ghetto or at least a restricted or minority group phenomenon and therefore elicited far less concern for our society at large.

WHAT BROUGHT ABOUT THIS CONDITION?

What happened to change this picture? How did the problem balloon in size to its current proportions? Two obvious reasons are greater availability of drugs and increased association of young people with other drug users. Or putting both of these points together, drugs were simply easier to obtain. However, other more profound changes were to take place during the late 1950's and early 1960's, changes based on sociophysiological trends, which cast the drugs in a different light and increased the likelihood of persons experimenting with mind-altering substances.

At the more general level of social changes, we find a more drawnout period of adolescence, in which young people simply need more time and many more diversified experiences to achieve a healthy, integrated personality. As our society becomes more congested, more interrelated by communication, transportation, and mobility, young people need more time for trial-and-error experimentation and exploration to avoid the conformity and drabness they fear. Greater social, educational, and intellectual pressures are placed on young people than ever before. With or without realizing it, they as well as we must perform, produce, and achieve in the context of larger and larger institutions. An economy of abundance has resulted, but the hard work ethic continues to dominate our ideals, if not our aspirations. The absence of striving and the alternative to keeping one's nose to the grindstone is unfortunately not the creative use of leisure but is for many the appearance of a low-grade malaise, a bored or dull feeling, increasing the unpleasantness by not providing for refreshment and renewal where expected. If we add to all of these conditions the discontent with the direction our country is taking—adopting policies which have not been able to keep pace with the rising expectations of minority groups, the periodic thrusts of the civil rights movements, and lastly, the outstanding achievements in technology with the comparative neglect of comparable social reforms—all of these provide for disenchantment with an alienation from our sociopolitical system. The point to be made here is that drugs, and a greater inclination to try them, either once or twice or sporadically, fit into these social changes very neatly either by manipulating moods such as a chemical tool, or by representing a feeling toward society, a protest, a challenge to society to find something better, and lastly, and the most important reason of all, by simply providing fun for the user.

The individuals who fit this picture are certainly not the hard-line addicts using heroin, morphine, paregoric, or barbiturates. Nor does this description fit the real acidhead or meth freak, who is a serious, continual abuser of drugs to the point where social changes cannot explain the behavior. What I have tried to do is to keep the discussion centered on broad trends rather than a very small percentage of pathological individuals. The broad trends are more adequately described in terms of drug use and abuse rather than drug dependence or addiction. Far fewer persons are actually dependent on drugs than abuse them, especially if we adopt a legal definition of abuse: the use of a prohibited substance.

THREE MAJOR TYPES OF DRUG PROBLEMS

Society appears to view the complexities of drug abuse as consisting of three primary types, all of which may be viewed as subgroupings under the heading of "drug effects" or, we should say, both intended effects and unintended effects.

The first type of drug problem arises from the unintended side effects of medically prescribed drugs and the over-the-counter preparations. These compounds are carefully controlled by the Federal Government as far as claims for efficacy and safety and experimental use in human beings. We obviously have a great need for compounds which will help to prevent or cure disease. Most of the "magic" aura of drugs comes from the use of these compounds by medical and paramedical professions to alleviate mankind's ills. There are, however, very large numbers of adverse reactions to these drugs, which are just as harmful to the individual and society as intentional misuse of drugs. They are more understandable, since the original need leading to the use of drugs was an ill or malady. The management of drugs for therapeutic purposes exposes many persons to increased risks of abuse; therefore, doctors and nurses show the highest proportion of professional groups who misuse drugs.

The second category of drug effects which concerns us is that of misuse, abuse, or addiction. It is loosely defined by the means by which a person acquires the drug and the purpose for which it is intended. Buying drugs from a street peddler to maintain a habit is the prototype of the abuse pattern, although examples of borderline cases can easily be drawn. Effects of drugs used in this class are not socially sanctioned but are brought about by individual decision and social pressure. And, more important, the effects sought are those of the high, the intoxication, or the escape from reality of the external or the internal world. The origin of this type of drug use is markedly different from the first pattern. Whereas the medical or thera-peutic use of drugs is directed primarily against a specific condition diagnosed by an expert, the effect of drugs when used for abuse is primarily to create a change in feeling, usually pleasure or at least the absence of an unwanted feeling. Research has not delineated the origins of the personailty dynamics for abuse, and there is a serious question about whether pre-dispositions or early personality signs of drug abuse proneness exist at all.

The drugs that are not diverted from legitimate channels very often contain contaminants or toxic matter of an immediate concern. "If a sizeable amount of DMT powder does not get you, a little strychnine thrown in may do the job." The sad part of this is that some users will interpret a harrowing experi-ence from which they barely return, "a wild trip." If one is looking for reasons why people should stay away from these drugs, the uncertainty as to content and effect on the body of illicit drugs are two very good reasons.

The third category of drug effects that are of interest may be termed the recreational use of drugs; or drugs for which no prohibition or social sanction against their use exists. They are, from the standpoint of law, neutral even though restrictions on their distribution decrease their abuse somewhat. Alcohol, tobacco, caffein, and cola are examples of recreational drugs, and some contend that marihuana is more of a recreational drug than a drug of abuse, although the evidence for this is scanty. Recreational drugs are those which the individual decides may be used for relaxation, fun, and to get away from the stresses and strains of life.

The comparison of drugs of abuse with recreational drugs reveals the lack of consistency in society's approach to both classes. A person may be a confirmed alcoholic and be regarded as "sick" in our society. If he habitually uses marihuana, i.e. is dependent on its psychologically, he will be viewed as a criminal, not a sick person. The social liability of both persons is much the same. The attitude of many people is that we do not need either one in society, but we already have six million alcoholics so why create a comparable class of potheads? And so the arguments go on. It is well to remember that what is called a recreational drug here has both a legal and an informal social base. And at some point the law will begin to reflect the behavior and attitudes of people.

While such a scheme as this necessarily oversimplifies a great deal, it does characterize the general attitude of many, if not most persons in Western society, that the drugs a doctor pre-scribes for you are "good" even if serious side effects occur; drugs self-administered in private are thought to be "bad," per se, even if some of the consequences are beneficial; and lastly, recreational drugs are not called drugs, because we do not like to admit that directly changing our moods or feelings has some social benefits as well as liabilities.

REFERENCES

1. BERG, DOROTHY F.: Extent of Illicit Drug Use: A Compilation of Studies, Surveys, and Polls. Bureau of Narcotics and Dangerous Drugs, United States Department of Justice, May, 1969.
2. SHILSTONE, BILL: Youngsters Use Liquor. *Palo Alto Times,* July 16, 1969.

Chapter Twelve

HAPPINESS: SOME FINDINGS BETWEEN NON-DRUG-USING AND DRUG-USING TEENAGERS

EDWARD M. SCOTT

W E ALL WANT TO be happy. Yet this desideratum is the most neglected of all psychological research. The professional literature is almost silent on this topic. Some books have appeared with happiness in the title as, for example, *This Way to Happiness* by Narramore[1]. Recently a thirteenth century treatise on happiness was translated from Latin into English.[2] Numerous definitions of happiness have appeared. A few will be selected to indicate the nonuniformity.

Among the many letters Freud[3] wrote to his friend, Wilhelm Fleiss, is the following:

My dear Wilhelm:

All sorts of little things are happening: dreams and hysteria are fitting in with each other even more neatly. These details are now standing in the way of the great problems touched on in Breslau. One must take it as it comes, and be glad that it does come. I send you herewith the definitions of happiness (or did I tell you a long time ago?)

Happiness is the deferred fulfillment of a prehistoric wish. That is why wealth brings so little happiness; money is not an infantile wish.

All sorts of other things keep dawning on me and driving their predecessors into the shade. It is not possible to piece it all together.

Your Sigm.

Gotschalk[4] describes different kinds of happiness: "There is the happiness of the healthy bullfrog with his lifelong gestalt of immediate satisfactions and the happiness of the willfully superstitious. Lately many have known the happiness induced by intellectual tranquilizers, which supply sedatives to troubled nerves by artificial cheeriness."

The need for research on happiness appeared more and more a necessity. Two years ago, I published an article[5] on happiness, based upon responses to a questionnaire given to 120 high school students, 60 boys and 60 girls. The results, sufficiently encouraging, compared 60 nondelinquent girls with 60 delinquent girls.[6] Some significant and important results were obtained. Hence it occurred to the present writer that a study comparing drug-using and non-drug-using teen-agers would be informative.

The research population consisted of 120 high school students, 60 boys and 60 girls, who were "normal," at least non-drug using. This is the population used two years ago in my original research on happiness. The 60 drug-using teen-agers (30 boys and 30 girls) were recorded from a variety of sources: our clinic patients, their friends, or teen-agers known to be on drugs by staff members, especially Mr. Charles Paulus. The important factor is that each of the 60 teen-agers were constant or regular users of drugs, principally marihuana, one of the amphetamines ("speed") or one of the hallucinogens (usually LSD).

All of the teen-agers were given individual questionnaires, asked to be as frank as possible, and assured that their identity would be unknown. The questionnaire consisted of eight questions. The responses to each question were tabulated into classifications and compared. Since previous research indicated some differences between boys and girls, a comparison was conducted between non-drug-using girls versus drug-using girls, and non-drug-using boys versus drug-using boys.

Question I: Describe in detail the most happy event you can recall. Explain as best you can.

Content	Non-Drug-Using Girls (N=60)		Drug-Using Girls (N=30)	
	No.	%	No.	%
1. Achievement (winning a prize, good grade, etc.)	8	13	1	03
2. Election (to a office, rally squad, etc.)	9	15	3	10
3. Romance (first date, kissed, etc.)	11	18	12	40
4. Religion (feeling close to God, etc.)	8	13	0	
5. Possession	0		0	

6. Experience of self (growth potential, feelings of confidence, etc.)	9	15	2	07
7. Family closeness	6	10	4	13
8. Friendship	5	08	1	03
9. Meaning of life	3	05	2	07
10. Don't know	1	02	0	
11. Drug use (marihuana, LSD, amphetamine, etc.)	0		4	13
12. Employment	0		1	03

One verbatim example of each group will be given in this report.

A nondrug using girl wrote:

The happiest event in my life was our family's vacation at Florence, Oregon. I enjoy myself more at this time than any other. Being near the lake and the sand dunes gives me a wonderful feeling—it's stimulating to get up in the cool, crisp morning and splash creek water on your face. The days seem long and are packed with fun and exciting events. It's hard to say how long this lasts because each time I reflect back upon it, I feel happy again.

A drug using teenaged girl reported:

I went to Lair Park and had the best time. I was free for a while, free to sing, to live and to be with the people I have learned to love. They return this love in many ways, mostly by just being there. They give me something I have never had. I have never been able to find it anywhere else. I was and still am given this love at home, but it's selfish.

A glance at the comparisons reveals that non-drug-using girls selected as most happy events and in greater frequency achievement, election to office, religious experience and experience of the self. Achievement most likely reflects a girl's feeling as she reaches some goal—election to an office, a feeling of popularity; whereas religious experience indicates the importance of this factor in a girl's life. Experience of the self as a category is a little difficult to explain; by and large it is used here when the teen-ager feels herself expanding, or growing, or "enlarging" as a person.

The category which the drug-using girls most often referred to as the most happy event is that of romance. Just what this indicates is a bit difficult to say, most likely it indicates quicker growth, and awareness of the other sex and hence a desire to give up the girl role for the woman's role. Anna Freud[7] observes that one distinguishing factor of a delinquent is a desire to grow up too soon; they do not permit, ". . . a gradual detachment from the parents to take place. . . ."

We might speculate that since many of the "rewards" of an adolescent period are not experienced (achievement, inner growth, religion, etc.), they "turn away" and reach for the next page.

There is then some beginning evidence for an adolescent gap, namely, groups of teen-agers differ widely among themselves.

Question II: Describe the most sad event you can recall. How did you feel? How did you experience this event?

Content	Non-Drug-Using Girls (N=60)		Drug-Using Girls (N=30)	
	No.	%	No.	%
1. Death (of relative or friend)	26	43	13	43
2. Death of animal (pet)	4	07	5	17
3. Illness of loved ones	5	08	1	03
4. Breakup of romance	9	15	3	13
5. Family problems			4	13
6. Maturing			1	03
7. Self-awareness (of self-weakness)			2	07

Here we note that death is the most frequently chosen sad event for both groups. The break up of romance is in second place.

A non-drug-using girl stated, "I felt like dying when my parents thought me untrustworthy."

A drug using girl said: I think I was saddest when I was in junior high in the sixth grade and realized I was growing up. I felt like trying to preserve my childhood, but knew I never could. I felt very sad and cried every night. I felt the fun in my life was gone and could never be replaced. I cried every night for about a week when I laid in bed. I think I even try to still be a child in actions.

Death of a relative or friend is a final verdict—representing an experience which cannot be changed, only endured or felt.

We might ask ourselves, "How do we, as a society, prepare our young people for the death of a loved one?" It seems as though we do not.

A non-drug-using teen-aged girl wrote, "I wouldn't live a normal life if my parents distrusted me and were ashamed of me. This is a basic principle of life. It's more important than becoming a concert pianist."

Question III: Which event (happy or sad) was the deepest, most meaningful experience? Why?

Content	Non-Drug-Using Girls (N=60)		Drug-Using Girls (N=30)	
	No.	%	No.	%
Happy event most meaningful	26	43	9	30
Sad event most meaningful	31	52	21	70
Can't decide	3	05	3	10

A drug-using girl stated her deeper event was, "when the last trip I had was real bad and ever since then I've felt in a shell and I don't know where I stand most of the time, I mean all the time and I need help."

The findings in this category are intriguing and informative. For instance, does the personality of the drug-using girls—or is it their life situation which caused them to feel that the saddest event was the more meaningful, more deeper event.

One reflection on the present finding is that some of the girls said they were able to use the sad event as a learning experience— unlike some patients who repeatedly complain and ruminate about a sad, traumatic event in their life—unable to grow, or forget it, but remain fixated, impaled to pathology.

Lastly, of course, one can speculate that the non-drug-using teen-aged girls who felt the happy event as more meaningful did not have to resort to drugs for "happiness."

Question IV: Do you experience more happy or sad events?

Content	Non-Drug-Using Girls (N=60)		Drug-Using Girls (N=30)	
	No.	%	No.	%
Happy events	44	73	20	67
Sad events	8	13	7	23
Don't know	8	13	3	03

The resounding reply for both populations was in favor of happy events. A variety of reasons were offered, one of which was, "I definitely experience more happy events. I can't help but believe that all normal human beings must, because to experience a majority of sad things seems almost impossible to me," wrote a non-drug-using girl.

A drug-using girl wrote, "I experience more happy events but remember more the sad. The happy events fade away faster and aren't quite as clear as the sad."

The above quotations are somewhat confirmative of an idea which struck me some years ago which prompted the original research—namely, people differ sharply on how they experience happiness and sadness in their lives. It is an hypothesis of mine that by and large patient populations come from those individuals who cling closely to the sad events in their lives, masochistically marooned, unwilling to find new moorings.

From the present question we observe that both groups of girls experience more happy events than sad events. Would this hold true twenty years from now? As we become older do we grasp at the depressive events? Is this one factor in the generation gap?

Question V: How does one go about seeking happiness?

Content	Non-Drug-Using Girls (N=60)		Drug-Using Girls (N=30)	
	No.	%	No.	%
1. Mental attitude	10	17	9	30
2. Don't know	5	08	2	07
3. Optimistic outlook	12	20	3	10
4. Seek it	4	07	5	17
5. Kindness to others	11	18	2	07
6. Good (moral) life	4	07	0	
7. Being one's self	4	07	2	07
8. Enjoy yourself	2	03	1	03
9. Looking for good mothers	4	07	1	03
10. Know what happiness is	1	02	1	03
11. Can't	1	02		
12. Doing one's best	2	03	1	03
13. Fantasy			1	03
14. With Family			2	07

The answer to this question, as might be expected, received a rather wide range of replies.

A non-drug-using girl stated, "The key to happiness is facing each problem life throws at one."

A drug-using girl said, "I go about seeking happiness by going someplace in which no one else knows about. You may call it fantasy land. I call it my land."

In comparing the two groups of girls, one notes that the differences occur in "optimistic outlook" and kindness to others. Perhaps this reflects the notion that non-drug-using girls attempt to be more optimistic, brew their own happiness. It's a bit surprising to me at least to find non-drug-using girls selecting "kindness to others," as an avenue to happiness. It has been my impression that drug-users, verbally express great concern about "others," and love.

The drug-using girls are more vague in their responses—"mental attitude."

Other differences can be noted but they are rather small. It might be interesting to observe that four non-drug-using girls felt that leading a good moral life lead to happiness, but none of the drug-using girls chose this entry.

By and large, all the girls seem to be saying that happiness is a mental set, or manner of approaching life and its tasks. If this mental set is present, happiness is present in the very process of working toward a goal.

Question IV: Was there any period of time (say 2-3 years) in which QuestionIV: you felt most happy?

Content	Non-Drug-Using Girls (N=60)		Drug-Using Girls (N=30)	
	No.	%	No.	%
1. Recently	25	42	8	27
2. None (no particular period)	23	37	10	33
3. Grades 1-3	1	02	2	07
4. Completion of 8th grade	4	08		
5. Summer	3	05		
6. High school	3	05	3	10
7. Real early in life	1	02	4	13
8. Future			1	03
9. Don't know			2	07

A non-drug-using girl wrote, "Now! Actually, all of my high school years, more probably because the experiences are so fresh in my mind. I believe I have always been basically happy. I have a good family."

A drug-using girl, "Age 4-5 because I did a lot of fun stuff at those ages, that I still remember."

A glance at the results indicate that by and large non-drug-using girls feel that the recent and present is a happier times of life; whereas, the drug-using girls fail to designate any special period. Once again it is tempting to theorize that drugs are used for (as) happiness pills.

A drug-using girl remarked, "The communications gap between me and other people. I want people to know how I feel, but it's so hard to say it."

It seems that for the most part the girls feel that the hurdles

Question VII: What is the biggest problem you feel you have to overcome in order to be more happy?

Content	Non-Drug-Using Girls (N=60)		Drug-Using Girls (N=30)	
	No.	%	No.	%
Personality Problems				
1. Worry	6	10	1	03
2. Shyness	7	12	2	07
3. Jealousy	2	03	1	03
4. Depression	3	05	1	03
5. Laziness	1	02		
6. Selfishness	2	03	1	03
7. Self-knowledge	3	05	1	03
8. Lack of honesty	1	02		
9. Being one's self	1	02	2	07
10. Inadequate	7	12	2	07
11. Pride	0		2	07
12. Self-conscious	0		2	07
Philosophy of Life	9	15	1	03
Social Problems				
1. Boy friend trouble	2	03	1	03
2. Need for girl friend	1	02		
3. Getting along with people	3	05	5	17
4. Too readily influenced	2	03		
Family Problems				
1. Sibling rivalry	2	03		
2. Parents	2	03	2	10
3. None	4	07		
4. Don't know	4	07	2	07

to happiness are within in the sense that they have to do something about it. So it appears that teen-aged girls can identify what the problems are; what bothers them is the solution. More adequate counseling in high school, geared toward a solution of "the known" might pay dividends. Counseling, therapy, operant conditioning, paranalysis, or anything else ought to be geared toward solutions and not explanations or excuses.

Question VIII: What kind or type of people are most happy?

Content	Non-Drug-Using Girls (N=60)		Drug-Using Girls (N=30)	
	No.	%	No.	%
A. Philosophical Attitude				
Good philosophy of life	17	28	9	30
B. Personality				
1. Generous	5	08	0	
2. Secure feelings	1	02	4	13
3. Mentally ill	1	02	0	
C. Religious				
1. Good Christians	11	18	1	03
2. Morally courageous			0	
D. Economic				
1. Well fed	1	02	0	

E. Social				
1. Have deep friendships	8	30	7	23
2. Not too many pressures	2	03	2	07
F. Family				
Good family	5	08	1	03
G. Romance				
In love	0		4	13
H. Hippies	0		2	07

A non-drug-using girl wrote, "The happiest people are those who are sincere and true. I think this is because they can have an honest look at themselves."

A drug-using girl stated, "People who don't really care what is going on in this world. People who go out on the town and have a really good time and don't even care what is going to happen the very next minute, or day, or week, or year."

These are some differences between the non-drug using teen-aged girls and the drug-using girls, namely that for the latter it seems that God is dead in the sense of leading one to happiness at least in this life.

Both groups, however, agree on deep friendships as a source of happiness, especially the drug-using girls. Another sharp difference is the place of romance, this was not mentioned once by the non-drug-using girls, but four times by the drug-using girls.

A good philosophy of life is generally agreed by most as essential to happiness. We might ask ourselves:

1. Who teaches this—parents, clergy, teachers, peers?

2. How is it taught?

Many centuries ago Plato remarked that we know who teaches math, rhetoric and the arts, but "who are the teachers of virtue?" Perhaps we are still searching for that answer. There are often individuals, or groups of individuals, who arise, claiming they are the teachers. Some caution in this regard is made by Wood[8] in his book, *Yoga*: "One should know a guru very well before blindly obeying any instructions he may give—know his character and motives especially, and if possible his effect on earlier students." Wood further suggests, ". . . care has to be taken not to be caught by teachers who are not conscientious, but who are merely setting up in this field to get rich quickly, *or to feel* important. And he must beware as the sage Ramakrishna said, of unripe gurus."

What now follows is a comparison of 60 non-drug-using teen-aged boys with 30 drug-using teen-aged boys.

Question I: Describe in detail the most happy event you can recall. Explain as best you can.

Content	Non-Drug-Using Boys (N=60)		Drug-Using Boys (N=30)	
	No.	%	No.	%
1. Achievement	27	45	8	27
2. Romance	4	07	6	20
3. Religion	0		2	07
4. Possession (car, etc.	7	12	5	17
5. New experience	4	07	1	03
6. Experiences of the self	7	12	1	03
7. Family closeness	5	08		
8. Friendship	1	02		
9. Job	1	02		
10. Poetry			1	03
11. Drugs (Marihuana, LSD, amphetamines, etc.)	4	07		
12. Election to office	1	02		
13. Travel			2	07

A non-drug-using boy wrote, "I felt wild and excited as I came in with the waves. I let out screams and rebel yells of wild joy."

A drug-using teen-aged boy said, "The time I saw the light on LSD in Eastern, Oregon."

We note, by comparison, that drug-using boys, refer to romance (engagement, going steady, sex) as the most happy event, more frequently than non-drug-using boys.

It is somewhat of a surprise, at least to me, that the non-drug-using teen-aged boys report the experience of the self as the most happy event more often than drug-using boys. The quote above, by the non-drug-using boys is but one example—he felt "something" inside and as a result "grew."

For both groups, achievement is the most frequently entered category and, as such, differentiates the boys from the girls. This is in keeping with the findings of Adelson and Douvan.[9] These authors write, based on their research of 1,045 boys (age 14-16) and 2,005 girls in grade six through twelve:

"The girls self-esteem is anchored to interpersonal relations more often than to achievement, work, or skill. Compared to boys, they are more likely to give popularity, acceptance by others, and adult recognition as the things that make them feel important and useful.

Popularity and glamour appears as dominant concerns in answers to a number of questions. Achievement is the major worry of boys and physical appearance and popularity are the center of girl's concerns."

Lederer[10] notes that, "From action comes impact with reality, and thus definition of the self; from willed, effective action comes realization of the self as an effective, mature agent and from effectiveness comes meaning and purpose." Our study seems to confirm the opinion of Lederer, especially for boys.

I recall one rather significant statement of a drug-using teen-aged boy, during a therapy session, "I have had a lot of insights while on trips from drugs, but I've never been able to put them into action—I guess I'll have to stop drugs and get going, put the insights into action."

Question II: Describe the most sad event you can recall. How did you experience this event?

Content	Non-Drug-Using Boys (N=60)		Drug-Using Boys (N=30)	
	No.	%	No.	%
1. Death (relative or friend)	25	42	6	20
2. Death of pet	3	05	6	20
3. Illness of loved one	5	08	1	03
4. Breakup of romance	2	03	2	07
5. Problem with parents	4	07	1	03
6. Loss of possession (car, etc.)	6	10	1	03
7. Loss of sports event	5	08	3	10
8. Loneliness	2	03	0	
9. Moving	2	03	2	07
10. Bad experience on drugs	0		2	07
11. Loss of job	5	08	0	
12. Divorce of parents	0		2	07
13. Useless death (JFK, etc.)	0		2	07
14. In jail	0		2	07

Death of a friend or relative is the most frequent entry for both groups; while death of a pet is higher for the drug-using group.

Some other differences, indicate that loss of a job was a blow to the non-drug-using boys (5 times) but not once did the drug-using boys mention this event. We should note that, "in jail," was chosen twice by drug-using boys.

Other differences occur, which can be easily noted.

We note a difference in that the non-drug-using boys most often felt the sad event was deeper, whereas the drug-using

Question III: Which event (happy or sad) was the deeper, more
meaningful experience?

Content	Non-Drug-Using Boys (N=60)		Drug-Using Boys (N=30)	
	No.	%	No.	%
1. Happy event more meaningful	22	37	17	57
2. Sad event more meaningful	31	51	10	33
3. Can't decide	7	12	3	10

group chose, more frequently the happy event. This finding is difficult to explain, to reality, or reaction.

A drug-using boy wrote, "When my friend died, I felt sad. I couldn't believe he was dead."

A non-drug-using boy chose the sad event because, "Sadness seems to carry more insight. It is remembered longer where happiness may be soon forgotten."

Is it possible that the non-drug-using boys are more reflective and hence choose the sad event; or is it that the drug-using boys take a "lighter attitude" as well as making attempts to utilize the happy events in their life.

Question IV: Do you experience more happy or more sad events?

Content	Non-Drug-Using Boys (N=60)		Drug-Using Boys (N=30)	
	No.	%	No.	%
1. Happy	46	77	15	50
2. Sad	6	10	9	30
3. Don't know	8	3	6	20

Here we find agreement in both groups; namely, both experience more happy than sad events—so also for the girls. A non-using-drug boy said, "Events are not happy or sad, only their interpretation. I am basically serious-minded. I try to find deeper meaning and reason in all events."

A drug-using boy wrote, "More happy events. I find happiness in simple events and these are so many it keeps me pretty happy."

There might be a lesson for all of us to try and look for the positive and the good, instead of the negative and the bad. Do we as adults lose this ability? Do we lose our bounce? If the lack of "bounce" occurs in adolescence, it appears we are observing a sick individual.

Both groups of boys feel that a good mental attitude is

Question V: How does one go about seeking happiness?

Content	Non-Drug-Using Boys (N=60)		Drug-Using Boys (N=30)	
	No.	%	No.	%
1. Mental attitude	14	25	12	40
2. Don't know	9	15	4	13
3. Optimistic outlook	9	15	7	23
4. Being active	8	3	1	03
5. Friends	3	05	0	
6. Seek it	4	07	0	
7. Religion	4	07	0	
8. Self Sacrifice	4	07	0	
9. Acceptance of others	2	03	0	
10. Kindness to others	2	03	0	
11. Doing one's thing	1	02	5	17
12. Meditation	0		1	03

essential for happiness. Just how one acquires this attitude, is a bit difficult to explain.

One non-drug-using boy stated that happiness was sought by "setting your sights on a goal and sacrificing to achieve this goal."

A drug-using boy wrote that happiness was sought "by wine, women and women and women."

We observe some differences between the two groups: non-drug-using boys more frequently (1) mentioned activity as producing happiness; perhaps the drug-using boys feel more meditative, and (2) mention religion and self-sacrifice; whereas the drug-using boys mention doing one's thing and being optimistic.

The important element emerging from this particular question, it seems to me, is that happiness is a mental set, or a manner of approaching life. How do we track this?

For both groups the entry most frequently chosen was "none." A non-drug-using boy felt his present life was happiest because ". . . there are so many interesting things to do."

Question VI: Was there any particular period of time (say 2-3 years) in which you felt most happy?

Content	Non-Drug-Using Boys (N=60)		Drug-Using Boys (N=30)	
	No.	%	No.	%
1. Recently	21	35	5	17
2. None (no particular period)	24	40	15	5
3. Early life (before scare?)	2	3	5	17
4. Grades 1 to 3	1	2	1	03
5. Grades 7 to 9	5	08	1	03
6. Don't know	7	12	3	10

"I can't explain that, because ever since I kicked drugs, life is becoming a wonderful experience."

This particular teen-ager, was on marihuana for two years (14-16). He began to use it as an experience; then when he learned that his mother was going to die of cancer, he took marihuana, "to relieve the pain. I could pretend she wasn't going to die." Following his mother's death, he continued to use marihuana for six months since he was somewhat dependent on it. His studies became more and more of a burden, as he was quite listless. Six months ago he stopped taking marihuana and he felt much better, as stated above.

There emerges from the response to this question a trend which indicates the non-drug-using boys feel happy in the present, whereas the drug-using boys do not express this same judgment. A quick, seductive, inference is to assert that drugs are used to make the drug-using boys happier. We might, however, be observing some inconsistency. In Question III drug-using boys felt the happiest event in their lives was deeper and more meaningful, unlike the non-drug-using boys—as well as both groups of girls. Just what this implies is difficult to say.

Question VII:	What is the biggest problem you feel you have to overcome in order to be more happy?			
Content	Non-Drug-Using Boys (N=60)		Drug-Using Boys (N=30)	
	No.	*%*	*No.*	*%*
Personality Problems				
1. Worry	12	20	5	17
2. Shyness	7	12	2	07
3. Jealousy	5	08	3	10
4. Depression	5	08	3	10
5. Laziness	2	03	1	03
6. Selfishness	1	02	1	03
7. Indifference	3	05	2	07
8. Loneliness	1	02		
9. Inadequate	2	03	3	10
10. Guilty conscience	3	05		
11. Temper			1	03
12. Pride			2	07
13. Narcissism			1	03
Philosophy of Life				
	2	03	3	10
Social Problems				
1. More social life	1	02	1	03
2. No driver's license	1	02		
3. Lack of money	1	02		

Family Problems

1. Parents	4	07	1	03
2. Don't know	5	08	1	03
3. None	5	05		

A non-drug-using boy wrote, "I don't like people as well as I should. I can't let myself have fun,"—regarding his biggest problem.

A drug-using boy said, "I feel I must be better than everyone else, which has its problems."

By and large, the differences between the two groups as to their biggest problem which has to be overcome to be happier is about the same. It is somewhat refreshing to note that personality problems occupy the category most often mentioned. Hence, the hurdles are felt to be within—self-erected, if you will.

We learn that teen-agers can recognize their problem—what is needed is help, solutions, not mere recognition. Suggestions made in the reference to the girls responses to this question are applicable for the boys.

A non-drug-using boy felt the happiest people are those "who are highly intelligent, friendly, have high moral standards and a deep regard for their fellow-man and a respect for religion."

Question VIII: What kind or type of people do you think are most happy?

Content	Non-Drug-Using Boys (N=60)		Drug-Using Boys (N=30)	
	No.	%	No.	%
A. Philosophical				
1. Good philosophy of life	17	28	13	40
B. Personality				
1. Intellectual	1	02	2	07
2. Not intellectual	1	02	1	03
3. Secure feelings	15	25	5	17
4. Generous	1	02	0	
5. Active	3	05	0	
C. Religion				
1. Good Christians	7	12	2	07
2. Morally courageous	2	03	0	
D. Economic				
1. Rich	2	03	3	10
E. Social				
1. Have friends	1	02	2	07
2. Popular	2	03	2	07
3. Happily married	2	03	0	
4. Good Family	0		3	10
F. MISCELLANEOUS				
1. Pre-school	2	03	0	
2. Don't know	4	07	1	03
3. Oriental people			1	03

A drug-using boy said, "The average married man who has got a healthy family, a good position in the working world, and is very much in love with his wife."

The entry which most frequently occurred is that of a good philosophy of life. The boys are attempting to balance their life with a well-rounded orientation, realizing that this is essential. Blos[11] writes:

> One typical roadblock encountered in traversing postadolescence is what I shall refer to as the "rescue fantasy." Rather than living in order to master life tasks, the adolescent hopes that life circumstances will master the task of living. In other words, he expects that the solution of conflict can be alleviated or side-stepped altogether by the arrangement of a beneficient environment.

It appears in the population sampled that there is some evidence that one's own thoughts are crucial and the expectation of a larger playpen is unrealistic.

Let us attempt to summarize some of the findings and offer tentative suggestions:

1. One major finding is that boys and girls from both groups feel that a good philosophy of life is necessary for happiness. It seems to me that this is significant. Philosophy as such is no longer taught to the teen-agers—yet obviously these youngsters (as well as others) and certainly their teachers or guru's have a philosophy about what they are teaching, whatever the subject. Yet, this is often overlooked. It is my opinion that the work of Kalin[12] and his associates can be utilized appropriately at this juncture. These investigators found this significant—termed it meaning control, in the TAT stories. This occurred regularly and significantly in the setting in which alcohol was used but not in the dry social setting. They comment:

> It is a newcomer to theorizing about the effects of alcohol and contains the first hint as to why people indulge in small amounts of alcohol in social settings of this kind. It apparently starts to allow or encourage them to think in contrasting terms about large or existential life issues. Many of the themes had a meditative and ironic twist to them, as in such poetic statements as "paths of glory lead but to the grave," or "to be or not to be, that is the question." One can think of these contrasts as involving primary process thinking—that is—entertaining contradictory thoughts or feelings of life's basic issues

(success, future life, death, pleasure, etc., which is encouraged or released by alcohol in small quantities under social conditions.

It would seem that using either alcohol or drugs, *in small amounts*, allows the young person a "time-out," to think about things which he or she is either too busy or too shy or fearful to think about, without these "aids" or crutches. Apparently, other young folk do not need these "aids." In order to arrive at a good philosophy of life, either through meditation or reflection, a time out to think is required.

2. Teen-agers need a mature counselor, or therapist, not an "unripe guru."

3. Drug users are attempting to grow up too quickly.

4. Non-drug-using teen-agers appear to have a sense of growth in the self; perhaps as a result they do not need "aids."

5. Some of the teen-agers (in both groups—boys and girls) can utilize sad events as occasions of growth, others cannot. I would speculate the latter will be tomorrow's patients.

6. All teen-agers report more happy events than sad events. Would this hold true for adults? Perhaps this is one factor in the generation gap.

7. Most teen-agers can identify the obstacles to happiness in their lives. As a result, it would seem that therapy (counseling, operant conditioning—or whatever one chooses to term it) needs to aim directly at the solutions rather than poking around at explanations.

Blachly[13] offers some specific suggestions in his chapter on this topic. For instance, Blachly suggests that discussion should be geared "to why people hurt themselves, their friends, and relatives." Another discussion topic would revolve around, "how people change habitual form of behavior." The discussions should include specific topics (for instance, incompatibility of two mutually exclusive behaviors. Substitutions of nonseductive for seductive behavior, e.g. Antabuse taking and alcohol drinking, cyclazocine taking and heroin use. Whenever possible, experiments should be conducted. Schultz[14] writes:

> The current interest in LSD and other psychedelic drugs has a relation to the joy techniques. The aims are similar—to make the experience of life more vital. The joy methods attempt to achieve

this without drugs. How similar the experiences are I don't know personally, but several people who have experimented feel there are some close similarities.

8. I am in agreement with Adelson and Douvain,[9] who state, "The normal adolescent holds, we think, two conceptions of himself—what he is and what he will be—and the way in which he integrates the future image into current life will indicate a good deal about his current adolescent integrations." These authors feel so keenly about this concept that they state, "Throughout this book and in all our work with adolescents, we have made one key theoretical commitment. We have assumed that adolescent adaptation depends on the ability to integrate the future to their present life and current self-concept."

If we assume that the statements of Simons and Winograde[15] are correct when they write that one characteristic about drug users is a heightened attention to the present and little or no concern for the future, it appears as though the non-drug-using teen-agers, as a group are more normal— presumably, more happy—than drug using teen-agers.

9. Rollo May[16] presents the concept that this generation is a schizoid one. If so, drugs might well be used as a means to feel, to experience, to be alive.

10. We have noted a wide range among the subjects of this study. For instance, one young teen-aged girl claimed she was atheistic, while a drug-using boy claims to have seen in a vision that, "I was in God's arms and He saved me," and later he related he was given the gift of tongues—glossolalia.

In other words, there is an adolescent gap among the teen-agers themselves. Recently I have had fruitful experiences with group therapy for drug-using and non-drug-using teen-agers where they could bridge the gap.

Perhaps a fitting conclusion to this paper is indicated by the words of one drug-using teen-aged girl, explaining her most happy event:

> I felt extremely full and rich. I felt I was experiencing life beautifully. I am in tune with everything. It was fascinating to see everything working together like parts of a machine. People were

allowing their emotions to come to the surface, not being ashamed of them. It recharged my battery for a long time to come. I was very slightly stoned. It was unfortunate that I wasn't more stoned. The experience would have been more intense, that's a key word. I'm not even sure that I was stoned on grass at all. I had had so little that it should have been worn off. I was stoned another way though— naturally. It's groovy when life makes you stoned without artificial aids. That's the best kind of way to be stoned.

REFERENCES

1. NARRAMORE, CLYDE M.: *This Way to Happiness.* New York, Pyramid, 1969.

2. AQUINAS, T.: *Treatise on Happiness.* Englewood, (Trans.) Oesterle, J. New York, Prentice-Hall, 1964.

3. FREUD, S.: *The Origins of Psychoanalysis.* (Letters, Drafts and Notes to Wilhelm Fliess). Ed: Bonaparte, Marie; Freud, Anna, and Kris, E.), New York, Doubleday, 1957.

4. GOTSCHALK, O.: *The Quest for the Good Life.* New York, Philanthropic Library, 1963.

5. SCOTT, EDWARD M.: Happiness: Protocols of teenagers. *Guild Catholic Psychiat Bull,* April, 1967, p. 69-82.

6. SCOTT, EDWARD M.: Happiness: a comparison between delinquent and non-delinquent girls. *Psychotherapy: Theory, Research and Practice,* 4:78-80, 1967.

7. FREUD, ANNA: Adolescence. *Psychoana Stud Child,* 13:255-278, 1958.

8. WOOD, E.: *Yoga.* England, Penquin Books, 1959.

9. DOUVAN, ELIZABETH, AND ADELSON, JOSEPH: *The Adolescent Experience.* New York, John Wiley, 1966.

10. LEDERER, WOLFGANG: *Dragons, Delinquents and Destiny.* Psychol. Mono #15. New York, International University Press, 1964.

11. BLOS, PETER: *On Adolescence.* Glencoe, Free Press of Glencoe, 1963.

12. KALIN, RUDOLPH; McCLELLAND, DANIEL, AND KAHN, MICHAEL: The effects of male social drinking on fantasy. *J Personality Soc Psychol,* 1:441-452, 1965.

13. BLACHLY, PAUL: Seductions as a Conceptual Model in the Drug Dependencies. Presented in part at the 31st Annual Meeting of the Committee on Problems of Drug Dependencies, Div. of Medical Sciences, Natural Academy of Sciences, National Research Council, Feb. 20, 1969, Palo Alto, Calif.

14. SCHULTZ, WILLIAM C.: *Joy.* New York, Grove Press, 1967.

15. SIMONS, T., AND WINOGRAD, B.: *It's Happening.* Santa Barbara, Marc Laird, 1967.

16. MAY, ROLLO: Love and will. *Psychology Today,* August, 17-64, 1969; (Adapted from the forthcoming book, Love and Will, to be published by Morton & Co.).

Chapter Thirteen

STUDENTS AND DRUGS: TRIP OR TREAT?

JOHN I. MAURER

Last year a senior came to me because he was concerned about his increasing use of the drug marihuana. When I asked him how it got started he said, "Well, last summer I was drinking a lot, but it was expensive, hard on my stomach, and gave me hangovers. Then I switched to pot which was a lot cheaper, didn't bother my stomach, and gave me no hangovers. It seemed to me to be the perfect way to relax every evening without suffering the next morning."

I saw Pete six times over the next six weeks, during which time we explored his rather nomadic background, familial pattern of escape, and current insecurities. Luckily it was not difficult to get him to stop using pot, since it is not an addicting drug, and he was using it as a tranquilizer. I merely substituted another tranquilizer. His insecurity about his academic performance and social behavior was relieved by a combination of our therapeutic contacts, his acceptance in graduate school, and the appearance of a young lady on the scene.

For me, this episode illustrates several points about marihuana. For one thing it is an excellent tranquilizer, and in a shy, insecure individual like Pete, can easily come to occupy a central substitutive and therapeutic position in his life. What makes it dangerous is the fact that it has few drawbacks. It is cheap, nonfattening, and produces no toxic hangover. Although it is not addicting, because it has so few drawbacks, psychological dependency develops all too easily.

THE SETTING

Marihuana has been around for thousands of years, and yet only in the last five has it had a sudden popularity. In order to

195

understand why, I think we need to take a look at the society, the times, and today's youth. I will not attempt to make any definitive statement about our society today. Many others far better qualified have described it accurately. I will say, however, that to me it appears to be an age of contrasts. The "American Dream" particularly has been realized in all its fantastic limits. The extraordinary wealth and power of this country and technological competence which now has placed men on the moon contrasts with our appalling failures: poverty, racism, and senseless waste. To the fresh mind of a youngster these contrasts are even more absurd. In addition to being a society of contrasts, this is indeed a society of miracle drugs and escapes. In 1968, Americans spent 794 million dollars in amusement parks. They spent 30 billion dollars on vacations, and 14.5 billion dollars on alcoholic beverages, 420 million dollars on headache remedies and smoked 500 billion cigarettes.[1] Tranquilizers were the most prescribed drugs during 1968. It indeed is a society in which the pursuit of escape by chemical and other means is a well-entrenched value. In many ways the "hippie" philosophy of a few years ago is the most extreme example of this escapism. The hippies tried to create a dream culture with drugs and a sort of permanent vacation. The drugs provided not only the miracle attainment of the "American Dream" but also the escape from the failure of our culture to realize it.

We must next ask, "Why now?" and again perhaps our answer comes from modern American know how. Affluence and transportation has provided ready availability of any and all drugs on virtually any street corner. Recently it was estimated that there are ten thousand drug dealers in the San Francisco Bay area alone. Marihuana and a grab bag of other drugs are available easily to any high school student.

In our age of miracles we have come to expect instant answers. Whether it be instant entertainment, instant coffee or instant cure for our ills, Americans born since 1946 have not learned to defer gratification as their parents did during the Depression and the Second World War. Today's youth seek instant orgasm by mainlining Methedrine and instant insight by dropping acid. Along with the postwar affluence there has also disappeared the "struggle for survival" characteristic of the individuals and indeed of the country in the thirties and forties. A teen-ager achieves no satisfaction or identity from providing for himself financially. The old goals are irrelevant, and our new ones are not established. Directionlessness characterizes a vast majority of our youngsters. In the college we see it as the "amotivational syndrome" often occurring during the second or third year. Many, mostly boys, by this point have discarded much of the values and objectives they brought to college from their families. They see before them only years of drudgery and increasingly confining routine. The draft robs them of the opportunity to take a psychological moratorium from school, so many find themselves swept along toward decisions that they do not want to make or grasping at ways to temporarily step off the treadmill.

Our society, though firmly based on a Protestant ethic, has recently developed peculiar ways of rewarding weakness. We rush in with men and money to clean up the ghetto *following* riots. We grant and perform a legal therapeutic abortion for a pregnant single girl if she can show us that she is emotionally unstable. We grant draft deferments to boys who show emotional maladjustment or irresponsible behavior. These indeed are absurd paradoxes for our youngsters today.

It has been said many times that our technology has out-stripped our emotional maturity and social ability to handle it. I can only underline this and point out the ambiguity which this provides for our youth. The mass media have all too successfully reported this. Before the days of television, youngsters were far less aware of the world and its problems. It was easier then for parents and teachers to dole out clear predigested information and values to eager young fresh minds. Only gradually did full awareness of life's complications develop, and then, when experience could temper its impact. Today's television delivers un-interrupted raw data to the viewer whether he be equipped to interpret it or not. As a result, a youngster of twelve or thirteen, if he pays attention, can have virtually as much data on the world available to him as anyone, and he must decide whether he wishes to attempt to cope with this and grow, or turn off and escape.

There is much more that can be said about society and the

dilemma of today's youth. I would like to move on though to describe the characteristics of the young people who get into trouble with drugs.

THE USERS

A recent report of the Bay area showed that 50 percent of high school senior boys have experimented with some sort of drugs,[2] and our latest data at Stanford shows that 69 percent of the students have tried marihuana or another drug at least once. The vast majority of this experimentation is brief and out of curiosity, and the majority of the youngsters move on without difficulty.[3] Some, however, do not.

One youngster who often gets into trouble is the emotionally immature youngster. Passive, dependent, and unable to cope, he blames others, is easily discouraged and depressed. Drugs for him can cause a loss of inhibition and timidity and the attainment of fantasies of achievement and a sense of adequacy. To the emotionally immature, drugs are extremely seductive, for they provide the instant pseudo-experience of success in a world otherwise experienced as threatening and frightening in the sober state.

A second youngster liable to severe involvement with drugs is the impulsive, angry youngster. The defiant youngster, who seeks ways of antagonizing the authority, takes drugs because they are illegal. Marihuana for him provides an excellent example of how repressive and ignorant his elders are in legislating against a mild drug. He finds pot not to be dangerous and addictive and uses it as an example of how the Establishment lies, deceives, and represses. The laws concerning marihuana certainly lend credence to his claim that legislation concerning drugs is in some cases inappropriately punitive.

Another group that runs a high risk of difficulty with drugs are the borderline individuals. These strange, seclusive, shy individuals, labeled schizoid by psychiatrists, find in the drugs a magical cure for their shyness. The drugs may dissolve their inhibitions to enter personal contact and provide them with the subjective feeling of intimacy and the illusion of closeness.

For an isolated, lonely youngster the drugs may provide his first or only experience of closeness.

The existentially lost, depressed, alienated youngster may turn to drugs also. Frequently those showing the "amotivational syndrome" fall in this category. Rather than facing and coping with the world of reality, it is only too easy to escape into the world of fantasy drug dreams.

A fifth group, certainly far less common in today's affluent youth, but still present in the ghettos and minorities, are those youngsters from deplorable life situations. To some, a drug-induced delirious high with its consequent anesthesia is a far less painful state than the sober reality of their real lives.[4]

Adolescence is a time of particular stress and susceptibility anyway. Peer group pressure is probably more influencial at this time than at any other. The college student who has newly broken from his home and has yet insufficiently developed internal and social restraints is more likely to impulsive and irresponsible behavior. Adolescence is characterized by active drives which can be highly anxiety producing. Many of the drugs may neutralize these drives temporarily and provide relief from their pressure. These drugs seem particularly seductive to young people because they promise to provide answers to the various questions that trouble many of this age. The introspective youth sees in LSD the road to instant analysis. The philosophy student sees answers to his existential search. The lonely isolated youngster gets promise of intimacy and closeness, and all users enter the "cool" world of peer acceptance.[5]

THE DRUGS

I will not dwell on the various drugs themselves except briefly. Basically there are the expanders, the contractors, the uppers and the downers.[6] The expanders or psychedelic compounds such as LSD, DMT, and so forth, seem to be decreasing in popularity on the university campus. News of chromosome damage and a few glaring examples of brain damaged individuals have decreased their popularity. Availability and purity has also decreased. Mescaline alone or in combination with marihuana or amphetamines seems to be the most popular at present.

Among the contractors, narcotics such as heroin and opium are most representative. They have not attracted much following among the college students. However, high school students who have less awareness of their dangers have recently shown some interest in heroin.

Among the uppers, Methedrine or "speed" is the most dangerous and prominent. Because of vigorous educational campaigns by most of us involved in the treatment of drug problems, at least the colleges have happily shown only a small amount of Methedrine. In my opinion it constitutes the greatest danger both physically and with regard to dependence.

The "downers" are gaining wide use in the Bay area high school scene. Seconal and, of all things, alcohol particularly are being used in increasing amounts. The ready availability through the family medicine cabinet and liquor closet apparently provide the more accessible source to the high school student in the current situation.

The basic drug still, however, at least on the campus, is marihuana. For the vast majority of users it is used as a social catalyst and weekend euphoriant. Most experience no ill effects whatsoever. The occasional "bad tripper" on marihuana simply quietly stops using it, and the individuals who use the drug excessively or abuse it usually show emotional disorder of sufficient magnitude to explain their difficulty. Pot merely acts as a catalyst for their already present disorder.

THE EFFECTS

On the campus ill effects of drugs definitely fall into two categories: acute and chronic. The acute reactions are relatively benign and easy to handle. The so-called bad trip can be anything from mild apprehension to intense panic, paranoia, or toxic delirium. Generally, external controls, knowledgable talk, and the use of injectable tranquilizers is sufficient to abort bad trips of these sorts in the vast majority of cases. We often place individuals who are on bad trips in our Student Health Infirmary overnight and almost invariably they are sheepish and repentent, but fine, the following morning. On occasions one of these drugs may trigger a psychotic episode, but usually it is in an individual who was borderline or prepsychotic anyway, and the drug merely serves to tip the scales into frank psychosis.

The effects that are of more concern to me are those that result from long-term, regular or heavy usage of the drug. Some fail to confine their use to weekends and gradually experience a shift of life focus from school and intellectual pursuits to the drugged state. Loss of interest in academic, social, sexual, and athletic endeavors follows and its consequent deleterious effects on grades, social relationships and physical health. This sort of pattern becomes self-perpetuating, since the drug then is utilized to escape from an ever worsening real situation. Three cases represent various aspects of this effect and are worth reviewing.

THREE CASES

Rich grew up in a successful, wealthy, vibrant home. His father is an energetic executive who drinks, lives, and fights with his wife at the same enthusiastic pace. Rich's mother is an active, pill-swallowing, chain-smoking, somewhat dominant, but extremely bright, woman. From an early age, Rich who was the oldest was encouraged to succeed in athletics. He worked diligently and successfully at his sport during high school and by his senior year had reached the pinnacle of success in his sport. He was an international champion and world record holder. Following this he entered college and seemed to pass his peak. Though still nationally prominent in his sport, he no longer won every race, and younger competitors began to gain on him. By his junior year he discovered marihuana during the off season and began to "turn on" regularly and thereby recapture chemically the "peaks" he had experienced from his athletic triumphs a few years before. His increasing use of drugs decreased his will, motivation, and ability to perform athletically, and he gradually lost competence as well as confidence. His interest in school lagged and finally he quit his sport and dropped out of school. Therapeutic attempts to reverse his drug abuse were fruitless. Past his peak by the age of twenty, Rich continues to attempt to recreate his past triumphs through chemical highs.

Vince too was once a promising athlete, a golfer through high school and into early college. He was always haunted by fears of inadequacy and insecurity. Through marihuana and later LSD, he discovered and lived in a haze of chemical pseudocompetence for approximately two years. During this time he lost interest and ability in his sport and dropped out of school, finally ending up in a mental hospital for a month. Now at the age of twenty-six, he is reentering school, shaky, depressed, unsure of himself, but determined not to again return to his previous chemical answers. Only after his hospitalization was Vince able to recognize and accept his own insecurities, isolation, and depression. The drugs had for several years provided him with an excellent way to deny awareness of his internal turmoil.

Jerry is the oldest of three boys of a Navy captain. His father, an extremely competent, successful, and admirable man, raised Jerry with a strong but sensitive ability with which he managed the men under him in the Navy. Mother's weakness and fragility added backing to father's strength by threatening Jerry with guilt if he should fall by the wayside. He, himself, futher added to his problems by showing genius intelligence and tremendous potential. His college entrance board tests were both in the high seven hundreds, placing him clearly among the most gifted in the country. As a senior in high school he found the work extremely easy and began to learn that he could get by on good intentions, his potential, and his glib tongue. As a freshman at Stanford, released from the strong control of his family, he discovered marihuana. His entire first year was a series of drug highs, incompleted courses, and academic manipulations which left him with less than a C average and many incomplete courses at the end of the year. As a sophomore he resumed his previous pattern and moved to Methedrine, a drug which gave him the racing euphoria and illusion of super intelligence which his teachers kept saying he possessed. As his real list of accomplishments dwindled and failures increased, his use of the drug redoubled. Finally dragged to my office by several worried friends, he entered into a three-month struggle with me to conceal and continue drug use while convincing me of his reformation. Despite or perhaps because of his extreme intelligence, Jerry shows very little emotional maturity. An almost psychopathic capacity to lie and manipulate had assisted him through three years of drug activity, and he was not about to abandon it at the request of a mere "shrink." Our struggle escalated until I had to hospitalize him, at which point he went on a sit-down strike, refusing to do anything. He received a medical leave from school and the last I heard was continuing his drugged existence. His pattern was particularly frightening because it resembled closely the pattern displayed by narcotics addicts werein the pursuit of the drugged state becomes the all-pervasive goal in life, and all activity becomes secondary to that goal.

THE RESPONSES

What can be done? Obviously the answers are not easy. For parents the dilemma is most difficult. The mid-ground between neglect and overprotection seems extremely small today. Obviously, maltreatment, abuse, overcontrol, as well as overpermissiveness, overprotection and unrealistic indulgence, all can create an atmosphere in which the child is insufficiently equipped to cope with today's world. However, the majority of parents can not be said to be guilty of any of these sins. I think that children who grow up in an atmosphere which is challenging but not overwhelming, managable but not boring, and exciting but not frustrating, find little appeal in drug abuse. Certainly the parent who drinks to excess, abuses tranquilizers, pep pills, sleeping pills, or cigarettes has an impossible task in pursuading his children to desist from drug usage. The parent who has no knowledge of drugs and their effects and simply mouths outmoded cliches will have little to say when the youngster turns to drugs. Though today's world is complicated and extremely challenging, if the youngster sees his parents successful in their marriage, happy and willing to confront today's challenges without the crutch of chemicals, and confident enough in their parenting ability to allow the child to grow freely when he is ready, he will tackle the challenges of life enthusiastically and with little need to escape.

The schools too have an important role in regard to drugs. The use of intoxicants, though labeled by many as "mind expanding," indeed do not facilitate psychomotor functioning; they do the opposite and are contrary to the goals of the educational process. The school, therefore, in order to be consistent should condemn the use of drugs. The primary goal of the school is to educate, and indeed with regard to drugs the school should educate. They should supply, as they do in all areas, unbiased, undistorted information about the drugs and their effects. The school can provide counsel for the user and, if issues of confidentiality are of concern, the school should provide access to a school psychologist or psychiatrist who has the advantage of privileged communication. Most important, however, the school must attempt to relieve the alienation and joylessness that pervades so many of our young people who become involved with drugs. The school must provide goals that are appropriate to the times. The school should attend more to the education of the senses and emotions as well as the intellect, and finally the school must set appropriate and adequate limits on behavior where the society fails to do so.[7]

SUMMARY

Basically, the drug user is saying by his action, "'the technology of today's world has provided chemicals with which I can cope with awareness. The society has not provided me with the emotional competence to cope with that world without the chemical." In a world of war, pollution, overpopulation, and poverty, we need to help our young people cope soberly with this awareness without the need to "blow their minds."

REFERENCES

1. *Statistical Abstracts of the U.S. 1968.*
2. The Narcotics Advisory Committee: The use of five mind altering drugs reported by San Mateo County, California high school and junior high school students. *Preliminary Release,* 1969.
3. BLUM, R. H., *et al.*: *Students and Drugs,* 2:49-100, San Francisco, Jossey-Bass, 1969.
4. COHEN, S.: *The Drug Dilemma.* New York, McGraw-Hill, 1969, pp. 107-109.
5. BLAINE, G. B.: Why intelligent young people take drugs. *J Iowa S Med Soc,* 59:37-42, 1969.
6. SMITH, D. E.; FORT, J., AND CRATON, D.: Psychoactive drugs, *Drug Abuse Papers 1969.* Berkeley, University of California, 1969, pp. 1-16.
7. COHEN, S.: *The Drug Dilemma.* New York, McGraw-Hill, 1969, pp. 115-126.

Chapter Fourteen

MARIHUANA: AN ATTEMPT AT PERSPECTIVE

CONRAD J. SCHWARZ

A 1934 EDITORIAL IN THE *Canadian Medical Association Journal* contained the following statements:

> . . . the use of Indian Hemp is no longer confined to the 'Mystic East' but has become a real menace in Canada and the United States. . . . The first intimation that the drug was being introduced into this country was . . . when it was discovered that Marihuana cigarettes were being sold in Walkerville, Ontario, at $1 each. . . . It can be seen that the traffic in Indian Hemp has attained the proportions of an industry with widespread ramifications. . . . Fortunately, our Narcotics Act fully covers the matter.
>
> The above tale, though told only in outline, will sufficiently indicate the excellent work done by our Narcotics Division with the efficient aid of the Royal Canadian Mounted Police in laying bare the existence of this nefarious traffic. Much has been done already to dash the ardour of the traffickers and some salutary punishment have been imposed by the Courts. Probably much more yet remains to be done but there is no doubt that eventually the traffic will be still better controlled and, we hope, ended. The menace is a serious one, for the experience of all countries is that the Hashish habit has a special appeal to the young, not necessarily that they crave for the drug, at least at first, but they use it with the desire to appear "smart." Then comes the urge for more and a dangerous habit is created. It would appear also that most of those indulging in Hashish represent new fields for exploitation, they not having been at any previous time addicts to Morphine, Heroin or Cocaine.

Those familiar with the history of marihuana in the United States will recognize in this Canadian statement a reflection of the similar American preoccupation with the drug which culminated in the Marihuana Tax Act of 1938, which incidentally was fifteen years after Canada had made it illegal.

Now, in 1969, thirty-five years after the editorial comments cited, one finds very similar statements appearing in the Western medical and lay press, together with more extreme assertions imputing a wide range of dangers to the drug. In apparent contrast to the 1930's, however, there is currently proceeding a wide dissemination of literature which minimizes the dangers of marihuana, at times to the point of claiming it to be harmless and favoring legalized distribution of it.

Like all extremists, those who promulgate either of the two polarized views undergo similar psychological processes in maintaining their positions. Whether one argues that marihuana is totally dangerous or that it is totally harmless, one is basing such a conclusion on a combination of complex idiosyncratic emotional factors and plain old-fashioned ignorance.

The ignorance falls into two broad categories: firstly, a lack of knowledge of what information is actually available on marihuana, and secondly, an equally important failure to realize the significance of some of the gaps in our knowledge of the drug.

For example, it is not generally realized that the English language medical literature on marihuana over the past thirty-five years contains reports on direct experimental observation of the effects of the drug on only a total of about 150 Western subjects and some 200 Eastern subjects. This literature contains reports on about two or three thousand individuals with a history of having used the drug, but many of the studies are lacking in scientific balance, and one can only approximate to this balance by reading widely and selecting commonly repeated observations which are not clearly contradicted elsewhere.

In this paper I propose to present the kind of balance I have achieved from my own clinical experience, from a conscientious search of the literature, and from many discussions of the type stimulated by this kind of conference. It is not intended to be a final exposition on the subject, but rather my own interpretation of the state of medical knowledge of marihuana at this point in time.

SOME CHARACTERISTICS OF INDIAN HEMP

The plant from which marihuana and hashish are derived is commonly known as the Indian hemp plant (*Cannabis sativa* L).

It is a universal weed which will grow in almost any climate in the world. However, the characteristics of the plant vary markedly in different locations to such an extent that the very appearance of the plant may be so altered as to cause major difficulties in its recognition. In earlier centuries, the plant formed the basis for a major part of the rope and textile industries in certain countries because of the tough fibrous qualities inherent in it. Such commercial use has gradually declined with the introduction of more easily manufactured products.

The ability of the plant to produce substances which when ingested by human beings cause psychological effects has been recognized for many centuries, particularly in countries where the plant can be grown under hot, dry conditions. It is under these conditions that the plant secretes the greatest amount of resin as a protection against heat, and it is in the resin that the active psychic ingredients seem to be most concentrated. However, the ability of the plant to produce active psychic ingredients also varies widely, even in plants grown in the same field and, in addition, the time at which the plants are harvested is a significant factor in the strength of the product. Even after it has been harvested, the potency of the substance deteriorates with time, although its outward appearance may not change that much.

The Indian hemp plant yields roughly three grades of intoxicating substances, but these overlap with each other, and there are no clear boundaries between them. The purest substance, known in the East as charas, consists of the resin scraped off the plants. This substance is known to have such deleterious effects that it is universally banned even in India where it used to have some spiritual significance, and its illicit use is restricted to a few small areas there. The second rough grade of substance produced by the plant is known as hashish, and this is a medium-strength preparation consisting generally of a mixture of various parts of the plant with whatever resin happens to be attached to them. The third grade is generally known as marihuana and is the weakest preparation, consisting of the dried matured leaves and tops of the plants. Marihuana is about one eighth as strong as hashish and about one twentieth as strong as charas.

During the nineteenth century and early part of the twentieth century, various chemical extracts of the plant were used in

Western systems of medicine in attempts to treat a wide variety of conditions. These "cannabis extracts" were eventually discarded because they had no specific effects, were variable in potency, deteriorated with time, and produced irregular effects on patients to whom they were administered. In practice, they were used, for example, as sedatives, but each patient had to be titrated to find his own appropriate dosage level, much in the same way that physicians formerly used digitalis leaf extracts, i.e. each patient had to be given increasing doses of the extract until he had literally been given too much and then the dose was cut back a step or two. Because of the unreliability of the preparations, this process had to be repeated each time a new bottle of the extract was introduced into the same patient.

The number of references in the medical literature on cannabis runs into the thousands, largely because of the many attempts to determine the chemical structure of the ingredients rather than because of direct observations on human beings. Despite these many attempts, the chemical structure at the present time is not clearly known. For many years it was assumed that certain substances such as cannabinol were the active ingredients, but these have more recently been shown to be inactive. In recent years, attention has been focussed on a group of substances called the tetrahydrocannabinols. It must be recognized, however, that so far about eighty of these substances are suspected of being present in Indian hemp. At the present time, the chemical structures of only about six of these have been worked out, only three to four have been manufactured synthetically, and only one has so far been administered to human beings in an experimental situation. This leaves us a long way from being able to justify the statement that "THC is the active ingredient of marihuana." In fact, there is some suspicion that the psychic potency of marihuana may be dependent on the ongoing chemical interaction of various tetrahydrocannabinols in the plant or in its derivatives.

From the above discussion, it can be seen that even before we consider the effects of these substances on human beings, there will be major research problems in attempting to define the substance that is being used and its strength at the time it

is being used. Added to this, one must take into consideration
the fact that in the Western usage inhalation is a method of
choice, and even the method of inhalation is more difficult than
that of inhaling ordinary tobacco, so that the level of toxic substance in the blood stream may be difficult to assess, since at the
present time, we do not have any direct methods of determining
it. It is also known that some individuals will develop psychological reactions to inert substances so long as they are convinced
that these contain marihuana. Finally, there are major problems
in attempting to standardize individuals and the settings in
which experiments are conducted.

Thus, in trying to answer the question, what does marihuana
do to human beings, one can only reply that it does many things
to different human beings, and all one can do is list the major
observations that have been made in different settings using
different substances and hope that from this mass of information
one might be able to derive some clues as to what sort of things
are likely to occur and what are not.

SHORT-TERM EFFECTS OF MARIHUANA

It should already be obvious that the effects of marihuana
will vary from individual to individual, but even in the same
subject fluctuations will occur during the span of any particular
exposure to the substance. The duration of effect is generally
from one-half to four hours, but in some individuals, the intoxicated state may last up to twelve hours with residual effects
persisting for a few days or even weeks.

In general, when a naive subject is exposed to marihuana,
his reactions to it are usually ambiguous and may even be quite
unpleasant. In practice, he may have to be cajoled by more
experienced users into persisting with his efforts, and if he is to
become a regular user, he will have to learn to ignore the unpleasant effects or to accept them as being the inevitable tribula-
tions of getting high. Among the more commonly reported effects
are intense thirst, increased appetite, headache, dizziness, faint-
ing, and perspiration. Increased pulse rate and palpitations with
a sensation of tightness in the chest may occur. Nausea is quite

common and, in fact, several observers regard it as usual. Vomiting has also been reported not infrequently and, less frequently, diarrhea or constipation may occur.

A characteristic feature of marihuana usage is dilatation of the blood vessels in the conjunctivae of the eyes, giving a general reddening appearance which may persist for several days afterwards.

Marihuana itself is an irritant inhalant and has to be smoked in a particular way in order to achieve the presence of a toxic substance in the bloodstream. In fact, what happens is that the individual has to inhale the smoke as deeply as possible into his lungs and hold it there for as long as possible. Such a procedure may produce a spasm of coughing, dry throat and acute bronchitis. Under the influence of marihuana, the individual may feel an urge to pass water frequently, and he may, in fact, pass so much more water than usual that it has been suggested that marihuana might have a potential use as a diuretic to rid the body of excess fluid.

If the substance is smoked properly, and a toxic derivative does get into the system at a sufficient level, the individual will not infrequently show some incoordination of movement, tremors and twitching, and will tend to have a staggering gait. Enlargement of the pupils of the eyes is sufficiently frequent to be regarded as usual, and this may to some extent explain the intolerance of light which subjects under the influence of marihuana experience. The ability to perform complex tasks requiring coordination deteriorates, and in particular, driving competence is generally considered to be impaired.

The predominant psychological effect of marihuana is an emotional high which is difficult to describe. In practice, it appears to incorporate elements of relaxation, euphoria, and feelings of well-being, confidence, and adequacy. The individual may feel that there is nothing he cannot achieve. He may appear quite exhilarated, laughing and giggling at trivial matters. On the other hand, he may appear quite calm and composed and wrapped up in his own inner thoughts without paying too much attention to what is going on around him.

Most frequently the individual will experience a distortion of the sense of time and distance, and his perception of color and sound may be considerably intensified. His ability to think clearly may be interrupted by fragmentation of his thought processes. Difficulty in recalling what happened immediately before, loss of contact with reality and confusion all occur. Paradoxically, the individual may subjectively be convinced that his thinking is much clearer, and he may claim major insights into problems with which he has been wrestling for some time. He may experience distortions of his body image and may be aware of parts of his body being split off from the rest. He may misinterpret inanimate objects as having living characteristics, and he may feel that he is being persecuted by those around about him.

On a behavioral level, the individual may appear relaxed to the point of being sedated, but on the other hand, he may also become hyperactive and restless and irritable. It is quite false to state that assaultive behavior never occurs under the influence of marihuana. In fact, there are fairly frequent reports of such behavior in the literature, and the individual may also show self-destructive or self-mutilative tendencies.

There is a wide divergence of opinion on the relationship between the use of Indian hemp and more serious behavioral disorders, such as personality deterioration, addiction to other drugs, criminal behavior and psychosis. In general, it would appear to be a fair interpretation of the literature to state that Eastern observers of long-term regular users of the stronger preparations in the hashish range tend to see a significant relationship between the use of the drug and these conditions while at the same time making some allowances for predisposing personality, cultural, and economic factors. In West Africa, Morocco and parts of India, the use of Indian hemp is considered to be a significant factor in up to 26 percent of admissions to mental hospitals in these areas.

LONG-TERM EFFECTS OF INDIAN HEMP

Again, there appears to be a significant difference between Eastern and Western assessments of the possible long-term physical and psychological effects of derivatives of Indian hemp.

Social, economic, personality, and cultural factors are acknowledged as being of equal, if not greater, importance than the drug. The chronic physical effects range from insomnia, headaches, persistent chronic injection of the blood vessels of the conjunctivae, increased susceptibility to infection, and a higher incidence of tuberculosis. Gastrointestinal features are not uncommon with prolonged use of stronger preparations and include dyspepsia, anorexia, and chronic diarrhea. As might be expected with an irritant inhalent, chronic laryngitis, chronic bronchitis, bronchial pneumonia, and emphysema have been observed in chronic users. Most observers tend to discount aphrodisic effects from the drug, despite a widespread belief in these powers, and prolonged regular use of the heavier preparations can be associated with sexual impotence.

There is general agreement that cannabis is not physically addicting in the same sense as opium and heroin are, and most observers state that there is no tolerance to the drug, no need to increase the dosage, and no serious physical withdrawal syndrome. However, few observers deny that there can be a psychological dependence which might be severe, particularly in regular users. This is characterized by intense resentment when the user is deprived of the drug, a persistent intent to return to use, even despite unpleasant reactions, and also moderately severe psychological withdrawal symptoms, including anxiety, restlessness, irritability, depression, aggressive outbursts and even psychotic episodes. It has been pointed out by several observers that some regular users show the major characteristic of psychological dependence in that they are unable to feel well or to function adequately without regular use of the drug. Progression to the use of the so-called hard narcotics is thought to be rare by some observers, and a serious danger by others. Such progression is generally seen as being through mechanisms of association rather than through any physiological procedure relative to the nature of the drug itself.

Prolonged hospitalization may be precipitated in unstable personalities who use the drug, and gradual personality deterioration is again more heavily emphasized in the Eastern reports but has also been noted in Western reports, with the general tendency to pass through phases of irritability, inadequacy, reduced work capacity towards an apathetic way of life.

SUMMARY

This review of the current state of medical knowledge of Indian hemp presents some points which may be of assistance in obtaining a clearer perspective on the subject in the midst of the heavy wave of emotionality surrounding it.

Marihuana itself is a poorly defined intoxicant, which varies in potency, deteriorates with time, and has widely variable effects on different individuals or even on the same individual at different times. It is not an easy drug to use, and because of minor irritating physical and psychological effects which are a necessary accompaniment of achieving the state of intoxication with it, it seems likely that only a small percentage of Westerners will persist with the masochism necessary to reach the stage of regular usage.

In addition to this, at the present time the chemical composition of this drug is not known, despite the present publicity being given to tetrahydrocannabinols. The very few synthetic products of this nature so far made are quite unstable and are not suitable for widespread use.

Although the plant itself will grow in almost any climate, there are certain conditions necessary, particularly a hot, dry, sun-drenched climate, together with particular soil conditions, for the production of Indian hemp with an adequately potent amount of resin in it. Even the Mexican variety is generally considered to be poor quality in comparison with the range of hashish preparations available in the Middle East and Asia.

From a practical point of view, those who argue for the legalization of marihuana fail to face up to the natural characteristics of the drug itself. With the variability in potency and the deterioration in time, procedures for standardization, or even storage, of the drug would require considerable elaboration and refinement before it could become a commercially marketable product, and it seems unlikely that this could be done on any large scale, especially with the weak North American variety of produce. In order to find a really potent preparation, one would have to move into the hashish range and obtain supplies from the Middle East, where the climatic and soil conditions contribute to the production of high-grade cannabis. However, with the variety of international agreements which have been built up over the past fifty years, culminating in the Single Convention of the United Nations Organization of 1961, all the source countries in Africa, Asia, and the Middle East have made it illegal to produce Indian hemp or to sell or distribute it. The law forbids exportation. Thus, if a Western Country wished to make the substance legally available, in order to obtain a reasonably potent substance, that country would have to involve itself officially in international smuggling, since there is no legal way of obtaining it from the source countries.

It seems unlikely that such an idea would be acceptable to the Western mind, but in any event, the argument may well be settled by the Western palate. There is already available in the West alcohol, a substance which can be used for a wide variety of purposes, and which, if necessary, can be used to become intoxicated. Marihuana can only be used to produce a state of intoxication, and seldom is claimed to have any other function than that of getting high, stoned, or—in simple terms—drunk with sensory misperceptions. But in order to achieve this state, the individual must be prepared to accept the minor irritating physical and psychological effects described above. It would appear unlikely that these are going to be tolerated by the majority of Westerners, just as in the same way, it is unlikely that the majority of Westerners would wish to be drunk two or three times weekly.

Despite the serious problems caused by the abuse of alcohol, one should not lose sight of the fact that while indeed it may result in intoxication or addiction, most of the alcohol used in the world is used for a variety of acceptable pleasures—quenching thirst, sharpening appetite, complementing food, or rounding off a meal. Such versatility offers much more than marihuana, which, like all so-called psychedelics, might be appropriately classified as a "soltoxicant," i.e. a substance whose psychological effects are solely dependent on the individual reaching a stage of intoxication with it.

In conclusion, while hopefully this kind of critical examination of Indian hemp will remove some of the emotionality surrounding the drug, it should not obscure the fact that there is cause for concern that many young people, whether or not they use marihuana, see nothing unhealthy about it. Even if it is a practical impossibility to legalize the drug, and even if, because of the innate unpleasant features in its use, it is liable to fade into the drug scene background in a few years, as it did in the 1930's, society may be left with at least two complications unless it can counteract the current atmosphere of acceptance.

The first of these is already familiar to those who work with youth; it is a growing chronic population of young drug users who are committing mental suicide by taking a multiplicity of mood-altering drugs. The progression to these other drugs may be paradoxically related to marihuana in that they provide an easier or a less unpleasant intoxication. It is easier to swallow a tablet of LSD, and it is less unpleasant to float along in the stable heroin state than it is to persist with the unpleasant effects of marihuana only to achieve a fluctuating "high."

The second effect of failure to deal with marihuana now may be the perpetuation and even broadening of the drug-oriented society which already requires urgent attention. Though each drug must be considered as it takes the center of the stage, the real problems lie in the attitudes of individuals and society towards artificially-induced states of intoxication.

REFERENCES

1. WALTON, R. P.: *Marihuana: America's New Drug Problem.* New York, J. B. Lippincott, 1938.
2. BROMBERG, W.: Marihuana: a psychiatric study. *JAMA, 113*:4-12, 1939.
3. *The Marihuana Problem in the City of New York.* Lancaster, Jacques Cattell Press, 1944.
4. BOUQUET, R. J.: Cannabis. *Bull Narcotics, 4*(2):14-30, 1950 (Part I) and *1*(3):22-45, 1951 (Part II).
5. BECKER, H. S.: Marihuana use and social control. *Social Prob, 3*:35-44, 1955.
6. BENABUD, A.: Psycho-pathological aspects of the cannabis situation in Morocco: statistical data for 1956. *Bull Narcotics, 4*(9):1-16, 1957.

7. CHOPRA, I. C., AND CHOPRA, R. N.: The use of cannabis drugs in India. *Bull Narcotics, 1*(9):4-29, 1957.

8. AMES, F.: A clinical and metabolic study of acute intoxication with *Cannabis sativa* and its role in the model psychoses. *J Ment Sc, 104*:972-999, 1958.

9. MURPHY, J. B. M.: The cannabis habit: a review of recent psychiatric literature. *Bull Narcotics, 1*(15):15-23, 1963.

10. LAMBO, T. A.: Medical and social problems of drug addiction in West Africa. *Bull Narcotics, 1*(17):3-13, 1965.

11. SOUIEF, M. I.: Hashish consumption in Egypt with special reference to psychosocial aspects. *Bull Narcotics, 2*(19):1-12, 1967.

12. SCHWARZ, C. J.: LSD, Marihuana and the law. *Brit Columbia Med J, 9*:274-285, 1967.

13. BLOOMQUIST, E. R.: *Marihuana.* Beverly Hills, Glencoe Press, 1968.

14. SCHWARZ, C. J.: Towards a Medical Understanding of Marihuana. *Canad Psychiat Ass J, 14*:591-600, 1969.

15. Editorial: Marihuana. *Canad Med Ass J, 31*:544-546, 1934.

Chapter Fifteen

THE GENERAL PRACTITIONER VIEWS DRUG ABUSE

RICHARD E. LAHTI

THE QUESTION OF illicit drug use and drug abuse may be illustrated by discussing just one drug, marihuana. Marihuana is the obvious choice, of course, because it is probably the most popular and enjoys the most widespread use. Some of the generalities that I make about the use of marihuana may be applied to almost any drug that is being abused ranging from nicotine and alcohol to heroin.

I approach this as a discussion of an intoxicant. I do not believe that this is an isolated problem. I do not believe that we can take drug abuse and examine it alone. I think it is a manifestation of a much wider, deeper problem of unrest; the evolution that our society is going through at the moment.

The definition of intoxicants in *Webster's* is, "something used to excite, stupify, inebriate, or poison." Now my *Webster's* is old, but I think that probably nowadays the definition should include some reference to emotional escape: to take a trip. Since we are not going to discuss these drugs as medicines, we are going to discuss them in terms of intoxicants, we will not discuss the pharmacology or the physiological effect in terms of therapeutics.

There has been much written and a lot said about marihuana and about the relative safety of marihuana when compared to our culture's standard for intoxicants—a substance we must compare all intoxicants with—alcohol. And I think that one of the keys to my approach is that we are comparing the relative "merit" of two intoxicants. One intoxicant compared to another, one poison compared to another, if you will. Now those of you who are involved in pharmacology or in similar related sciences, of course, understand any discussion of the effects of drugs must depend upon and is related to the dosage used and the route of administration. What I have to say about marihuana and alcohol is in relationship to a light to moderate dose, the common method of using it.

When marihuana is smoked and inhaled, the effect is rapid, the onset of action is in a few minutes. The greatest effect occurs in one to two hours, and then it gradually tapers off up to six to eight hours, dependent on the dosage and the quality of marihuana used. Most users describe the feeling in marihuana intoxication as one of a high feeling, a euphoria, a sense of well-being, contentment, and sociability. Usually at the end it wears off, and there is a feeling of drowsiness. In common with other intoxicants there is a marked loss of inhibition, and this is similar, of course, to alcohol. This may be the reason that some people feel that marihuana is a sexual stimulant. More likely it merely releases inhibitions. The effect of the drug in some people is peculiar in that it must be learned; people must learn to use this thing, and much of the effect is said to depend upon the attitude or the expectations of the user—and this characteristic is not confined to marihuana. This aspect of effect of drugs is not unusual. In many people, drugs produce effects which the subjects expect to feel. I well recall, and perhaps some of you recall, the Coke® and aspirin routine of a previous generation. In my day there was a fair number of intoxicated "trips" taken on that combination, and probably all it did was relieve headaches. A year or so ago we had a high school student brought into our clinic who was obviously on a trip. She was grossly intoxicated and had in her possession several packages of white powder. She had taken one and had a rather violent episode on the front steps. The powder was analyzed at the crime laboratory, and it was basically baking soda. There was a fellow selling the little packets of white powder for one dollar a packet. The girl still believes she had taken an hallucinogenic drug. Marihuana has been given to experimenters without their knowledge, and these subjects reported they felt nothing. This was a very light dose, however.

Many people will say that marihuana increases one's awareness, sharpens one's acuity, both in hearing and vision and other senses. One study indicated that the drug increased auditory acuity, and other studies deny this. I have read studies in which there has been an attempt to measure the effect on intellectual functions, and most of them indicate that though the subject feels as if he is more creative and that he is more intelligent, actual objective tests fail to bear this out. This, again, I would like to point, out is similar to alcohol. I am aware of the person who, under the influence of a drink or two, becomes the life of the party and suddenly is quite witty. At any rate, the feeling of enhanced creativeness under the influence of marihuana is probably for the most part a myth.

The primary effect, then, of marihuana is intoxication, and since at the moment marihuana is an illegal drug, this then becomes a difficult thing to evaluate. Intoxication is a difficult parameter to translate into the scientific terms like temperature and blood pressure, and the use of the drug is illegal so therefore it is difficult to get any pure drug or group of people to study.

Probably the most important effect, at least to me, of the use of marihuana and similar drugs is the sociological and psychological. I think these are far more important. The drug in light doses has little real physical or addicting property. I think the most important thing is, therefore, its deep-seated sociological and psychological effects.

Some of the other effects that people talk about are the distortion of time and space, and again as I understand it, this has not been scientifically established. People describe an enhanced appreciation of beauty. Unfortunately, this quality is neither constant nor consistent. One cannot take a given dose of marihuana and consistently appreciate Pablo Piccaso, for example. There is no physical addiction. There is a potential for tremendous psychological dependency and this dependency is not necessarily limited to the quality of the drug. I see this emotional dependency on many things. I think this is a quality of people as much as it is a quality of the drug concerned. And I am as concerned with the dependency I see in my patients on diet pills and nicotine. I think this is just as important. I have had obese people demand "diet pills" from me which they have been taking for years from other sources. Obviously, they have not lost weight but are using this as a means of rationalizing their dependence. This is evading the truth. This is an escape from reality by using drugs as much as the use of marihuana.

One of the things that complicates the picture in the use of marihuana is the way in which it is used. Being an illegal drug, of course, its use has to be fairly secret. Intoxication with marihuana, or for that matter, any drug, lowers inhibitions and increases the chances of using something else. I had a young man in the office last week who plays in a high school pop group and had been introduced to marihuana by his best friend. Unfortunately, this led during the use of marihuana to the use of some LSD and other drugs, and this young man had an unfortunate response. He had a bad trip and was still having the effects of it some three months later. He is not even sure what all he took that particular time. So this presents, I think, a real danger, just as I think someone intoxicated from alcohol is liable to do some rather stupid things.

Some young people today have no fear of drugs. They will take anything, inject anything, use anything. I was called early one morning to see a teen-age girl, the daughter of a very good friends of mine, who was wildly hallucinating. She had heard from her best friend that one could take a trip on Merazine®, which is a remedy for seasickness which can be purchased without a prescription. So she bought two bottles and took them. And she did have a trip. This is difficult for me to comprehend. I know this girl well. She is a very intelligent and, I thought, well-adjusted young lady. But she spent three days in the hospital in restraints. This situation is being seen with increasing frequency. I had another young man, brought in by his father, obviously semiconscious. He and his friends had climbed a fence around a manufacturing plant and found a fifty-gallon drum full of solvent, of an unknown type. They poured a Mason jar full of it and inhaled it to unconsciousness. We were unable to identify the solvent at the time and neither could the boys. Episodes such as these are expressions of a real social problem.

I think one of the aspects of chronic marihuana use that must be considered is that production of an euphoric state is incompatible with the desire to produce useful effort. I will quote three different reports, one is from the Mayor's Report[1] of New York City in which marihuana users are described as subjects which "did not have desire or urge to occupy themselves creatively in a manner which might prove socially useful. They showed a tendency to drift along in a passive fashion and gave a good portion of their attention to relatively unimportant matters. These men were poorly adjusted." Maurer and Vogel[2] report, "most of them appear rather indolent, ineffectual young men and women who are on the most part not very productive. Most habitual users suffer from basic personality defects." Goodman and Gilman[3] describe the typical marihuana user in the United States as "usually a person 20-30 years of age, idle, lacking in initiative, with a history of repeated frustrations and deprivations. He is often maladjusted, seeks distraction, escape, and sometimes conviviality." Now, let me add a little bit here. I think these descriptions are somewhat outmoded. They were taken before the widespread popularity of this drug. I do not believe that currently all drug users and all the marihuana users are maladjusted, and I do not believe they all come from the deprived areas of our society. It is very obvious that drug dependency involves any area, any social status. However, most of the literature indicates that this tendency toward passiveness is characteristic of a chronic marihuana user. I think that in discussing the effects of this drug, one should consider the attitudes of the nations which have the most experience with it. In India, Morocco, Algeria, and other Near East nations, it is illegal to smoke marihuana. India allows the drinking of bhang, which is a weak brew, probably with as much potency as our beer. In most of these nations the cultivation of marihuana is theoretically under government control. The drug grows so easily and so widely over there, governmental control is probably more wishful thinking than actuality. These nations have moved more recently to a more punitive attitude toward drug use. For example, I believe it is Nigeria that executes convicted pushers. I think it is evident that these nations fear the effect of the drug enough to legislate against it. Sociologists of these nations feel the passiveness and lack of productivity produced by widespread use of marihuana has been a significant factor in the lack of advancement of their countries. The study by McClelland[4] says, "It is probably no accident that the society which most consistently encourages the use of these substances (India) produced one of the sickest social orders ever created by mankind in which thinking men spent their time lost in the Buddha position under the influence of drugs, while poverty, disease, social discrimination and superstition reached their highest and most organized form in all history." Mellon says, "Insight with drugs is easy and passive, and while it may help an individual to understand himself, *it cannot be translated into action or creation,* nor can intoxication from anything for that matter."[5] He further says, "group uses of drugs among non-Indians represent a trend towards passivity in our society. A highly dangerous trend since the passive societies in the midst of active ones are always destroyed." And I might point out that most marihuana societies were subjugated by alcohol societies at one time or another. For example, the opium wars in China.

I have spent many hours talking to student groups, high schools and grade schools. Initially I was talking to large assemblies, but I have given it up, since for the most part I think it is very unproductive. These kids have had it up to their ears from the establishment standing up and telling them, don't, don't, don't. And I must admit that some of the propaganda that they have been forced to swallow is rather poor. Some of the movies and slides and things are an insult to any intelligent person. I think our approach has been entirely wrong. I have garnered the following impressions in talking to these young people: I find the high school student is quite well informed, and let me emphasize here that I feel strongly that the average young person in this country has a pretty good head. And I think he is thinking deeply about his problems, about all our problems. I have the feeling that the young person is concerned less about drug abuse than he is about other social problems, much more than his teachers or his peers are. Unfortunately, it appears that many of them are concerned over what I consider merely another symptom, drug abuse, instead of the real problems. Now why do high school students use drugs? I hesitate to imply that I have any answers. One of the most important factors is the herd instinct. Many, many kids try these things simply because the others did it. They do not want to be classed as an outsider or a square, and so to fit in, they try drugs. I do not believe they intend to become drug addicts nor that they will become drug addicts. I think that the fact that they have inhaled some marihuana is not going to mark them for life. I do not feel that experimenting with this drug or alcohol, for that matter, is going to destroy their productivity in the future. I think this is a fairly normal expression of their age. Obviously reasons for drug abuse range all the way from the simple herd instinct to psychosis. There is no one pattern. I have told you about the young man who was a patient who did it because his best friend offered it to him. This was not an overt desire on the youngster's part to use drugs. It was just a desire to belong. He would have done the same thing for a beer or loud shirts, or you name it. Unfortunately, this boy got into more drug difficulties.

Another common factor in inducing youngsters to try these things is conveniently lumped under the term *rebellion.* Now a good share of the rebellion is induced by the adult society. For example, they have a hard time, the youngsters, relating our association with alcohol, our use of alcohol, and our treatment of alcohol to social uses of a drug in light doses such as marihuana. They are told, and rightly so, that it is no worse than alcohol, that it is not as bad as alcohol. But they are losing sight of the fact that what they are doing is comparing one intoxicant with another. One bad thing with another bad thing. This argument does not imply that marihuana is good or that alcohol is beneficial. It implies that our society is stuck with the use of intoxicants, with drug dependency, and that it is merely a question of trying to decide which one we want. It probably would be more pertinent and more intelligent to try to develop a society that was not as drug dependent. Most of the youngsters eagerly throw it up to you that you use the alcohol—why can't I use marihuana? And you tell me it does not harm me physically. And most of us trip over our guilt complexes and have no real good answer for this. And I am not sure that I do either. But one approach and one answer is to point out that because the established society has not done so well and because the established society has exhibited marked tendencies to become drug dependent, perhaps it would be better for the younger society to move in a different direction, rather than make the same mistake we have been making for centuries with alcohol, except to substitute marihuana. Perhaps it would be better for all of us if we tried to move away from drug dependence. And that includes diet pills, tobacco, and sleeping pills. I wonder if we really must as a society accept drug dependence as inevitable. Can we as a society move away from drug dependence?

Most of the students consider marihuana and other intoxicants in the light of the individual rather than in the light of society as a whole. They point out that the drug is nonaddicting, not harmful, and yet I am sure that many of you are aware of the studies in Lexington where they say something like 82 percent of all the heroin addicts used marihuana first. I do not attach personally a cause and effect relationship to this statistic. But what this does represent to me is that of the group of people who use drugs, and by that I include the hallucinogens, there are those who could not handle them. These are the alcoholics of the drug society. And if our great standard of intoxicants, alcohol, has produced a large segment of our population that is costing us billions a year, then it seems logical to me that the encouragement of widespread use of another intoxicant would merely produce another group of people who are dependent on society. The implication is given that we can substitute marihuana for alcohol, and I think there are some very good reasons why this would never happen. There are economic reasons, and I think that there is even some work which indicates that drug users are not interested in alcohol, and vice versa.

The youngsters point out all these "good things" about marihuana: it does not cause crime, does not cause cirrhosis, and it does not cause lots of things. But it does not *do* anything beneficial. They are confusing these claims as being statements justifying the use of it. One of the biggest arguments I have had with the youngsters is the concept of the individual versus society. The concept that we cannot moralize for each other. This is a big debate, and there is room to consider both sides of this. Most societies have laws, all societies are restrictive to individuals, and in a sense there is a large body of laws in any society that represent an attempt to moralize for each other. It becomes a question then, whether we aim at an ordered society or not. This is the concept "that I can do anything that I wish as long as I don't hurt anyone else." Idealistically this is wonderful but this considers only the individual and not the group as a whole. It is vital in an ordered society to consider the net result of any action and, if necessary, restriction of individuals for the good of all must be done. Young people exhibit a high sense of injustice. And they feel that many of their cohorts have been penalized unjustly for the possession of a drug that is harmless, or relatively so, and yet alcohol users go free. I am sure that most of you are aware that we have made attempts in Oregon to change this and avoid the inequity.

I would hope in closing that we as a society can move away from drug dependence of all types and perhaps pay more attention to rehabilitation and education of those that have these problems.

REFERENCES

1. *Mayors Committee on Marihuana, New York City.* Lancaster, Jacques Cattell Press, 1944.
2. MAURER, D. W., AND VOGEL, V. H.: *Narcotics and Narcotics Addiction.* Springfield, Illinois, Charles C Thomas, 1962.
3. GOODMAN, L. S., AND GILMAN, A.: *The Pharmacological Basis of Therapeutics.* New York, MacMillan, 1955, p. 171.
4. GORDON, N.: The hallucinogenic drug cult. *The Reporter,* Aug. 15, pp. 35-43, 1963.
5. MELLON, C.: Reflection of a peyote eater. *The Harvard Review, 1*: No. 4, pp. 63-67, 1963.

Chapter Sixteen

THE PSYCHOTHERAPEUTIC DRUG SCENE IN SAN FRANCISCO

GLEN D. MELLINGER

T HIS PAPER IS based on findings from a cross-section sample survey of adults (ages 18 and over) in San Francisco. The survey was conducted in late 1967 and early 1968, and one of its main purposes was to obtain information about the use of psychotherapeutic drugs (such as stimulants, tranquilizers, sedatives, and hypnotics) which are intended to alleviate various psychic or somatic symptoms.

It should be noted at the outset that the paper will not have much to say about drug abuse. In fact, we have deliberately avoided the concept of *abuse* in our studies and have concentrated instead on prevailing patterns of psychotherapeutic drug *use* in the general population.

Which of these many possible patterns one chooses to regard as abuse is very much a function of the values of the observer. To some, any use of a chemical substance to alter one's physiological or emotional state is regarded as abuse. To others, such use is legitimate, provided it takes place under proper medical supervision. Still others would want to consider the nature and intensity of the individual's problem or need and also the availability of acceptable alternative ways of coping with distress.

In short, drug abuse is a complex and emotionally loaded concept that reflects a great variety of values and is applied to many different types of behavior. Accordingly, there is a real need in our present limited state of knowledge to step back and take an objective look at drug use within the context of the individual's perceived needs and values. Those who are involved professionally in dealing with drug abuse problems may find this approach disappointing or even disconcerting. Hopefully, however, an overall view of prevailing drug-use patterns will provide a useful perspective for discussions of drug abuse.

The paper will begin by describing the background of the study and some of the broader issues with which we are concerned. Later, it will present a few of our findings with respect to how many people are using stimulants, sedatives, tranquilizers, and other psychotherapeutic agents, where these drugs are obtained, what they are used for, and how they are used.

The study is part of a larger research program, the ultimate goal of which is to describe the extent and character of psychotherapeutic drug use in the United States. This program is being sponsored by the Psychopharmacology Research Branch of the National Institute of Mental Health, and the survey research aspect of the program involves two collaborating research teams: the Family Research Center of the Langley Porter Neuropsychiatric Institute, and the Social Research Group of George Washington University. The Family Research Center has been responsible for developing procedures and instruments for collecting data and for conducting surveys in California.[*1] The Social Research Group recently carried out a methodological study on the validity of survey data on drug use.[†2] The latter group has also obtained some preliminary data on a national basis and will shortly undertake a more detailed nationwide survey patterned after the study reported here.[3]

The impetus for this research program came primarily from the growing importance of psychotherapeutic drugs in medical practice, combined with the fact that very little is known about "the history of the pill bottle" once it leaves the pharmacy. There is no need here to document the increasing use of these drugs, but it should be emphasized that any figures used to do so should be viewed with caution. The extent of increase may easily be maximized or minimized if one has a particular axe to

---

[*] The studies in California are being conducted under research grant MH-12591.

[†] The validity study compared interview information on drug use with information about the data people obtained from prescription records.[2]

grind. In evaluating the increase in use of tranquilizers, for example, it is easy to overlook the fact that much of the increase took place at the expense of the sedatives, such as phenobarbital. Further, the enactment of the Drug Abuse Control Amendments in 1965 creates certain problems in comparing information obtained prior to that date with information obtained subsequently. Nevertheless, there has clearly been an increase in the use of psychotherapeutic drugs.

Accompanying the increase, there has been growing concern about the medical and social implications of the so-called revolution in psychopharmacology.[4] Medically, there has been concern about the demonstrated potential for physical dependency on the barbiturates, amphetamines, and tranquilizers—concern that led to the Drug Abuse Control Amendments of 1965. There is also concern about the use of these drugs without medical supervision or for purposes not intended by the practicing physician. At the same time, a committee of the American Medical Association has pointed out that physicians themselves may contribute to the problem by, "Utilizing prolonged and unsupervised administration . . . for symptomatic relief, often without adequate diagnosis or knowledge of the patient's past experience with medications or attitudes toward drugs.[5]

In any case, the increasing reliance of physicians on psychotherapeutic drugs has been matched (if not surpassed) by the popularity of and demand for these drugs among the lay public. Moreover, there is a growing rift between traditional medical conceptions of what drugs should be used for versus quite different conceptions which are emerging, especially among the younger generation. Traditionally, the use of drugs in medical practice has been restricted to the treatment of disease, that is, to conditions which the physician and patient both recognize as disabling. Now there is no question that emotional distress can become disabling, and most physicians would agree that the use of psychotherapeutic drugs is appropriate in these circumstances. The trouble is that emotional distress cannot be neatly calibrated, and often times may be vague and diffuse and appears to the physician, at least, to be a case of "dys-ease" rather than disease. In these cases, the patient is apt to leave the doctor's office disappointed, if not incensed, if his need has been dismissed and his request for drugs denied.

The rift between patient and physician is even more pronounced when the patient is actually functioning reasonably well and simply wants a drug to help him function better. Take, for example, the student who wants to stay awake to study for finals, or the executive who wants to "be at his best" for an important meeting, or the housewife who is "uptight" over the impending arrival of her mother-in-law. These needs are clearly outside the realm of disease, but the fact is that psychotherapeutic drugs provide a simple and effective way of dealing with these needs in today's fast-moving and high-pressured society. This conflict between the desires of the patient and the professional standards of the physician raises some intriguing questions about what goes on in the transaction between the physician and the patient who comes seeking a drug. Although these questions unfortunately are beyond the scope of our study, we do have evidence that one way patients sometimes resolve the conflict is to simply bypass the physician and obtain drugs from other sources.

In addition to its implications for medical practice, the enthusiastic public acceptance of psychotherapeutic drugs is also viewed by some as a vivid indicator of widespread malaise in modern American society and as a harbinger of changing cultural values. The extent of psychic distress in the population has been well documented in recent studies by Gurin and others.[6] And one gets the impression from many sources that traditional values of self-denial and acceptance of suffering are going out of style, not just among young people, but among many of their elders as well. In fact, some students of the psychedelic drug culture among young people trace that development, in part, to the readiness of parents to seek instant, magic relief in pills.[7, 8] If we are indeed becoming a "drug-seeking society," as is sometimes claimed, the explanation surely involves the widespread need for relief from everyday tension in a culture which increasingly views physical and emotional distress as an impediment to adequate functioning—rather than a moral test of virtue.

These, then, are some of the interests and concerns that led to this study of the use of psychotherapeutic drugs. The methods we used to obtain our data are described briefly in the following section.

STUDY METHODS

The data were obtained by means of personal interviews with 1,104 adults selected by strict probability sampling methods to represent adult residents of San Francisco.* Although there have been many interesting and useful studies of drug use based on medical or prescription records, these records deal with only one aspect of drug-using behavior. For our purposes, it is important to consider the entire range of the individual's psychotherapeutic drug use, regardless of where the drugs were obtained. We are interested in people who obtain medical care from physicians as well as those who do not. We are interested in people who "shop around" among various physicians to obtain their drugs, in those who obtain prescription-type drugs from various illicit or informal sources, in those who are willing to settle for over-the-counter drugs such as No-Doz, Sleep-Eze, and Compoz®, and (incidentally) in those who never use drugs at all. Most important, we are interested in relating various patterns of drug acquisition and use (including nonuse) to the needs, values, and other characteristics of the individual. There is no one set of records, to our knowledge, that contains this kind of information on any group of individuals, let alone a cross-section sample of an entire community. The only feasible way to obtain such information is by sample surveys.

The main point to emphasize about our study methods is that the interviewing procedures were carefully and extensively pretested before the study began. We were aware that some respondents might be reluctant to discuss their use of psycho-

---

* A probability sample is one in which each person in the population has an equal (or known) opportunity of being selected into the sample. The main advantages of this type of sampling are (1) probability theory may be used to deduce how closely estimates based on the sample will agree with the results that would have been obtained if the entire population had been surveyed, using the same data collection procedures; and (2) the likelihood of selecting any given individual is not influenced by the characteristics of that individual, i.e. the sample is not biased.

therapeutic drugs or find it difficult to recall and identify drugs they had used. Pretesting demonstrated that these problems were not as serious as we had expected and that they could be largely overcome by, first, establishing good rapport with respondents before raising the subject of drugs and, second, by using photographic aids to help them recall drugs used.

I say "largely overcome" because our estimates are not and can never be 100 percent reliable. However, results from the validity study being conducted by the Social Research Group indicate that the estimates of drug use we are reporting are within a very few percentage points of the estimates we would get if there were no underreporting or memory loss by respondents. We also have the strong impression from our own study that most persons who use psychotherapeutic drugs are not only willing to discuss the matter, but actually enjoy the opportunity to do so—if only to air the guilt feelings that many of them seem to experience when they use psychotherapeutic drugs.

FINDINGS

Let us turn now to the psychotherapeutic drug scene in San Francisco. Table 16-I is designed to show the proportions of men and women in San Francisco who have *ever* used psychotherapeutic drugs, and the proportions using such drugs *during the past year*. In this table, we have classified drug users according to whether they have used prescription-type drugs, over-the-counter drugs, or both.

TABLE 16-I
PROPORTION OF ADULTS IN SAN FRANCISCO USING
PSYCHOTHERAPEUTIC DRUGS

Drug Type	Ever Used		Used Past Year	
	Women %	Men %	Women %	Men %
Any psychotherapeutic drug	60	51	45	33
(Rx only)†	(34)	(20)	(32)	(18)
(Rx & O.T.C.‡)	(15)	(14)	(6)	(5)
(O.T.C. only)	(10)	(18)	(7)	(9)
None	40	49	55	67
	—	—	—	—
Total %*	100	100	100	100
(No. of persons)	(634)	(470)	(634)	(470)

* Percentages may add to slightly more or less than 100 because of rounding.
† Rx = prescription.
‡ O.T.C. = over the counter.

The main findings in this table are as follows:

1. Six out of ten women have used at least one psychotherapeutic drug at one time or another, as compared with five
   out of ten men.* (According to data not shown in the
   table, slightly over one half of the drug users have used
   two or more different drugs.)
2. Forty-five per cent of the women and 33 percent of the
   men have used one or more drugs during the past year.
3. Note that while women are more likely than men to have
   used prescription drugs—probably because they go to a
   doctor more often—the reverse tends to be true for over-
   the-counter drugs ever used.

Two comments should be made about the finding that women
are more likely to have used prescription psychotherapeutics
than men. One is that these drugs represent only one of many
alternative ways of coping with emotional distress or "dys-ease."
The most popular alternative, of course, is alcohol. And studies
of drinking practices show that men are more likely to drink
than women and they are much more likely to be heavy
drinkers.[9, 10] Apparently, it is more acceptable in our society for
men to use alcohol to relieve tensions than it is for women, but
it is less acceptable for men to admit they are sick enough to
go to a doctor. In any case, it is evident that the kinds of needs
that lead alternatively to drugs or to alcohol seem to be fairly
common among both men and women, and that both are likely
to do *something* to alleviate these needs.

The other comment is that even though our survey finds the
prevalence of drug use to be greater among women than it is
among men, the difference is not as great as one would expect
from studies based on medical or prescription records.[11, 12, 13]
Any differences in the findings from our study, as compared with
other studies, may be due in part to the character of San Fran-

---

* The multistage sampling design used in this study underrepresented
persons in direct proportion to the number of adults in the households selected.
This underrepresentation was corrected by appropriate weighting, and all
percentages shown are based on weighted data. However, the number of cases
referred to are the actual number of interviews (in Table 16-I) or the actual
number of "drug mentions" (in later tables).

cisco. However, these differences are probably due in greater measure to the fact that studies based on medical records do not take account of the nonmedical sources from which prescription drugs are sometimes obtained. As will be seen later, these non-medical sources are more likely to be used by men than by women. But first, let us consider Table 16-II which shows the various kinds of drugs that respondents told us they have used.

TABLE 16-II

PROPORTION OF DRUGS MENTIONED AS "EVER USED"

Drug Class	Drug(s) Mentioned Most Often in Class	%
Rx Drugs		
Stimulants, Anorexants	Dexedrine®, Dexamyl®	29
Minor tranquilizers	Librium®, Miltown®, Equanil®	14
Hypnotics	Nembutal®, Seconal®, Doriden®	11
Sedatives	Phenobarbital	8
Antispasmodics and/or antiemetics	Donnatal®, Compazine®	5
Major tranquilizers	Thorazine®, Stelazine®	3
Antidepressants	Tofranil®, Elavil®, Ritalin®	2
(Total Rx-type drug mentions)		(72)
OTC		
Stimulants	No-Doz®	12
Sleeping pills	Sominex®, Sleep-Eze®	11
Tranquilizers	Compoz®	5
(Total O.T.C. drug mentions)		(28)
Total percent		100
(Number of drugs mentioned as "ever used")		(1699)

The percentages in this table are based on the number of specific drugs mentioned as having been used by respondents. For example, if a respondent told us he has used Librium®, that is counted as "one mention"—regardless of the number of times he used it. If the same respondent also told us he has used Miltown®, that is counted as another "mention."

In all, 634 of our 1,104 respondents mentioned at least one drug (in the sense just described). These 634 respondents mentioned having used (at one time or another) a total of 1,699 drugs, or an average of 2.7 different drugs per drug user.

Of the 1,699 drugs mentioned, 72 percent were prescription-type drugs, and the remainder (28%) were over-the-counter drugs. Among the prescription drugs, the stimulants (mostly amphetamines) were mentioned twice as often as any other single class—much more often than is usually found in studies based on medical prescriptions.[11, 12, 13]

There are now two important respects in which our survey data differ from the results of studies done in medical settings: first, we find somewhat more men who have used psychotherapeutic drugs than we expected; and second, we find stimulants being reported much more often than we expected. Some of the reasons for these differences will become apparent in the following tables.

TABLE 16-III

DRUG TYPES AND SOURCES FROM WHICH DRUGS WERE OBTAINED
(Based on Psychotherapeutic Drugs Used Last Month or Last Time)

Drug Type	Source	Men %	Women %	All %
Rx	Medical	34	60	50
Rx	Nonmedical	24	15	18
	(Friend)	(14)	(10)	(11)
	(Spouse)	(4)	(*)	(2)
	(Relative)	(2)	(2)	(2)
	(Other)	(4)	(2)	(3)
O.T.C.	All	41	23	30
	(Store)	(33)	(17)	(23)
	(Friend)	(5)	(2)	(3)
	(Spouse)	(2)	(*)	(1)
	(Relative/Other)	(1)	(3)	(3)
Any	Not ascertained	1	2	2
	Total %	100	100	100
	(No. drug mentions)	(346)	(552)	(898)

* Less than 0.5 percent.

In Table 16-III we restricted the analysis to drugs that were used during the past month or, if not during the past month, to the drug that was used most recently. The purpose of this restriction was simply to maximize the reliability of certain of the detailed information we wanted to obtain regarding drugs—in particular, where the drug was obtained, what it was used for, and so on. By limiting these kinds of detailed questions to the drug used most recently (or to any drug used during the past month), we concentrated on experiences with drugs that the respondent was most likely to remember accurately.

This table reflects, in a different way, the earlier finding that women are more likely than men to use prescription drugs, and that men are more likely than women to use over-the-counter drugs.

More important, notice that 18 percent of all the drugs used last time were prescription-type drugs that were obtained from nonmedical sources.* Another way of stating this finding is that 27 percent of the prescription-type drugs—more than one fourth of them—were obtained (the last time they were used) from some source other than a physician. Notice, too, that nonmedical sources are more likely to be used by men than they are by women. This fact will not show up, of course, in data based on prescription records, and it is one important reason why studies done in medical settings tend to underestimate the number of men who have actually used psychotherapeutic drugs.

Another interesting finding in the table is that the non-medical source mentioned most often (both by men and women) is someone described by the respondent as "a friend." In most cases, this designation can probably be taken at face value. Respondents often described the friend as a roommate, a boyfriend or girl friend, and so on. In other cases, the relationship of the friend to the respondent was not quite so clear. We were curious, naturally, about the possibility that the friend might be "the friendly neighborhood pusher." However, other parts of the interview were really more important for our purposes, so we resisted the temptation to ask respondents to be more explicit. In short, we do not know how many of these drugs were obtained through truly illicit channels. Suffice it to say that a good many of the prescription drugs are being obtained through channels that we can at least describe as "informal."

Another interesting point is that the spouse is seldom mentioned as one of the nonprescription sources for obtaining prescription drugs. When a spouse is mentioned, it is usually the wife who is the source rather than the husband, probably because she is more likely than he is to get drugs from a physician. For

---

* This finding does not necessarily suggest that these respondents *always* obtain the drug from a non-medical source, but only that the last time the drug was used, it had been obtained without a prescription. It may also be noted that the drugs used last time (or during the past month) account for more than one-half of all drugs mentioned by respondents. In some (although relatively few) cases, the drug used last time had not been used for a period of years.

whatever implications it may have, it also appears (data not shown) that the drugs men obtain from friends are usually stimulants, whereas the drugs they obtain from their spouses are usually tranquilizers.

We have seen, then, that the likelihood of obtaining a prescription-type drug from a nonmedical source is related to the sex of the user. The same fact is evident in Table 16-IV which considers only prescription-type drugs. As in the previous table, these data are based on the drug (or drugs) used during the past month or last time.

TABLE 16-IV

PROPORTION OF PRESCRIPTION-TYPE DRUGS OBTAINED
FROM NONMEDICAL SOURCE

(Based on Psychotherapeutic Drug(s) Used Last Month or Last Time)

	Men		Women		All	
Age of User	%	(Base)*	%	(Base)	%	(Base)
Under 30	60	(56)	41	(108)	51	(164)
30 to 44	27	(55)	17	(108)	24	(163)
45 or older	19	(87)	6	(195)	10	(282)
All	41	(198)	20	(411)	27	(609)

Even more important, Table 16-IV shows that the likelihood that a prescription drug was obtained from a nonmedical source is clearly highest if the user is in the youngest age group. Of the prescription-type drugs mentioned by men under thirty, almost seven out of ten were obtained last time without a prescription. The figure is considerably lower for drugs used by men over thirty, but even in the age group forty-five or older, two out of every ten prescription drugs were obtained last time from a nonmedical source. We find the same pattern for the drugs mentioned by women, except that, in general, the probability of using a nonmedical source is only one-half as great for women as it is for men.

Thus, it is very evident that younger people, especially men, are bypassing the medical system to a considerable extent in obtaining psychotherapeutic drugs.

As suggested earlier, the likelihood of using the medical system to obtain drugs will also depend on the condition or need

---

* Base: total number of prescription-type drugs used last month or last time by persons in each age-sex group.

the drug is to be used for. This point is clearly illustrated in Table 16-V.

TABLE 16-V

DRUG TYPE AND SOURCE ACCORDING TO PURPOSE
FOR WHICH DRUG WAS USED

(Based on Psychotherapeutic Drug(s) Taken Past Month or Last Time)

MEN

Drug Type	Source	Used for:					Get High %
		Physical %	Weight %	Tranquil. %	Sleep %	Stimulat'n %	
Rx	Medical	96	81	62	41	7	—
Rx	Nonmedical	4	19	17	12	25	100
O.T.C.	All	—	—	21	47	68	—
	Total percent	100	100	100	100	100	100
	(No. of drug mentions)	(24)	(16)	(54)	(92)	(119)	(8)

WOMEN

Rx	Medical	86	87	70	48	27	—
Rx	Nonmedical	13	13	13	13	20	—
O.T.C.	All	1	—	17	39	53	—
	Total percent	100	100	100	100	100	—
	(No. of drug mentions)	(59)	(100)	(143)	(111)	(101)	(—)

In this table, we have distinguished between drugs obtained via three distinct drug distribution systems or channels: the medical system for prescription-type drugs, the nonmedical system for prescription-type drugs, and the over-the-counter system. Which system was used depends very much on what the drug was used for. The first column represents drugs used primarily for physical problems such as gastrointestinal disturbances, and muscular tension. Most of these drugs were obtained through medical channels. The next column represents drugs used for weight control. Four out of five of the drugs used by men for this purpose were obtained through the medical system, as were almost nine out of ten of the drugs used for weight control by women. Thus, problems pertaining to weight and other physical symptoms clearly fall under the heading of "disease," and the physician is generally used as the source for drugs to treat these problems.

The medical system is much less likely to be used to deal with sleep problems and particularly the desire for stimulation.

Among men, only 7 percent of the drugs used for stimulation or energy (which includes staying awake) were obtained last time from a medical source. Of these drugs 68 percent of the over-the-counter variety, mainly No-Doz, and 25 percent were prescription-type drugs obtained from nonmedical sources. There were relatively few cases in which the respondent explicitly told us he used a drug to get high. All of those we did get were reported by men and all of them were prescription drugs from non-medical sources.

TABLE 16-VI

PATTERN OF DRUG USE ACCORDING TO TYPE AND SOURCE OF DRUG

(Based on Psychotherapeutic Drug(s) Taken Past Month or Last Time)

Sex of User	Pattern of Use	Drug Type/Source Rx/Med.	Rx/Nonmed.	O.T.C.
Men	Only a few times	28	63	81
	Occasionally	12	28	11
	Daily <1 month	18	6	4
	Daily ≥1 month	42	3	4
	Total % (Men)	100	100	100
	(No. of drug mentions)	(128)	(70)	(145)
Women	Only a few times	16	80	80
	Occasionally	21	8	17
	Daily <1 month	19	7	3
	Daily ≥1 month	44	5	*
	Total % (Women)	100	100	100
	(No. of drug mentions)	(347)	(64)	(132)

Having demonstrated that a sizeable proportion of the prescription drugs used last time were obtained from nonmedical sources, it is now important to consider how these drugs are being used as compared with prescription-type drugs obtained through medical channels and with over-the-counter drugs. The last table thus shows the pattern of drug use according to the source from which the drug was obtained. The drug use patterns include the following categories: "only a few times," "occasionally, but never more than a day or two at a time," "daily, for a period of less than one month," and "daily for one month or longer."

The main point to be made from Table 16-VI is that the prescription-type drugs obtained from medical sources are much more likely than other drugs to be used on a continuing or

---

* Less than 0.5 percent.

"chronic" basis. About four out of ten of the medically obtained drugs were used, both by men and women, on a daily basis for a month or longer. Drugs obtained from the other two systems tend to be used much more casually and infrequently. The reverse side of this coin is that the overwhelming majority (over 90%) of the drugs used regularly and continuously were obtained from a physician.

SUMMARY AND CONCLUSIONS

In summary, data from a cross-section sample of adults in San Francisco indicate that the following:

1. The use of psychotherapeutic drugs to deal with various kinds of emotional needs and distress is very widespread, and there is little reason to believe that these drugs will be used any less widely as time goes on.
2. If people cannot, or choose not to, get these drugs from physicians, the fact is that they are getting them elsewhere. Among young people, especially, there appears to be a considerable deterioration in the physician's traditional role as gatekeeper in the drug distribution system. However, drugs obtained from nonmedical sources appear, for the most part, to be used on a relatively casual and infrequent basis.
3. The extent to which the physician is still the primary source of drugs depends not only on the age and sex of the user, but also on the need for which drugs are sought. In a society which places great value on energy, it is a rather interesting paradox that the medical system apparently is not viewed, either by its practitioners or its clients, as an appropriate place to obtain energizing drugs.

In closing, it is our belief that any discussion of the drug problem must consider two exceedingly important issues. First, *why* are people using these drugs? If certain patterns of drug use are "bad," then are they not symptomatic of a more fundamental problem, i.e. the pressures and tensions of society which create emotional distress? And second, what acceptable *alternatives* does society provide to the use of psychotherapeutic drugs? We have seen that the desire for energy and stimulation is syphoned off to some extent by the relatively innocuous over-the-counter drugs. But the younger generation recognizes that these drugs are not really very potent, and they have learned where to find more effective alternatives. The pressing question we must try to answer is what do we have to offer them that is better?

REFERENCES

1. MANHEIMER, D. I.; MELLINGER, G. D., AND BALTER, M. B.: Psychotherapeutic drugs: Use among adults in California. *Calif Med, 109*:445-451, 1968.
2. PARRY, H. J.; BALTER, M. B., AND CISIN, I. H.: Primary levels of under-reporting psychotropic drug use (with and without the use of visual aids). Social Research Group, George Washington University, May 1969. (Mimeographed)
3. PARRY, H. J.: Use of psychotropic drugs by U. S. adults. *Public Health Rep, 83*:799-810, 1968.
4. JARVIK, M. E.: The psychopharmacological revolution. *Psychol Today, 1*:51-59, 1967.
5. A.M.A. Committee on Alcoholism and Drug Abuse: Dependence on barbiturates and other sedative drugs. *JAMA, 8*:673-677, 1965.
6. GURIN, G.; VEROFF, J., AND FELD, S.: *Americans View Their Mental Health.* New York, Basic Books, 1960.
7. NOWLIS, H. H.: *Drugs on the College Campus.* Garden City, Anchor Books, Doubleday and Co., 1969.
8. BLUM, R. H., *et al.*: *Students and Drugs.* San Francisco, Jossey-Bass, 1969.
9. CAHALAN, D., AND CISIN, I. H.: American drinking practices: summary of findings from a national probability sample: I. Extent of drinking by population subgroups. *Quart J Stud Alcohol, 29*:130-151, 1968.
10. KNUPFER, G.: The epidemiology of problem drinking. *Amer J Public Health, 57*:973-986, 1967.
11. SHAPIRO, S., AND BARON, S. H.: Prescriptions for psychotropic drugs in a non-institutional population. *Public Health Rep, 76*:481-488, 1961.
12. GREENLICK, M. R.: A comparison of general drug utilization in a metropolitan community with utilization under a drug prepayment plan. Unpublished dissertation, University of Michigan, Ann Arbor, 1967.
13. BARON, S. H., AND FISHER, S.: Use of psychotropic drug prescriptions in a prepaid group practice plan. *Public Health Rep, 77*:871-882, 1962.

Chapter Seventeen

WHERE DO WE GO FROM HERE?

GEORGE SASLOW

THE PLANNING COMMITTEE of this Second Institute of Drug Problems would like me to attempt a statement that relates various components in the problems of drug use, drug dependence, and drug abuse to one another, taking account of our present ability to identify these rather different components, and also taking into account the possibility that we can set ourselves tasks for the immediate future that are relevant to these identified components. How effectively one can carry out such an assignment remains to be seen. This is an invitation to look ahead into the future. In 1967, the magazine *Daedalus* published an entire issue called, "Towards the Year 2000: Work in Progress," a publication by able students from a great variety of fields summarizing several years' attempts to imagine what life would be like in the year 2000. One of the striking contributions was that, if one made a similar attempt by looking backward in history to see how well major features of life in 1800 had been anticipated in 1767, or in 1900, if you were living in 1867, very few of the major scientific, technologic, or political changes had been foreseen thirty-three years ahead of the new century. That is a humbling reminder of how feebly we have been able to forecast the future in our society. Probably we will do even less well now than we did in the earlier centuries.

Nevertheless I accepted in good faith the assignment of the committee and thought I would proceed on this plan: to try to build with you step-by-step a statement taking into account the various components I mentioned. I will do this by enumerating a number of propositions that start with the individual user of drugs and end with some large-scale contemporary sociocultural issues.

The first proposition is this: Drug dependence and drug abuse are now massive social health problems (although there are several different categories of drug users). Just as important is the fact that the use of drugs, dependence, and abuse are not confined to any one social or educational level or class but involve a considerable number of not only able young people in our society but often, by our customary criteria, the ablest. In Western society, when we have been faced in the past with such large-scale health problems as warrant the term *massive,* we have not solved them by doing what seems so natural and obvious. That is, by increasing the number of individual healers, doctors, or treaters who then attend to the needs of the large number of distressed individuals. Rather, to take one example, we learned to reduce the size of the health problem due to typhoid fever by widespread sanitation control measures before we even knew what caused the disease. To take another example, we reduced the size of the health problem due to poliomyelitis by procedures of vaccination and immunization based upon years of research in the field of infectious disease. These problems are examples of the way in which we have in actuality solved massive health problems in our culture. They have been mastered by large-scale procedures of a public health kind, the result of careful observation, of experiment or of both. It seems to me therefore that it is not probable that new treatments, no matter how optimistic they sound, such as the methadone treatment you heard about during the conference, or cyclazocine and other drugs which will be used, which require individualized administration, will deal effectively with the large number of persons and with the ever increasing and changing number of drugs that clearly are involved over time. Such treatment procedures will have definite usefulness, but that usefulness will probably be limited because of the availability of new drugs and of the size of the problem.

The second proposition is important for those who try to treat persons who are overinvolved with drugs. In overcoming his dependence, the importance of the drug user's motivation, of his intentions, of his will, and of his understanding have been much overemphasized in relation to his actual drug-using be-

havior and what can influence that behavior in a constructive
way. Many professionals in this field believe, for example, that
a drug user such as an alcoholic, must be "motivated" for treatment if he is to be helped. It is not well known that a careful
study conducted several years ago[3] demonstrated that three-
quarters of the professional personnel engaged in treating alcoholics in the St. Louis area believed that unless the chronic
alcoholic was highly "motivated" to do something to help himself,
treatment would be unsuccessful. Analysis of the data obtained
by the research group showed that although this idea sounded
plausible and was used by the majority of professional helping
personnel, there was no agreement on how to define the "motivation" of the unfortunate chronic alcoholic. The term really turned
out not to be based upon a shared definition. It appeared rather
to be used as a name-calling device to explain that you had failed
with a particular alcoholic. You could always say, "Well, he
wasn't sufficiently motivated." But there was no way of defining
motivation. The research group pointed out the serious consequences of this insistence upon an explanatory term which did
not have an explicit shared definition. You stopped thinking of
alternative ways of influencing constructively the behavior of
an alcoholic to the end that he might have more control over
his dependence on the drug, such as the social setting in which
he lived, and his satisfactions and dissatisfactions in it, whether
he had an occupation which gave him satisfaction, whether he
had stable or satisfying family relationships, and so forth. The
preoccupation with, "Is he motivated or not?" thus resulted in
underuse of other approaches to influencing favorably the
damaging drinking behavior. Yet the question turned out to be
unanswerable even by the criteria of the professional personnel
themselves. To turn to the self-understanding theme, many drug
dependent persons have a fairly good understanding of how they
came to start their dependence on drugs. They have what we
call adequate insight into how this came about. But all studies
of the outcome of treatment of persons in relation to adequacy of
insight as a major factor have been very disappointing. Thus
understanding what the antecedent circumstances were in the
development of drug dependence does not seem to be very help-

ful in modifying the person's life by creating a life style that is less dependent or not at all dependent upon particular drugs.

Finally I would like to remind you that dependence can occur accidentally through prescription for a limited period by a doctor or nurse of drugs that at one point are medically advisable or necessary. It can also occur accidentally as one tries a drug just to see what the experience with it is like. It may be just as difficult to stop such accidental drug dependence as when it occurs deliberately. The factors I have been noting (motivation, insight) therefore need much *less* emphasis than they have been receiving. We need to look in different directions for constructive outcomes of attempts to modify drug dependence.

This leads me to the third proposition: that some recent treatment efforts that do not depend so much on will, understanding and motivation appear more successful than earlier ones. Examples that many of you have heard about are the Synanon groups, and a plan developed in Puerto Rico in which former addicts seek out current addicts and work with them, describing their own experiences in the hope of influencing them to do some controlling of the drug dependence. You heard at this Institute from Doctor Jaffe about combinations of Synanon-like group influencing procedures (where drug use is forbidden) with the methadone treatment to help change the dependence on the more dangerous drugs. Such treatment efforts as these face the drug abuser vigorously and confrontively with the consequences of his drug abusing behavior. He can continue belonging to a given human group like one of those in Chicago or the Synanon group only by stopping his drug dependence. Often drugs are forbidden in these groups, and in the process of attempting to accept this constraint, he has found himself able to do it only as he develops a personally rewarding style of life which is at the same time acceptable to the group in which he is living. These recent efforts need more adequate documentation. The ones in Chicago are receiving careful study. The Synanon procedures have *not* been adequately documented. What is striking about all of them is that the participants do not fall into the patterns that the researchers at Washington University pointed out were so traditional, persistent, tempting yet futile in outcome: they place little emphasis on *understanding* how the drug abuse came about. They place little emphasis on *education about the dangers* of drugs, which has not been found very effective. They place no emphasis at all on sympathetic bailing out of the drug abuser when he has to face the consequences of his drug abuse in the form of some kind of legal, social, or interpersonal dilemma of one kind or another. These are rather different approaches which attempt to influence the behavior we call drug dependence without calling into play dimensions of the person's functioning which sound very plausible but have gotten us practically nowhere, but utilize rather the important observation that the consequences of behavior influence powerfully the nature of future behavior.

The fourth proposition is this: As you come to know persons who are drug dependent, no matter who they are or from what segment of society they come or in what country for that matter, the style of the daily life of many drug users is grossly unusual by comparison with the pattern of nonusers of similar subcultural or cultural membership. Their rhythm of awake time to sleep time, their rhythms of exercise and rest, their nutritional, personal, and social recreational patterns, the relationship between meaningless and meaningful occupations or interests, or between short-term and long-term human contacts, tend to be in considerable disorder. As an extreme example of the deliberateness with which this is fostered, let me quote from one of the underground newspapers circulated among drug users in London called *The International Times* (November, 1966). The quotation is, "We'll not merely stay out all night but campaign for a wide-open 25-hour a day city so as to change the waking, sleeping and no doubt sexual political habits of life not only in London but everywhere else in the world where the dreary always sleep through the dark habits prevail." Anyone who has at times lived in a fairly regular way with regards to the various dimensions that I mentioned, sleep, exercise, rest, nutrition, recreation, interest in activities of one kind or another, long-term as well as short-time relationships, and at other times has lived very irregularly with regard to these same features of his or her life, realizes how differently he feels during these two different styles of living. You feel vaguely uneasy and uncomfortable in quite a variety of ways which are individual from person to person. Drugs are one way, often prescribed by a doctor such a person goes to, of reducing the discomforts, the vague uneasinesses, the biological malfunctions which produce discomforts, that appear to be generated by an irregular life style and are absent from one that is more regular. Our understanding of these differences in our state of well-being is very feeble. All of us have known of a few people, some of them very well known for their achievements, such as Thomas Edison, who lived very irregularly.

Apparently most of us cannot live so irregularly and feel well over time or function well over time. One wonders what the explanation might be. I would like to throw out for your consideration some well-known observations which have been made in a variety of animal experiments. Some twenty years ago experiments were done on dogs in connection with the study of how high blood pressure develops. It was found that by appropriate procedures, you could get dogs to have very steady, low levels of blood pressure. These "basal levels" occurred when the dogs had to do exactly the same thing for so many minutes each day and then something else in exactly the same way for so many minutes, while their blood pressures were taken in a standard way by a particular person and a particular instrument. It took several months to train each dog to reach this state.[5] The researchers then discovered that if a very tiny change was made from the routinized procedure to which the animal had become accustomed, surprisingly large elevations of blood pressure occurred and lasted for hours. For example, another technician, just as skillful in working with another dog in taking blood pressures, replaced the first one by sliding under the sheet which covered the dog's head and just continued taking blood pressures at the same rate, in the same way, with the same instruments. That slight change, difficult to describe in objective terms, produced tremendous rises in the systolic and diastolic blood pressure of an individual trained dog. They experimented with many changes like this, and the blood pressure responses were always similar and striking. They suggested that the explanation could be that an animal trained to great regularity about certain aspects of its life comes to function in many other ways with similar regularity. He also becomes excessively vulnerable to a slight disturbance from regularity, to which disturbance he responds with instability of various biological functions as well as of internal feeling states. One speculation about the kinds of uneasiness and malfunctions we go through when our lives are irregular as we pass early childhood is that in many instances we have gotten too used to living too regularly as part of our early rearing and cannot then overcome the discomforts of irregularity. If our pattern becomes too irregular for us sometime later, drugs are a very convenient way of reducing our discomforts and enabling us to function. Whether such a speculation is close to the mark or not—for the human drug abuser—is less important than the observation that those who are drug-dependent persons often live very differently from those who are not drug dependent but are otherwise demographically and socioculturally similar.

The fifth proposition is that the outcome of the struggle to give up drug dependence seems to be the better for the individual person the more intimately that drug user has participated or can continue to participate in his available sociocultural life (the sociocultural life of the dominant culture he is in). For example, in a study of the outcome of treatment of alcoholism in a group of business concerns in New York City, 80 percent of chronic alcoholics have been shown to go for three or four years with adequate control of their drinking or complete abstinence if they have had long-time employment, high seniority, families, and a desirable social position.[2] When they were faced with a loss of their jobs as a consequence of their continuous drinking, 80 percent of them did very well in the succeeding three years of follow-up. But these were people closely related to their subculture, functioning regularly, effectively and with recognition by other members of it. If you attempt to rehabilitate chronic alcoholics who have lost all their family members, have either driven them away by their behavior, have left them, have lost them by death, who are isolated, have no friends, have no work, no matter what you do, you can rehabilitate only about 12 percent of them and to a very limited degree. After years of effort they may become able to leave a protected, sheltered hospital floor and live on their own. But 88 percent can control their alcohol dependence only by living in groups in a specially provided hospital unit, from which they leave for work, and to which they return after the day's work.[1] The rate of rehabilitation from abuse of hard narcotics, to take another example that is closer to home, is very much higher among people like those in this audience, doctors, nurses, dentists, pharmacists, than of other groups. When you study the rate of rehabilitation from narcotics addiction among *unselected* groups, the rehabilitation rate in relation to drug dependence is the higher the greater any one drug user's educational experience up to the time he became drug dependent, the greater his work experience or work skills up to that time, and the more rich the social group memberships that he had before his drug dependence started.[4] So the phenomenon seems to be a general one: if you are dealing with persons who are drug dependent and you would like to rehabilitate them, the more stake they have in life and the more past satisfactions, the easier it is to help them. That is an old story remarked upon in the biblical statement that to them who have shall be given, and from them that have not shall be taken away the little that they have. The less help they need the easier it is to help them and the better the outcome.

The five propositions I have presented so far can be summarized as follows. The use of drugs for other than well-defined medical purposes is obviously related to multiple factors in one's life. I mentioned biological factors, psychological factors, interpersonal, social, occupational, and educational influences. One can become drug dependent intentionally or accidentally or simply through sufficiently frequent use by just fooling with a drug. One can stop drug dependence in a variety of ways—by voluntary personal effort, by special conversion experiences of one kind or another, by voluntary participation with others in some group treatment programs such as I have mentioned, or by the use of certain kinds of threats and social sanctions which force the drug dependent person to face consequences of his use of drugs which are simply not acceptable to others, such as his family or peers. Those who are more successful in controlling drug dependence appear to value their lives more than those who are less successful. They appear to value the rewards that they themselves can achieve in the future. They appear to value activities and persons in ways that are not related to drug use. In short, they find in themselves and in other people what at first they had been seeking from drugs. And that is like the remark that you have heard Doctor Blachly make, that it is helpful to think of drugs as people substitutes. Evidence supports these statements which I have made in summary.

The sixth proposition is that so diverse in their importance are the factors that have to do with whether a person can stop drug dependence or not, that we have no business expecting research studies on treatment to provide us with just one guideline as to what will be effective for a lot of people or even for a few. We are therefore in great need of research that will permit us to identify the particular factors that need to be modified for effective results in mastering such dependence of particular persons who use particular drugs and live in particular ways. Of this we know very little. We will accumulate such knowledge sooner, the more we make a research component in working on the drug dependence problem, not an afterthought or something we wish we had done, but a primary ingredient in any planned treatment program for drug users. You have heard how that is being done in the Chicago experiments described by Doctor Jaffe and in the methadone clinic that Doctor Blachly has just started.

The seventh proposition is this: All over the world there is evident on a scale that seems genuinely new a determination of people, young and old, men and women, to share in creating their own life style, in what you might call expanding their own egos, in ways in which their own wishes and feelings have a recognized place. Within one summer (1968) the following events occurred and will be remembered by all of you: the college student rebellion at Columbia University, the criticism of the Pope's encyclical on birth control by many Catholics both lay and religious, and the defiance by Czechoslovakia's Communist Party of the Communist Party of the U.S.S.R. These would seem to be rather unrelated events from some points of view. But they can be seen as related in terms of what I have just mentioned, that there is less willingness to be content with one's place in the world, no matter where you look, no matter what the ages of the people are, no matter what their sex, education, or economic circumstances. Not only young people, but people of all ages are acting in our time now as if they are dissatisfied with the technological world they see themselves in, a world that they cannot manipulate, that they cannot master. They seem to be dissatisfied with the quality of life offered them by the world they see themselves in. They do not relish the future which seems to be developing, no matter how affluent they themselves might become.

The eighth proposition has to do with the way in which Americans, in particular, seem to regard their present and future life. The United States is experiencing a technological revolution that many of us do not appreciate in relation to other changes going on in the world. Students of the subject estimate that the technological revolution going on in the United States (the "technetronic revolution") will in a few years, maybe in a decade or a decade and a half, separate us from other advanced industrial nations, such as those in Western Europe, as much as they are themselves now distant from the undeveloped countries. Something is happening here that is on a bigger scale than what is happening in what we think of as similarly advanced industrial countries. The United States technological revolution will probably change our mode of living more basically than occurred in previous revolutions (such as the October 1917 revolution in Russia), in which the chief change which seems to have occurred was a shift of social power and control from one social class to another. What we seem to be facing is a change of a much more drastic kind in the texture of our personal living as technology becomes so vital a part of our lives and thereby molds us. We must ask ourselves the question, "Are the changes in our style of living that seem to be on the horizon, and some of those already here, so uninteresting to young people, so unchallenging, that young people cannot project themselves into their own future?" Are these attitudes developing most rapidly in this country, in the United States, precisely because in this country scarcity—the main preoccupation of man up to now—need not be a problem any longer at all? Precisely because now, in this country, the quality of this life we could create is the major concern? Is this a country which in their eyes has created no human social life that appeals to them as they look ahead to their future? Is this a country which seems too little concerned with that thin covering of the planet, the biosphere, upon which all life depends? Are they saying that, as a nation, we are not concerned about these things upon which all life including their own lives depends?

The fact seems to be that many drug users appear totally pessimistic that these issues will be resolved in favor of a meaningful human life. They are not concerned with abstract ideas and intellectual controversies, scholarship, the culture of the past, or the future of society. As they observe older people, they see *them* not seriously concerned with man's dilemmas but watching television. They themselves look at colored stroboscopic lights. Older people smoke tobacco and drink alcohol; the drug users smoke pot, take LSD. The drug users consider sensation to be the essence of life. They regard any and all experience as enriching their lives. Practical activity in society is meaningless. These views have been given a name—they are called *apolitical systemicide*. That is to say, if you are that apolitical and live so much in the present, the whole social system upon which all of us depend is committing suicide.

This is a program for which man is invited to abandon the analysis of social and political problems and to take no part in active efforts to solve humanity's dilemmas. It sounds appealing to those who are seeking here-and-now intense immediate sensation and reject the future. We must ask ourselves in relation to certain of humanity's dilemmas, such as the population explosion, is it likely that man, no matter how sensation-seeking, can be immune from overcrowding? We know from overcrowding experiments on other animals (such as the rat) that when population is too great for a given space, cannibalism, deformity, and sterility are very frequent consequences for individual members of such a population. It is not likely that quiet, personal sensation seeking will be possible in a starving, overcrowded world. Nor can such behavior solve such a problem. As you reflect upon this one example, you can see the relevance of the term apolitical systemicide.

The ninth proposition is this: When here-and-now practical activity and the satisfactions one might create for one's own future life are not important, I think we should not be surprised at the curious kinds of behavior people show under those circumstances, such as their absorption in a search for current intense experiences to make them feel better, to make them feel like something, or to make them feel that life is worth something. It does not matter, in a certain sense, just what these experiences are. Some of them are apparently less destructive than others, as you have seen, and many have been tried in different centuries. They have been called a search for meaning, for truth; they have included dedication to a life of contemplation. All of these have had honorable histories in different times. But they can also include searches for current intense experiences under circumstances in which both the past and the future mean nothing. They can include the deliberate bringing about of humiliation of authority, which is behind a number of the student events in various universities throughout the world, destructiveness of various kinds, search for hallucinatory states, and for new sensations of all kinds. It looks as if, when long-term concern both for the past and for the future, and absorption in ongoing diverse overt activity are absent, the search for current immediate sense experience is highly amplified. But it is questionable whether man can live without current involvement in varied overt activity or without a long-term dimension in his life.*

One might reflect also that there is probably something profoundly wrong with a society (and here I mean not only our own) in which a considerable minority of the most talented young men and women feel they must turn to mind-altering drugs to find meaning, truth, commitment, or escape. It is very hard to see, if this is the pertinent context of drug dependence,

---

* Halleck has described such programs as "going to hell in style," in the November 1969 issue of *Psychology Today*.

how a prohibitionist approach, so congenial to the history and temperament of the United States, will be particularly effective. It has not been so far. It might be much wiser to try to separate the use of drugs from the dissatisfactions of the young with our society. We could perhaps try to ignore their behavior whenever it can be ignored. We could try to arrange it that, when they behaved in certain, defined, unacceptable ways, they would have to face the consequences of their behavior. At the same time we would have to be willing to make help available that can be shown to be effective. It is clear that we would like to have more ways of doing that than we now have. We could also be attempting, as alternatives to a prohibitionist approach, to identify and stop widespread social influences that condone, encourage, or even reward drug abuse. As one example, what do we, as a society, do about the estimated 500,000 dollars a day advertising expenditure to promote cigarette smoking?

The tenth proposition is that there is some evidence that even a small use of some drugs may alter a person's self-concept and his scale of values. He may, after X uses of a particular drug, come to prefer a withdrawn dreamy state, free of problems, of demands for action and of expectations, to a home, career, sustained affectional relationships, being part of a family. When this happens, he has been deprived by drug use (which he started for other reasons) of opportunities to make important choices about his life style. If this is what can happen with a number of current drugs (as with LSD, and probably marihuana too) a very important question becomes, what is our obligation to persons who can damage themselves in this way? They do not know that this might happen, and once it has begun to happen, it is as if part of their brain has been removed, with resulting impairment of subtle and long-term judgments. Do we treat persons who might damage themselves in this way, the way we treat very young children whom we protect in a congested traffic street? We do not ask them any questions. We do not ask them what they understand. We do not ask them whether their intention is *not* to get killed. We just pick them up and get them out of the traffic. We tell them we are going to keep on picking them up until they learn not to imperil their lives. We do not care what they say; we do not care how much they

scream. We behave in these controlling ways in order to save
their lives, having decided that they themselves do not know
how to do that, and might well, later on, wish that their lives
had been saved. Are we responsible for people who are not
young children, to whom there may occur this kind of damage
in their self-concept and in the kinds of ability necessary to make
complex choices about the life styles they could consider creating
for themselves? If we are responsible in this sense, how do we
discharge that kind of responsibility effectively as a society?

I summarize the last five propositions as follows. It looks
as if drug use has become entangled with adolescent dissatisfaction and revolt as well as with adult dissatisfaction and revolt,
and women's dissatisfaction and revolt. When a possibly worthwhile future exerts no influence on the present, one's life style
tends to become bizarre, uncomfortable, or both. One person
responds to this situation with some kind of biological malfunction, such as an overactive bowel, a stomach ulcer, or a
migraine headache. Others respond with social withdrawal,
antisocial behavior, or with drug use. The style of malfunction
is secondary, the constricted life view is primary. If life in
itself is not appealing, what difference does it make in what
particular way one functions badly or with distress or suffering?
What is of major importance is, what do we need to do, all of
us, to articulate a significant *future* dimension with the widespread current preoccupation of young and older people with
the sensations, desires and experiences of the immediate *present?*
Apparently these two modes of living stand to each other in a
surprising and unstable relationship. This is another way of
stating the main theme presented by Doctor Blachly (in
language different from the language of "seduction behaviors"
that he used), but it speaks to the same point. Another way
of focussing on the same issue is to ask the question, how can
we interest people in the quality of personal life that they
could create over a long period of time as well as in the enjoy-
ments of here-and-now seduction?

The eleventh proposition is that the present educational
system (in countries which study their educational systems)
generally and conspicuously fails to do enough to make the

present life of the young sufficiently diverse and involved, and their possible future more meaningful. Its overconcern with credentials and rules, its disinterest in individual pathways of students to self-discovery, which it habitually tries to cut down, its separation of students from the world of daily life now so much richer than it was before television, radio, and the present use of mass media, its technological backwardness and conservatism, all need serious examination in relation to this particular issue. How can you so modify the educational experiences of youngsters that they will be eager, as a consequence of satisfactions they have been getting today, to anticipate what they can create tomorrow and next week and the week after? How can you so construct an educational set of experiences that the future becomes meaningfully articulated with living in the present? This is something the educational system has hardly begun to ask except in rare schools or faculties. In this connection, recall how long it may take for relatively simple changes in human behavior on a mass scale to occur. Last year you read that in Sweden they shifted from driving on the left side of the road to the right, to join all other countries on the continent of Europe. It took twenty-two years from the time this first began to be discussed before the big shift was finally made last year. When we think how long it took to bring about a change so small, we have to ask ourselves, how can we include in the educational experiences we provide young people from the very beginning, the daily shaping of tomorrow's behavior, next week's, next year's, so that one can think with interest and commitment of social objectives that take years to mature? There are objectives far more complicated and more important than this, of course, that take as many years or more to bring about. Examples are a redistribution of wealth, or a more equitable tax system such as has just begun to be discussed by our own Congress. How do you build in that kind of interest in the future from the very beginning of the educational experience? It is evident that we have failed to do that effectively as our society has been undergoing its continual changes.

The twelfth proposition, and the last, is that such reexamination of our educational system is not likely to come about by itself. I think it is now impressively demonstrated that in all important human affairs in a more and more interdependent society, no group of experts can be considered wise enough to solve by themselves the problems generated in their own field of expertness. First it was pointed out that war cannot be left to the generals. This nation is now deciding that health care cannot be left to the doctors alone. Education cannot be left to the educationists alone either. We all have to be concerned. So to come back to the point that I want to make. The examination of our educational system may be a very vital part of improving matters in the problem you have been discussing this week. It is not likely to come about by itself. Nor are we entitled to optimism if changes are left to the educators, themselves, or to the educational institutions. All of us, including all of you who are here as professionals concerned initially with the brouhaha of drug abuse but must deal with the more central problems of dissatisfaction, revolt, and the lack of an appealing future in our society, are probably going to have to become more socially responsible and active in the political process if you want to see any improvements. We need not be surprised that this is necessary. There was an interesting similar precedent set last year by a group in our country that has habitually despised political activity, had believed that it is immune from having to deal with it, because its achievements would demonstrate the merits of what this group is doing. That group is the scientific community of the United States. They realized in 1968 through various congressional committee examinations of requests from the National Science Foundation and other such groups that, although they had been traditionally uninterested in political activity with Congress, they would personally and as a group have to get into the political arena to convince Congress that money to maintain our scientific and technological preeminence in the world will have to be asked for in competition with many other requests for funds from that total limited sum which Congress in any year is willing to vote at any one session. The scientific community, Congressmen interested in science told them, will *either* become active and skillful in this enterprise *or* they will see themselves participating in a steady erosion of the scientific professions and level of activity that have grown up here since World War II. Here then is a group which has suddenly realized that they have to participate in the political process in a different way. The professionals at this institute are going to have to think the same way.

At the present time (summer, 1969), two bills came under discussion in the United States Senate which were attempts to deal with the problem of drug dependence that you have been considering. They are very interesting with regard to how different they are. One of them looks upon drug abuse as a law enforcement problem. The general assumption underlying it is that if you stamp out drug abuse, you will get rid of the problem. I have already suggested that drug use or absence of drug use is not the central problem that has to be dealt with. Drug use is a symptom of some other kinds of problem. Further, we have no reason to be satisfied that we have been able to devise enforceable laws to control drug use with reasonable and meaningful penalties. If we add unenforceable laws and inappropriately savage penalties to this situation, it is probable that we will make the central problem worse. That is what we seem to have been doing since the days of the Harrison Narcotic Act. The other Senate bill looked upon the problem of drug dependence as one mainly of health and education. They are both in the early stages of committee hearings. Here then are two different ways of dealing with the problem you have been considering. One approach clearly does not look as if it is going to have much of a future except to make things worse. The other one at least does not make things worse and gives us the challenge of defining what we mean by effective health and education services as a way of going at the problem. I would then rather change the assignment I was given by the steering committee, "Where Do *We* Go From Here?" to ask *you* a question. In view of the way the central problem looks after a week's study and exchange of conversation about it, where are *you* going to go from here, economically, technologically, and politically? That's a question about which a conference like this ought to generate some action.

REFERENCES

1. MYERSON, D. J., AND MAYER, J.: Origins, treatment and destiny of skid-row alcoholic men. *New Eng J Med, 275*:419-425, 1966.

2. PFEFFER, A. Z.; FELDMAN, D. J.; FEIBEL, C.; FRANK, J. A.; CONEN, M.; BERGER, S., AND FLEETWOOD, M. F.: A treatment program for the alcoholic in industry. *JAMA, 161*:827-835, 1956.

3. STERNE, MURIEL W., AND PITTMAN, D. J.: The concept of motivation: A source of institutional and professional blockage in the treatment of alcoholics. *Quart J Stud Alcohol, 26*:41-57, 1965.

4. VAILLANT, G. E.: A twelve-year follow-up of New York narcotic addicts:
   I. The relation of treatment to outcome. *Amer J Psychiat, 122*:727-737, 1966.
   II. The natural history of a chronic disease. *New Eng J Med, 275*:1282-1288, 1966.
   III. Some social and psychiatric characteristics. *Arch Gen Psychiat* (Chicago), *15*:599-609, 1966.
   IV. Some characteristics and determinants of abstinence. *Amer J Psychiat* (Chicago), *123*:573-584, 1966.

5. WILHELMJ, C. M.; McGUIRE, T. F.; McDONOUGH, J.; WALDMANN, E. B., AND McCARTHY, H. H.: Emotional elevation of blood pressure in trained dogs. *Psychosom Med, 15*:390-395, 1953.

Appendix A

DRUG DEPENDENCE: ITS SIGNIFICANCE AND CHARACTERISTICS

NATHAN B. EDDY
H. HALBACH
HARRIS ISBELL
and
MAURICE H. SEEVERS

It has become impossible in practice, and is scientifically unsound, to maintain a single definition for all forms of drug addiction and/or habituation. A feature common to these conditions as well as to drug abuse in general is dependence, psychic or physical or both, of the individual on a chemical agent. Therefore, better understanding should be attained by substitution of the term drug dependence of this or that type, according to the agent or class of agents involved, in discussions of these conditions, especially interdisciplinary. Short descriptions, followed by concise listings of their characteristics, are formulated for the various types of dependence on at present widely abused major groups of substances.

INTRODUCTION

AMONG THE FUNCTIONS of the World Health Organization is the taking of decisions on the status of individual drugs under the relevant international treaties for narcotics control. This function has been established by international conventions and depends upon the competence of the WHO Expert Committee on Addiction-Producing Drugs. The conventions specifically direct that, in response to a notification from a government, the committee come to a finding as to whether or not the substance in question is or is convertible into one with addiction-producing

Reprinted from the *Bulletin of the World Health Organization*, 32:721-733, 1965, with permission of the World Health Organization, Publisher, and Nathan B. Eddy.

or addiction-sustaining properties similar to those of morphine or cocaine or cannabis. A positive finding by the committee is followed by a recommendation for appropriate international narcotics control. Pertinent to any conclusion or decision is the consideration of specific therapeutic effects, the liability of substances having such effects to produce drug dependence, and the evaluation of the risk to public health if such substances are used for medical purposes or abused. Obviously, such considerations depend upon the availability of dependable methods and critical evaluation of their application to the determination of both useful therapeutic properties and the kind and degree of dependence that may accompany drug use. WHO has already published a series of reports on these requirements.[3, 4, 5, 6, 14]

As a partial guide to its own deliberations and those of others, the WHO Expert Committee on Addiction-Producing Drugs[11] attempted to formulate a definition of addiction that would be applicable to drugs under international control. A revised definition* was proposed by the committee several years later, in its seventh report.[12]

In its seventh report the committee sought also to differentiate addiction from habituation and wrote a definition of the latter† which, however, failed in practice to make a clear distinction. These definitions gained some acceptance, but confusion in the use of the terms addiction and habituation, and particularly misuse of the former, continue. Both terms are frequently used interchangeably and often inappropriately. It is not uncommon to apply the term addiction to any misuse of drugs outside of

---

* Drug addiction is a state of periodic or chronic intoxication produced by the repeated consumption of a drug (natural or synthetic). Its characteristics include: (1) an overpowering desire or need (compulsion) to continue taking the drug and to obtain it by any means; (2) a tendency to increase the dose; (3) a psychic (psychological) and generally a physical dependence on the effects of the drug; (4) detrimental effect on the individual and on society.

† Drug habituation (habit) is a condition resulting from the repeated consumption of a drug. Its characteristics include: (1) a desire (but not a compulsion) to continue taking the drug for the sense of improved well-being which it engenders; (2) little or no tendency to increase the dose; (3) some degree of psychic dependence on the effect of the drug, but absence of physical dependence and hence of an abstinence syndrome; (4) detrimental effects, if any, primarily, on the individual.

medical practice, with a connotation of serious harm to the individual and to society, and often with a demand that something be done about it. Such broad use can only create confusion and misunderstanding when abuse of drugs is discussed from different viewpoints.

The difficulties in terminology become increasingly apparent with the continuous appearance of new agents with various and perhaps unique pharmacological profiles, and with changing patterns of use of drugs already well known. These developments must be considered in their relation to, but may not be adequately characterized by, current definitions of addiction. There is scarcely any agent which can be taken into the body to which some individuals will not get a reaction satisfactory or pleasurable to them, persuading them to continue its use even to the point of abuse—that is, to excessive or persistent use beyond medical need. Probably the only exceptions are agents that have incidental or side effects that prevent such use—for example, cumulative or early toxic effects, to which the individual does not become tolerant.

THE TERM "DRUG DEPENDENCE"

In order to try to clarify this situation, much thought and discussion have been devoted to finding a term that will cover all kinds of drug abuse. The component in common appears to be dependence, whether psychic or physical or both. Hence, use of the term *drug dependence* with a modifying phrase linking it to a particular type of drug in order to differentiate the characteristics associated with one class of drugs or another has been given most careful consideration. In its thirteenth report, the WHO Expert Committee on Addiction-Producing Drugs[13] has, in fact, recommended substitution of the term *drug dependence* for both of the terms drug addiction and drug habituation. This recommendation has been endorsed by the WHO Scientific Group on Evaluation of Dependence-Producing Drugs[14] and has been concurred in and supported, *inter alia,* by the Committee on Drug Addiction and Narcotics of the National Academy of Sciences—National Research Council (USA).*

---

* Twenty-sixth Meeting, Washington, D. C., 1964.

Drug dependence is a state of psychic or physical dependence, or both, on a drug, arising in a person following administration of that drug on a periodic or continuous basis. The characteristics of such a state will vary with the agent involved, and these characteristics must always be made clear by designating the particular type of drug dependence in each specific case; for example, drug dependence of morphine type, of barbiturate type, of amphetamine type, and so forth.

The specification of the type of dependence is essential and should form an integral part of the new terminology, since it is neither possible nor even desirable to delineate or define the term drug dependence independently of the agent involved. It should also be remembered that it was the desire to achieve the impossible and define a complex situation by a single term (addiction or habituation, respectively) which has given rise to confusion in many cases. Therefore, the description of drug dependence as a state is a concept for clarification and not, in any sense, a specific definition.

It must be emphasized that drug dependence is a general term that has been selected for its applicability to all types of drug abuse and thus carries no connotation of the degree of risk to public health or need for any or a particular type of drug control. The agents controlled by international treaties and by national narcotics laws continue to be those that are morphine-like, cocaine-like, or cannabis-like, the use of which may result, respectively, in drug dependence of morphine type, of cocaine type, or of cannabis type. Other types of drug dependence, such as those of the barbiturate and amphetamine types, continue to present problems, and their description under the general term of drug dependence, while it may help to delineate those problems, in no way suggests or affects the measures to be taken to solve them. Use of the general term will help to indicate a relationship by drawing attention to a common feature associated with drug abuse, but at the same time will differentiate, by more exact description, specific characteristics according to the nature of the agent involved.

Further to clarify our meaning, the nature and significance

of drug abuse may be considered from two points of view: one relates to the interaction between the drug and the individual, the other to the interaction between drug abuse and society. The first viewpoint is concerned with drug dependence and the interplay between the pharmacodynamic actions of the drug and the psychological status of the individual. The second—the interaction between drug abuse and society—is concerned with the interplay of a wide range of conditions, environmental, sociological, and economic. The committee tried to encompass both points of view when, in its definition of addiction, it listed characteristics of which some were pharmacodynamic and others psychological and socioeconomic, perhaps thereby compounding some of the existing confusion.

As already noted, individuals may become dependent upon a wide variety of chemical substances that produce central nervous system effects ranging from stimulation to depression. All of these drugs have one effect in common: they are capable of creating, in certain individuals, a particular state of mind that is termed *psychic dependence.* In this situation, there is a feeling of satisfaction and a psychic drive that require periodic or continuous administration of the drug to produce pleasure or to avoid discomfort. Indeed, this mental state is the most powerful of all of the factors involved in chronic intoxication with psychotropic drugs, and with certain types of drugs it may be the only factor involved, even in the case of most intense craving and perpetuation of compulsive abuse.

Some drugs also induce physical dependence, which is an adaptive state that manifests itself by intense physical disturbances when the administration of the drug is suspended or when its action is affected by the administration of a specific antagonist. These disturbances, i.e. the withdrawal or abstinence syndromes, are made up of specific arrays of symptoms and signs of psychic and physical nature that are characteristic for each drug type. These conditions are relieved by readministration of the same drug or of another drug of similar pharmacological action within the same generic type. No overt manifestation of physical dependence is evident if an adequate dosage is maintained. Physical dependence is a powerful factor in reinforcing the influence of psychic dependence upon continuing drug use or relapse to drug use after attempted withdrawal.

To reiterate, psychic dependence can and does develop, especially with stimulant-type drugs, without any evidence of physical dependence and, therefore, without an abstinence syndrome developing after drug withdrawal. Physical dependence, too, can be induced without notable psychic dependence; indeed, physical dependence is an inevitable result of the pharmacological action of some drugs with sufficient amount and time of administration. Psychic dependence, while also related to pharmacological action, is more particularly a manifestation of the individual's reaction to the effects of a specific drug and varies with the individual as well as with the drug.

Many of the drugs that induce dependence, especially those that create physical dependence, also induce tolerance, which is an adaptive state characterized by diminished response to the same quantity of drug or by the fact that a larger dose is required to produce the same degree of pharmacodynamic effect. Both drug dependence and drug abuse may occur without the development of demonstrable tolerance.

Drugs that are capable of inducing dependence may also be associated with psychotoxic effects that are manifested by profound alterations in behavior. These effects may occur with a single large dose or during the course of continued administration, or they may be precipitated by withdrawal of the drug following continued administration. The pattern of abnormal behavior is, within limits, characteristic for each drug type, but wide variation occurs in individual responses depending, among other things, upon the preexisting mental state of the person involved.

The characteristics of drug dependence show significant differences from one generic type to another, a situation that makes it mandatory to establish clearly the pattern for each type of drug dependence. Even though some variations occur among individual members of each generic group, the consistency of the pattern of pharmacodynamic actions and responses is sufficiently uniform to permit, at this time, the delineation of each of the principal types.

CHARACTERISTICS OF DRUG DEPENDENCE

Drug Dependence of Morphine Type

The outstanding and distinctive characteristic of dependence on morphine and morphine-like agents is that the major elements —psychic and physical dependence, as well as tolerance—can be initiated by the repeated administration of small doses and increase in intensity in direct relationship to an increase in dosage. This characteristic implies that dependence on drugs of this generic type may be created within the dosage range generally used for therapeutic purposes, and that its mechanism may be set in motion by the first dose administered.

The characteristics of dependence of the morphine type are the following:

1. Strong psychic dependence, which manifests itself as an overpowering drive or compulsion to continue taking the drug and to obtain it by any means, for pleasure or to avoid discomfort.

2. An early development of physical dependence which increases in intensity, paralleling increase in dosage. This requires a continuation of administration of the same drug, or an allied one, to maintain a semblance of homeostasis and to prevent the appearance of the symptoms and signs of withdrawal. Withdrawal of the drug or administration of a specific antagonist precipitates a definite, characteristic and self-limited abstinence syndrome.

3. Development of tolerance that requires an increase in dosage to obtain the initial pharmacodynamic effects.

With morphine, the abstinence syndrome appears within a few hours of the last dose, reaches peak intensity in twenty-four to forty-eight hours, and subsides spontaneously. The most severe symptoms usually disappear within ten days, although a residuum persists for a much longer period. The time of onset, peak intensity, and duration of abstinence phenomena vary with the degree of dependence on the drug[1] and with the characteristics of the specific agent involved. Administration of a specific antagonist during continuing administration of morphine-like drugs promptly precipitates a more rapid and intense abstinence syndrome that lasts only a few hours.

The unique feature of the morphine abstinence syndrome is that it represents changes in all major areas of nervous activity, including alteration in behavior, excitation of both divisions of the autonomic system simultaneously, and dysfunction of the somatic nervous system. The complex of symptoms and signs include anxiety, restlessness, generalized body aches, insomnia, yawning, lacrimation, rhinorrhoea, perspiration, mydriasis, pilo-erection (gooseflesh), hot flushes, nausea, emesis, diarrhoea, elevation of body temperature, of respiratory rate and of systolic blood pressure, abdominal and other muscle cramps, dehydration, anorexia, and loss of body weight.[7]

The generic type of morphine-like compounds for which morphine is used as the standard of reference comprises substances with different chemical constitutions but similar pharmacological profiles. They vary in potency from substances with low activity to others that are several thousand times as potent as morphine. These agents are alike in their ability to produce and maintain some degree of physical dependence, to maintain tolerance and physical dependence, and to prevent the appearance of abstinence phenomena. These agents are mutually interchangeable by substitution, although not on a milligram-for-milligram basis. Variations exist in the capacity of potent morphine-like substances to induce psychic dependence and to produce psychic satisfaction on substitution for one another.

Within the generic class of agents with pharmacodynamic features similar to those of morphine, making them capable of inducing physical dependence with sufficient dosage, there are some with a high degree of usefulness which, in therapeutic doses, are generally inadequate substitutes for morphine. Even in higher doses, these compounds are not completely satisfactory in sustaining an established morphine dependence; their effects are not usually sufficiently satisfying subjectively to induce significant psychic dependence. Codeine is generally recognized as a reference standard for this group.

A relationship between dose, pharmacodynamic properties, and intensity of physical dependence has been mentioned.

Regularity of administration at intervals well within the duration of action of the drug also hastens development of physical dependence. The time from the beginning of administration to the appearance of demonstrable physical dependence also varies with the agent. With morphine, this interval under clinical conditions of administration is two or three weeks; it is shorter for ketobemidone, probably longer for phenazocine and definitely longer for codeine, especially when this is administered orally.

Finally, with drug dependence of the morphine type, harm to the individual is, in the main, indirect, arising from preoccupation with drug taking; personal neglect, malnutrition and infection are frequent consequences. For society also, the resultant harm is chiefly related to the preoccupation of the individual with drug-taking; disruption of interpersonal relationships, economic loss, and crimes against property are frequent consequences.

Drug Dependence of Barbiturate-Alcohol Type

The signs and symptoms of barbiturate and of alcohol intoxication are similar, as are the signs and symptoms of abstinence from these drugs. Barbiturates will suppress alcohol abstinence phenomena, and alcohol will suppress, at least partially, the symptoms of barbiturate withdrawal. The two drugs are essentially additive and interchangeable in chronic intoxications; these similarities justify the term *dependence of barbiturate-alcohol type*, but there are psychological and sociological differences, so that barbiturate and alcohol dependence will be described separately.

Drug Dependence of Barbiturate Type

While dependence on drugs of the barbiturate type presents certain similarities to dependence on drugs of the morphine type, in detail there is a characteristically different picture both during the course of intoxication and during withdrawal. It is a state arising from repeated administration of a barbiturate on a continuous basis, generally in amounts that exceed the usual therapeutic dose levels. There is a strong desire or need to continue taking the drug, a need that can be satisfied by the drug taken initially or by another with barbiturate-like properties. There is a psychic dependence on the effects of the drug that is related to subjective and individual appreciation of those effects, and there is physical dependence requiring the presence of the drug for the maintenance of homeostatis and resulting in a characteristic and self-limited abstinence syndrome when the drug is withdrawn.

Tolerance to barbiturates does develop and, with relatively low doses, it will become evident within seven days. There is, in contrast with tolerance to morphine-like drugs, a limit to the dose to which a person can become tolerant. This limit is a characteristic of the individual patient and varies widely. Following withdrawal of barbiturates, tolerance is rapidly lost, and some patients may become more sensitive to barbiturates than they had been prior to chronic intoxication with these drugs.[2]

During the chronic intoxication of continuing administration, there is some persistence of sedative action, ataxia, and so forth, through the incomplete development of tolerance, which makes the individual accident-prone. There is also impairment of mental ability, confusion, increased emotional instability, and risk of sudden overdosage through delayed onset of action and perceptional distortion of time. The clinical manifestations of chronic barbiturism are similar to those of chronic alcoholism.[8]

The abstinence syndrome is the most characteristic and distinguishing feature of drug dependence of the barbiturate type. It begins to appear within the first twenty-four hours of cessation of drug-taking, reaches peak intensity in two or three days, and subsides slowly. At present there is no agent which is known to precipitate the barbiturate abstinence syndrome during continuation of drug administration. The complex of symptoms constituting the abstinence syndrome, in approximate order of appearance, includes anxiety, involuntary twitching of muscles, tremor of hands and fingers, progressive weakness, dizziness, distortion in visual preception, nausea, vomiting, insomnia, weight loss, a precipitous drop in blood pressure on standing, convulsions of a grand-mal type, and a delirium resembling alcoholic delirium tremens or a major psychotic episode. Convulsions and delirium do not usually occur at the same time; generally, a patient may have one or two convulsions during the first forty-eight hours of withdrawal and then become psychotic during the second or third night. With respect to the psychotic episodes, paranoid reactions, reactions resembling schizophrenia with delusions and hallucinations, withdrawn semistuporous state, and disorganized panic have been seen.

One would expect that the mechanism of physical dependence of the barbiturate type, as of that of the morphine type, would be set in motion by the first dose, but there is no evidence that this is the case. There is, indeed, no evidence that physical dependence develops to a detectable degree with continuation of the therapeutic doses usual for the production of sedation or hypnosis; the daily dose must be increased appreciably above the usual therapeutic level before abstinence signs will appear on abrupt withdrawal. Some degree of psychic dependence facilitating continuance of administration may occur with therapeutic doses, but such doses can usually be discontinued without serious subjective disturbance. Factors that may lead to increasing consumption and eventual overt physical dependence include, in addition to tolerance, the incomplete relief of emotional problems and tension, and impairment of judgment, so that larger doses are taken without regard to need.

In drug dependence of the barbiturate type, the detrimental effect on the individual stems in part from his preoccupation with drug-taking, but more particularly from the untoward effects of large doses of the drug: ataxia, dysarthria, impairment of mental function, with confusion, loss of emotional control, poor judgment and, occasionally, a toxic psychosis, and coma and death. The harm to society is also related to both the individual's preoccupation with drug-taking and the persistence of the effects of these drugs on motor functioning, emotional stability and interpersonal relationships, with proneness to accidents and to assaults on other persons as frequent consequences. By analogy, all agents which produce barbiturate-like sedation, because of the relief of anxiety, mental stress, etc., should produce some psychic dependence and, for the reasons enumerated for dosage increase, physical dependence when a sufficient concentration in the organism has been attained. This possibility has been confirmed for many sedative agents of different types, including barbiturates and the so-called nonbarbiturate sedatives such as glutethimide, methyprylon, meprobamate, chlordiazepoxide, bromisoval, chloral hydrate and paraldehyde, but there may be exceptions.

Drug Dependence of Alcohol Type

Drug dependence of the alcohol type may be said to exist when the consumption of alcohol by an individual exceeds the limits that are accepted by his culture, if he consumes alcohol at times that are deemed inappropriate within that culture, or if his intake of alcohol becomes so great as to injure his health or impair his social relationships. Since the use of alcoholic beverages is a normal, or almost normal, part of the cultures of many countries, dependence on alcohol is usually apparent as an exaggeration of culturally accepted drinking patterns, and the manifestations of dependence vary accordingly in a characteristic fashion with the cultural mode of alcohol use. Thus, in the USA, alcohol is frequently taken in concentrated forms as an aid to social intercourse, so that dependence on alcohol in the United States is usually characterized by heavy consumption of strong spirits during short periods of the day, by a tendency to periodic drinking, and by overt drunkenness. In some other countries, on the other hand, alcohol is customarily consumed in wine, usually with meals. In these countries, dependence on alcohol is characterized by the drinking of wine throughout the day, by a relatively continuous intake of alcohol in this manner, and by relatively little overt drunkenness. A similar pattern applies where beer is the common beverage.

Psychic dependence on alcohol occurs in all degrees. In the mildest grade, alcohol is missed or desired if not available at meals or at social functions. A moderate degree of psychic dependence exists when the individual feels compelled to drink in order to work or to participate socially and takes steps to ensure a supply of alcohol for these purposes. Strong dependence is present if the individual uses alcohol in amounts far exceeding the cultural norm, drinks in situations that culturally do not call for drinking and is obsessed with maintaining a supply of alcohol even to the extent of drinking unusual or poisonous mixtures.

As with other drugs, psychic dependence on alcohol results from an interplay between the pharmacodynamic effects of the drug and the personality problems of the user. The consciously verbalized reasons for the use of alcohol cover a wide gamut and may include a need to stimulate the appetite, to alleviate anxiety or fatigue, to remove boredom, or to induce sleep. Other reasons, not consciously verbalized, may include needs to express masculinity, to remove behavioral controls so that aggressive impulses may be expressed, and to blot out completely a hostile, threatening world.

Tolerance to alcohol does develop. During continuous drinking there is a slight but definite increase in the amount of ingested alcohol required to maintain a given blood level. In addition, some sort of physiological and psychological adaptation occurs so that the alcoholic appears less intoxicated and is less impaired in performance tests at a given concentration of blood alcohol than is a nonalcoholic. Tolerance to alcohol, however, is incomplete and never reaches the degree seen with morphine-like agents.

Physical dependence on alcohol definitely occurs, and the abstinence syndrome resulting when the intake of alcohol is reduced below a critical level is manifested by tremors, sweating, nausea, tachycardia, rise in temperature, hyperreflexia, postural hypotension and, in severe grades, convulsions and delirium. The last-mentioned condition is characterized by confusion, disorientation, delusions, and vivid visual hallucinations. The intensity of the alcohol abstinence syndrome probably varies with the duration and amount of alcohol intake, but as yet little quantitative information on this point is available. The mortality rate, when the alcohol abstinence syndrome is severe, averages at least 8 percent.

The harm to the individual resulting from dependence on alcohol can be quantitatively greater than that caused by any other type of drug dependence. Alcohol impairs efficiency of thinking and psychomotor coordination, leading to deterioration in work performance and to accidents. Judgment deteriorates, leading to all sorts of errors in business and to disturbances of relations with other people. Conscious controls of behavior are "dissolved," with resulting exhibitionism, aggressiveness, and assaultiveness. In addition, dependence on alcohol predisposes to and causes serious physical disease. The physical damage may be indirect, due to neglect of hygiene or to inadequate dietary intake and utilization, with resultant deficiencies, for example, in vitamins, minerals, and proteins. The most common serious complication of protracted alcoholism is fatty portal cirrhosis. Alcoholics are frequently injured because of impaired coordination and judgment.

Damage to society is great. The alcoholic squanders his resources to obtain his beverage, his productivity declines, and his family may be neglected to the extent that it has to be supported by society. Alcoholics are frequently involved in accidents, with property damage and injury to others. The economic burden of dependence on alcohol is enormous; even more important is the tremendous amount of human suffering endured by the alcoholic and all who are close to him.

The characteristics of drug dependence of the barbiturate-alcohol type are as follows:

1. Psychic dependence of varying degree that may lead to periodic rather than continuous abuse, especially with alcohol.
2. The definite development of a physical dependence that generally, however, can be detected only after the consumption of amounts considerably above the usual therapeutic or usual socially acceptable levels. Upon the reduction of intake below a critical level, a characteristic self-limited abstinence syndrome ensues, the symptoms of which, in the case of barbiturates, can be suppressed not only by a barbiturate-like agent but also, at least partially, by alcohol. The reverse situation exists in the case of alcohol.
3. The development of tolerance which is irregular and incomplete, so that there is considerable persistence of behavioral disturbance dependent upon the pharmacodynamic effects of the drugs. There is a mutual, but

incomplete, cross tolerance of some degree between alcohol and the barbiturates.

4. A frequent consequence of alcoholism is overt pathology in tissues, whereas a similar development with the barbiturates has not been demonstrated.

Drug Dependence of Cocaine Type

Cocaine is the prototype of the stimulant drugs that are capable, in high dosage, of inducing euphoric excitement and hallucinatory experiences. These properties rank it high in the esteem of experienced drug abusers and lead to the highest degree of psychic dependence.

Abuse of cocaine takes several forms. The most common is the centuries-old custom of coca-leaf chewing, which is practised habitually by certain Indians of the high Andes. The leaf, mixed with lime, ostensibly to release the alkaloid, is used almost continuously to reduce sensations of cold, fatigue, and hunger. With this form of abuse, release of the alkaloid and its absorption generally are too slow or quantitatively too small to induce mental changes that would lead to abnormal behavior, as described below.

Despite its vasoconstrictive properties, cocaine is readily absorbed through mucous membranes. At one time, the application of cocaine solutions to oral and nasal lesions was a very popular form of treatment, especially with those patients who appreciated the euphoric stimulation induced by the absorbed drug. Closely allied to such use or abuse is another form of absorption through the mucous membranes that is now less common than it was—namely, the snuffing of cocaine crystals. This is a concentrated form of administration that induces such great psychic effects as to border on those which may be obtained with intravenous administration.

Diminished need for cocaine as a local anaesthetic and control of the world supply has reduced the total illicit use of this drug, but coincidentally there has developed a most dangerous type of abuse—intravenous injection. In the most advanced form, this type of abuse involves administration at frequent intervals, as short as ten minutes, the user desiring the ecstatic thrills associated with this practice. This type of abuse appeals particularly to persons with psychopathic tendencies, which are often unmasked by the drug. The induced feeling of great muscular and mental strength leads the individual to overestimate his capabilities. This, associated with paranoid delusions and auditory, visual, and tactile hallucinations, often makes the user a very dangerous individual, capable of serious antisocial acts. Digestive disorders, nausea, loss of appetite, emaciation, sleeplessness, and occasional convulsions are commonly experienced by cocaine abusers of this type. Long-standing, continuing misuse of cocaine alone at a high level is rare, however. The user reaches such a state of excitement that he voluntarily seeks sedation. A frequent current practice is to antagonize the exciting effects by the alternate administration of morphine or some other depressant drug, or by the injection of the two types of drug in combination, the cocaine-heroin mixture ("speedball") being particularly popular.

No physical dependence on cocaine develops and, consequently, no characteristic abstinence syndrome is noted on abrupt withdrawal. But severe depression may occur and delusions may persist for some time after withdrawal.

Since cocaine undergoes rapid destruction in the organism, large quantities can be given during a twenty-four-hour period. Indeed, in man as much as 10 gm daily may be used when the drug is administered in relatively small doses at short intervals. This has led to the belief that tolerance to cocaine develops, a conclusion that is warranted neither by the facts nor by analogy with animal experiments. The criteria for tolerance (diminution in objective effects and elevation of the lethal dose) are not observed in animals even though it may be possible to administer several lethal doses within twenty-four hours, the total quantity varying with the detoxification capacity of the individual species. Although the acute lethal dose for man is unknown, it is clear that, given a constant blood level, no diminution of its subjective or objective effects is noted. These effects, in fact, become enhanced, a sensitization phenomenon that is also seen in animals. It is safe to conclude that man, like animals, does not develop tolerance to cocaine.

In summary, then, the characteristics of drug dependence of the cocaine type are as follows:

1. Strong psychic dependence.
2. No development of physical dependence and, therefore, absence of a characteristic abstinence syndrome when the drug is withdrawn.
3. Absence of tolerance; rather, there is sensitization to the drug's effects in some instances.
4. A strong tendency to continuation of administration, as in coca-leaf chewing, or rapid repetition of the dose, as in the current practice of intravenous administration. Quantitatively, the effects are strikingly different, according to the mode of abuse.

Cocaine is probably the best example of a substance to which neither tolerance nor physical dependence develops and with which psychic dependence can lead to a profound and dangerous type of drug abuse.

Drug Dependence of Cannabis (Marihuana) Type

It is not known with absolute certainty which of the chemical structures that have been isolated from *Cannabis sativa* L. is responsible for the typical cannabis effects, but these can nevertheless be described as constituting an entity that varies in degree according to the concentration of the active principle or principles in the plant and the preparations obtained therefrom, and to the mode of application. These effects are also producible by certain synthetic substances of similar chemical structure.

Among the more prominent subjective effects of cannabis, for which it is taken occasionally, periodically or chronically, are the following: hilarity, often without apparent motivation; carelessness; loquacious euphoria, with increased sociability as a result; distortion of sensation and perception, especially of space and time, with the latter reinforcing psychic dependence and being valued under special circumstances; impairment of judgment and memory; distortion of emotional responsiveness; irritability; and confusion. Other effects, which appear especially after repeated administration and as more experience is acquired by the user include lowering of the sensory threshold, especially for optical and acoustical stimuli, thereby resulting in an intensified appreciation of works of art, paintings and music; hallucinations, illusions, and delusions that predispose to antisocial behavior; anxiety and aggressiveness as a possible result of the various intellectual and sensory derangements; and sleep disturbances.

In the psychomotor sphere, hypermotility occurs without impairment of coordination. Among somatic effects, often persistent, are injection of the ciliary vessels and oropharyngitis, chronic bronchitis and asthma; these conditions and hypoglycemia, with ensuing bulimia, are symptoms of intoxication, not of withdrawal.

Typically, the abuse of cannabis is periodic but, even during long and continuous administration, no evidence of the development of physical dependence can be detected. There is, in consequence no characteristic abstinence syndrome when use of the drug is discontinued.

Whether administration of the drug is periodic or continuous, tolerance to its subjective and psychomotor effects has not been demonstrated.

Whereas cannabis often attracts the mentally unstable and may precipitate temporary psychoses in predisposed individuals, no unequivocal evidence is available that lasting mental changes are produced.

Drug dependence of the cannabis type is a state arising from chronic or periodic administration of cannabis or cannabis substances (natural or synthetic). Its characteristics are as follows:

1. Moderate to strong psychic dependence on account of the desired subjective effects.
2. Absence of physical dependence, so that there is no characteristic abstinence syndrome when the drug is discontinued.
3. Little tendency to increase the dose and no evidence of tolerance.

For the individual, harm resulting from abuse of cannabis may include inertia, lethargy, self-neglect, feeling of increased capability, with corresponding failure, and precipitation of psychotic episodes. Abuse of cannabis facilitates the association with social groups and subcultures involved with more dangerous drugs, such as opiates or barbiturates. Transition to the use of such drugs would be a consequence of this association rather than an inherent effect of cannabis. The harm to society derived from abuse of cannabis rests in the economic consequences of the impairment of the individual's social functions and his enhanced proneness to asocial and antisocial behavior.

Drug Dependence of Amphetamine Type

The capacity of the amphetamines and drugs with similar pharmacological properties to elevate mood and induce a state of well-being is probably largely the basis for their value and widespread use as stimulants and anorexiants. Since such therapy commonly involves continuous and prolonged administration, the users of these drugs may develop varying degrees of psychic dependence upon them. This fact establishes the basis for abuse, where the dosage may be increased in both quantity and frequency of administration in order to attain a continuing stimulation and state of elation. When carried to an extreme, the psychotoxic effects of large amounts of drugs of the amphetamine type may lead to aggressive and dangerous antisocial behavior.

The abuse of this class of drugs originates in and is perpetuated by the psychic drive to attain maximum euphoria; no physical dependence is created. Qualitatively, the psychological effects are in many respects similar to those produced by cocaine.

A unique feature of the amphetamines is their capacity to induce tolerance, a quality possessed by few central nervous system stimulants. Although tolerance develops slowly, a progressive increase in dosage permits the eventual ingestion of amounts that are several hundredfold greater than the original therapeutic dose. Apparently, all parts of the central nervous system do not become tolerant at the same rate, so that the user will continue to experience increased nervousness and insomnia as the dose is increased. Although an individual may survive the oral administration of very large quantities, such ingestion may produce profound behavioral changes that are often of a psychotic nature, including hallucinations, delusions, etc. These latter effects are much more likely to occur after intravenous injection than after ingestion. Indeed, the intravenous route is employed for the express purpose of obtaining bizarre mental effects, often associated with sexual functions, even to the point of orgasm. This type of abuse has been increasingly frequent in recent years with the changing patterns of drug abuse in various countries.

Although the amphetamines do not induce physical dependence, as measured by the criterion of a characteristic and reproducible abstinence syndrome, it would be inaccurate to state that withdrawal from very large dosages is symptomless. The sudden withdrawal of the stimulant drug which has masked chronic fatigue and the need for sleep now permits these conditions to appear in an exaggerated fashion. Thus, the withdrawal period is characteristically a state of depression, both psychic and physical, which probably reinforces the drive to resume the drug. In this regard, it is much less important and does not compare in magnitude with those that occur with morphine, barbiturates, alcohol and other drugs that create physical dependence. Withdrawal of drugs of the amphetamine type is never threatening to life and requires psychological rather than somatic therapy.

The use of amphetamines by self-administration has increased consistently in recent years, ostensibly as antifatigue agents in situations in which it is desired to remain mentally alert for long periods without sleep or rest or to permit increased physical performance. The use of amphetamines as stimulants has also increased markedly in persons who abuse alcohol and/or barbiturates; in many such instances there is dependence on more than one drug. In such cases, the prognosis is poor, the relapse rate is high, and continued dependence on one or more drugs is the rule, especially in prepsychotics or individuals with latent schizophrenia.

Thus, the characteristics of drug dependence of the amphetamine type are as follows:

1. A variable psychic dependence.
2. No physical dependence and, consequently, no character-

istic abstinence syndrome, though withdrawal will be followed by a state of mental and physical depression as the organism escapes from the persistent stimulation.

3. The slow development of a considerable degree of tolerance to many effects, but not participated in equally by all components of the cerebral system, so that nervousness and sleeplessness persist and psychotoxic effects such as hallucinations and delusions may occur.

Abusers of amphetamines are prone to accidents because of both the excitation produced by these agents and the excessive fatigue which may break through and manifest itself at an inopportune time. Abuse by intravenous administration, with its concomitant bizarre mental effects, may result in serious antisocial behavior.

Drug Dependence of Khat Type

Khat (*Catha edulis* Forssk.) is cultivated and consumed in circumscribed areas of East Africa and the Arabian peninsula. The common, and quantitatively most profitable, mode of application is by way of chewing the tender parts of the plant in as fresh a state as possible.

The active principle of the khat leaf is chemically and pharmacologically related to the amphetamine group of substances so closely that its effects are to be considered qualitatively identical with those of the latter group and quantitatively equal to these weaker members. These resemblances extend to the somatic as well as to the psychic effects, among which a usually moderate degree of central stimulation, with ensuing elation and removal of fatigue, is the effect most sought for by khat users, besides suppression of hunger and, sometimes, of libido. The quantitative difference between the effects of khat and those of the commonly abused amphetamine substances is enhanced by the limitation of the ingestion and absorption of khat due to its particular mode of application. The naturally limited dose of khat is assumed to prevent the occurrence of tolerance, of rebound phenomena after cessation, and of psychotoxic effects typical of the amphetamines when the latter are administered in pure form and in high dosage. There is no evidence of the development of a physical dependence on khat during chronic use.

Nevertheless, the pleasurable effects afforded by khat are a strong inducement for many to procure by any means the necessary supplies at least once a day or to repeat or prolong the periods of chewing, often at the expense of vital needs such as food. Such behavior is a manifestation of psychic dependence.

Drug dependence of the khat type is, under the circumstances of its traditional consumption by chewing, characterized by the following:

1. Moderate but often persistent psychic dependence as long as its maintenance is at all practicable.
2. Lack of physical dependence.
3. Absence of tolerance.

The habitual and, in particular, the exaggerated consumption of khat may also, on account of its nonamphetamine ingredients (tannins) damage the individual's health. The social and economic consequences of dependence on khat consist, in the main, of the alienation of the user's funds and the erosion of his working capacity and concern both the individual and his environment as well as the community.

Drug Dependence of Hallucinogen (LSD) Type

Drugs of this type include lysergic acid diethylamide (LSD), a semisynthetic derivative of ergonovine; psilocybin, an indole found in a mushroom ("teonanacatl," *Psilocybe mexicana*); mescaline, the most active alkaloid present in the buttons of a small cactus ("mescal," "peyote," *Lophophora williamsii*), and in the seeds of some morning glory varieties ("ololiuqui," *Rivea corymbosa* L. Hall f.; *Ipomoea violacea* L.), the active principle of which is closely related to LSD. The mushrooms, cactus buttons and the morning glory seeds are used by certain American Indian tribes in religious ceremonies or are employed by medicine men or women of these tribes in treating illness, usually in ritualistic fashion. Such religious and ritualistic use does not seem to lead frequently to drug dependence. The drugs have received wide publicity, however, and they possess a particular attraction for certain psychologically and socially mal-adjusted persons who have difficulty in conforming to usual social norms. These include "arty" people such as struggling writers, painters and musicians; frustrated nonconformists; and curious thrill-seeking adolescents and young adults. The drugs are taken for thrills ("kicks"), to alter mood, to change and clarify perception, to induce reveries, and to obtain "psychological insight" into the personality problems of the user. Generally, the drugs are taken orally and in the company of other users. Ingestion of a single dose or of several doses over a period of two or three days is the customary pattern; prolonged or continuous use is unusual. Periodic, rather than continuous, use is favored by difficulty in obtaining the drugs, rapid development and disappearance of tolerance, and lack of physical dependence on these drugs.

Drugs of the LSD type induce a state of excitation of the central nervous system and central autonomic hyperactivity manifested by changes in mood (usually euphoric, sometimes depressive), anxiety, distortion in sensory perception (chiefly visual), visual hallucinations, delusions, depersonalization, dilatation of the pupils, and increases in body temperature and blood pressure.

Psychic dependence on drugs of the LSD type varies greatly, but it usually is not intense. The thrill-seekers and nonconformists may enjoy the effects of these agents and may wish to repeat them, but if such agents are not readily available, these persons will either do without them or substitute another substance. A minority of users may develop such strong psychic dependence on those substances that they wreck their careers by persisting in using the drugs despite strong social condemnation.

No evidence of physical dependence can be detected when the drugs are withdrawn abruptly.

A high degree of tolerance to LSD[9] and to psilocybin[10] develops rapidly and disappears rapidly. Tolerance to mescaline develops more slowly. Persons who are tolerant to any of these three drugs are cross-tolerant to the other two.[10]

The chief dangers to the individual arise from the psychological effects. Impairment of judgment could lead to dangerous decisions or accidents. Occasional persons may become depressed, so that suicide is a possibility in users of these drugs.

REFERENCES

1. ANDREWS, H. L., AND HIMMELSBACH, C. K.: *J Pharmacol Exp Ther*, *81*:228, 1944.
2. BELLEVILLE, R. E., AND FRASER, H. F.: *J Pharmacol Exp Ther*, *120*:469, 1957.
3. BRAENDEN, O. J.; EDDY, N. B., AND HALBACH, H.: *Bull WHO*, *13*:937, 1955.
4. EDDY, N. B.; HALBACH, H., AND BRAENDEN, O. J.: *Bull WHO*, *14*:353, 1956.
5. EDDY, N. B.; HALBACH, H., AND BRAENDEN, O. J.: *Bull WHO*, *17*:569, 1957.
6. HALBACH, H., AND EDDY, N. B.: *Bull WHO*, 28, 139, 1963.
7. ISBELL, H., AND WHITE, W. M.: *Amer J Med*, *14*:558, 1953.
8. ISBELL, H.; ALTSCHUL, S.; KORNETSKY, C. H.; EISENMAN, A. J.; FLANARY, H. G., AND FRASER, H. F.: *Arch Neurol Psychiat* (*Chicago*), *64*:1, 1950.
9. ISBELL, H.; BELLEVILLE, R. E.; FRASER, H. F.; WIKLER, R., AND LOGAN, C. R.: *Arch Neurol Psychiat* (*Chicago*), 76:468, 1956.
10. WOLBACH, A. B., JR.; ISBELL, H., AND MINER, E. J.: *Psychopharmacologia* (*Berlin*), 3:1, 1962.
11. WHO Expert Committee on Addiction-Producing Drugs. Third Report. *WHO Techn Rep Ser*, 57:9, 1952.
12. WHO Expert Committee on Addiction-Producing Drugs. Seventh Report. *WHO Techn Rep. Ser*, *116*:9, 1957.
13. WHO Expert Committee on Addiction-Producing Drugs. Thirteenth Report. *WHO Techn Rep Ser*, 273:9, 1964.
14. WHO Scientific Group on the Evaluation of Dependence-Producing Drugs. *WHO Techn Rep Ser*, 287, 1964.

DIAGNOSIS AND TREATMENT OF DRUG DEPENDENCE OF THE BARBITURATE TYPE

ABRAHAM WIKLER

The basic principles in treatment of patients suspected of, or known to be, physically dependent on barbiturates, non-barbiturate sedatives, and/or "minor tranquilizers" are stabilization on pentobarbital in daily amounts and frequency of dosage sufficient to completely suppress barbiturate-type abstinence phenomena and produce minimal signs of barbiturate intoxication; and progressive reduction of pentobarbital dosage at the rate of not more than 100 mg a day after three to five days of stabilization.

According to the definitions proposed by the World Health Organization[18]:

Drug dependence of the barbiturate type is described as a state arising from repeated administration of a barbiturate, or an agent with barbiturate-like effect, on a continuous basis, generally in amounts exceeding therapeutic dose levels. Its characteristics include: 1) a strong desire or need to continue taking the drug; the need can be satisfied by the drug taken initially or by another with barbiturate-like properties; 2) a tendency to increase the dose, partly owing to the development of tolerance; 3) a psychic dependence on the effects of the drug related to subjective and individual appreciation of those effects; and 4) a physical dependence on the effects of the drug requiring its presence for maintenance of homeostasis and resulting in a definite, characteristic, and self-limited abstinence syndrome when the drug is withdrawn.

ALTHOUGH PATIENTS WHO display any or all of the first three characteristics are also in need of medical and psychiatric attention, the development of the fourth characteristic, physical

---

Reprinted from *American Journal of Psychiatry, 125*:758-765, 1968, with permission of the American Psychiatric Association, Publisher, and Abraham Wikler.

dependence, may be fraught with danger to life and therefore demands immediate and skillful treatment. This article will therefore begin with a discussion of the diagnosis and treatment of physical dependence on drugs of the barbiturate type.

PHYSICAL DEPENDENCE ON BARBITURATES

Understanding of the clinical course and predictable outcome of chronic barbiturate intoxication was greatly advanced by the experimental studies of Isbell and associates,[14] Wikler and associates,[17] Fraser and associates,[8, 10] and Belleville and Fraser.[2] Using former narcotic addicts without psychosis, epilepsy, or other central nervous system disease as subjects (all volunteered for the research), these investigators demonstrated that tolerance, though only partial, does develop to the effects of barbiturates on the central nervous system, and that abrupt withdrawal of secobarbital, amobarbital, or pentobarbital after prolonged (one or more months) continuous intoxication results in a characteristic abstinence syndrome. The severity of the latter is at least in part directly related to the daily dose level attained before drug withdrawal.

Table B-I summarizes the essential features of the "full-blown" barbiturate abstinence syndrome as it develops on abrupt withdrawal of the so-called short-acting barbiturates following chronic intoxication at daily dose levels of 0.8 to 2.2 gm. For convenience in discussion the clinical phenomena may be classified as "minor" (apprehension, muscular weakness, tremors, postural faintness, anorexia, and twitches) and "major" (seizures, psychosis).

As indicated in the table, the minor abstinence phenomena are observable within twenty-four hours after administration of the last dose of barbiturates and continue beyond the appearance of the major abstinence phenomena which, if they develop, emerge between the second and eighth days.

Among the minor abstinence phenomena, postural faintness (orthostatic hypotension) is of particular value in differentiating the developing barbiturate abstinence syndrome from ordinary anxiety states, but often the differential diagnosis is difficult to make at this stage. The presence of coarse, rhythmic intention

TABLE B-I

THE BARBITURATE ABSTINENCE SYNDROME

(After abrupt withdrawal of secobarbital or pentobarbital following chronic intoxication at dose levels of 0.8 to 2.2 gm per day orally, for six weeks or more)

Clinical Phenomenon	Incidence	Time of Onset	Duration	Remarks
Apprehension	100%	1st day	3-14 days	Vague uneasiness, or fear of impending catastrophe. Evident on mildest exertion.
Muscular weakness	100%	1st day	3-14 days	
Tremors	100%	1st day	3-14 days	Coarse, rhythmic, nonpatterned, evident during voluntary movement, subside at rest.
Postural faintness	100%	1st day	3-14 days	Evident on sitting or standing suddenly. Associated with marked fall in systolic and diastolic blood pressure, and pronounced tachycardia.
Anorexia	100%	1st day	3-14 days	Usually associated with repeated vomiting.
Twitches	100%	1st day	3-? days	Myoclonic muscular contractions; or spasmodic jerking of one or more extremities. Sometimes bizarre patterned movements.
Seizures	80%	2nd-3rd day	8 days	Up to a total of 4 grand mal episodes, with loss of consciousness and postconvulsive stupor.
Psychoses	60%	3rd-8th day	3-14 days	Usually resemble "delirium tremens"; occasionally resemble schizophrenic or Korsakoff syndromes; or acute panic states may occur.

NOTE: These data are based on a series of nineteen cases of experimental addiction to barbiturates. Four developed seizures without subsequent psychosis; one exhibited delirium without antecedent seizures. Three escaped both seizures and delirium.

tremors in the upper extremities is also a useful but less specific sign of barbiturate abstinence. Other minor abstinence phenomena include insomnia, profuse sweating, and tendon hyperreflexia. Even if overt major abstinence phenomena do not develop, paroxysmal discharges may be found in the electroencephalogram after the second day of abstinence in a majority of patients abruptly withdrawn from such dose levels.[5, 17]

When major abstinence phenomena do appear, the seizures are invariably of the clonic-tonic grand mal type clinically indistinguishable from those of idiopathic grand mal epilepsy. It is curious that in the experimental studies on which this discussion is based, no subject had more than four seizures, and the interseizure electroencephalograms were characterized by recurrent four per second spike-wave discharges. Also of interest is that none of the subjects having seizures could recall any aura.

The psychoses that develop as major barbiturate abstinence phenomena are more variable. In severe cases the psychosis is indistinguishable from that of alcoholic delirium tremens (also a withdrawal phenomenon), with disorientation, agitation, delusions, and hallucinations (usually visual, sometimes also audi-

TABLE B-II

SUMMARY OF DATA ON RELATIONSHIP OF DOSAGE OF SECOBARBITAL OR PENTOBARBITAL TO INTENSITY OF PHYSICAL DEPENDENCE

Patients No. Receiving					No of Patients Having Symptoms		
Total No.	Secobarbital	Pentobarbital	Daily Dose of Barbiturate, Gm.	Days of Intoxication in Hospital	Convulsions	Delirium	Minor Symptoms of Significant Degree
18	16	2	0.9-2.2	32-144	14	12	18
5	5		0.8	42-57	1	0	5
18	18		0.6	35-57	2	0	9
18	10	8	0.4	90	0	0	1
2	1	1	0.2	365	0	0	0

(Reprinted from *JAMA, 166*:126-129, 1958, by permission of the editor; see reference 10.)

tory). Rising core temperature is an ominous sign prognosticating a fatal outcome if not combated vigorously.[9] Milder cases may be characterized by hallucinations with relatively clear sensorium, a Korsakoff-like syndrome, or by extreme anxiety.

The data in Table B-II, also obtained in experimental studies on former narcotic addicts who volunteered for research, show the relationships between daily dose level and duration of intoxication on the one hand, and the incidence of major and minor abstinence phenomena following abrupt withdrawal of barbiturates on the other. It will be noted that of twenty subjects who were withdrawn from daily barbiturate dose levels of 0.4 gm or less, none developed major, and only one developed significant minor, abstinence phenomena. On the other hand, of twenty-three subjects withdrawn from 0.6 to 0.8 gm daily, three had convulsions, one displayed hallucinations, and fourteen showed significant degrees of minor abstinence phenomena.

It may be inferred therefore that chronic intoxication with barbiturates at daily dose levels of 0.6 to 0.8 gm for periods of thirty-five to fifty-seven days is sufficient to produce a clinically significant degree of physical dependence. The data in Table B-II also indicate that higher daily dose levels of barbiturates induce stronger physical dependence. Thus all of eighteen subjects withdrawn from 0.8 to 2.2 gm daily had minor abstinence phenomena, fourteen had convulsions, and twelve had delirium (some subjects had both).

Although there is a direct relationship between daily intoxication dosage and severity of barbiturate abstinence phenomena, more information is needed about the relationships that may exist between duration of chronic barbiturate intoxication per se (daily dose level held constant) and the severity of abstinence phenomena.

Initial treatment of patients chronically intoxicated with barbiturates is directed toward withdrawal of the drug in such a manner as to prevent the appearance of the major abstinence phenomena altogether and to minimize the severity of minor abstinence phenomena. To this end the procedure developed by Isbell[13] has proven to be safe, simple, and reliable. Essentially it consists of stabilization of the patient on a so-called short-acting barbiturate (eg. pentobarbital) at doses (0.2-0.4 gm, orally if possible, intramuscularly if necessary) at four- to six-hour intervals, regulated in such a manner that no abstinence phenomena and a minimal degree of barbiturate-type signs of intoxication are observed.

After two to three days of such stabilization the barbiturate is withdrawn *slowly* at a rate not exceeding 0.1 gm a day regardless of the daily stabilization dose level. If more than the mildest minor abstinence phenomena appear, the reduction schedule is suspended until these signs and symptoms subside, after which it is resumed at the same rate or a slower rate, e.g. 0.05 gm daily, if orthostatic hypotension, marked tremulousness, and/or persistent insomnia develop.

In clinical practice, initiation of this stabilization and reduction procedure will depend of course on the status of the patient on admission. Should the patient be grossly intoxicated or comatose on arrival, no barbiturates are given until these effects have receded completely, but if there is a clear history of chronic barbiturate intoxication or if this is strongly suspected on other grounds, one should not wait until severe minor or any major withdrawal phenomena are observed before instituting the "stabilization" procedure.

In doubtful cases a test dose of 0.2 gm of pentobarbital may be given after all signs of intoxication have disappeared, and if no signs of barbiturate effect (positive Romberg sign, gait ataxia, finger to nose incoordination, nystagmus, slurred speech, drowsiness) are observed one hour later, the same dose may be prescribed every six hours around the clock. During the next twenty-four hours the patient should be observed for signs of abstinence just *before* each dose and again for signs of barbiturate intoxication one hour *after* each dose.

If during this period clear abstinence phenomena and no signs of barbiturate intoxication are observed, the dose and/or the frequency of administration should be increased and then manipulated upwards or downwards until optimal stabilization is achieved. Often optimal stabilization takes more than twenty-four hours, but in no case should systematic reduction of daily dosage be initiated before the patient is stabilized.

On the other hand, if the patient reacts to the initial test dose of 0.2 gm of pentobarbital with gross signs of barbiturate intoxication, the diagnosis of physical dependence on barbiturates should be questioned. To be safe, it is usually advisable to continue the "assay" at reduced dosage—e.g. 0.1 gm of pentobarbital every six hours with the same observations before and after each dose as already described. If during the next twenty-four hours no abstinence phenomena are observed and especially if the patient shows signs of increasing barbiturate intoxication, the diagnosis of physical dependence may be rejected and barbiturates may be discontinued altogether.

This testing and stabilization procedure may also be applied to patients who on admission display minor abstinence phenomena. In the case of patients who have already had one or more seizures, the initial dose of pentobarbital should be somewhat larger (0.3 to 0.4 gm) and the stabilization procedure should be accelerated beginning with 0.2 gm of pentobarbital every four hours, and dosage and frequency manipulated thereafter as indicated.

The presence of delirium on admission calls for a somewhat different approach. This condition is not easily reversible in the sense that the stabilization state can be readily achieved. Rather, the aim should be to sedate the patient heavily so that agitation, insomnia, and above all hyperpyrexia are suppressed. To accomplish this, pentobarbital may have to be given intramuscularly or intravenously in whatever amounts may be found necessary for three to five days, after which the degree of sedation may be lightened gradually and slow reduction carried out as in stabilized patients.

Because of its longer duration of action, sodium phenobarbital may be preferable to pentobarbital. Indeed, the Danish workers[16] have used the very long acting barbiturate, barbital (Veronal) with excellent results in the treatment of alcoholic delirium tremens since 1909; probably this venerable agent would be equally effective in the management of barbiturate withdrawal delirium. However, the very long duration of action of barbital may be a disadvantage to physicians who had had little experience with it.

In addition to specific therapy as described, it is of course necessary to ensure that patients displaying barbiturate abstinence phenomena, and especially delirium, are protected from injury. They should be provided with very low beds or mattresses on the floor and should receive adequate fluids and electrolytes, calories, vitamins, and, when indicated, antibiotics.

While theoretically such drugs as paraldehyde or chloral hydrate should readily substitute for pentobarbital in specific therapy, there appears to be no valid reason for employing certain other agents that have been advocated from time to time. Thus neither diphenylhydantoin (Dilantin®) nor chlorpromazine (Thorazine) prevents barbiturate withdrawal seizures in the dog,[4, 6] and systematic studies on the effectiveness of meprobamate (Miltown, Equanil) or chlordiazepoxide (Librium) in the management of the barbiturate abstinence syndrome have not yet been made.

DEPENDENCE ON NONBARBITURATE SEDATIVES AND MINOR TRANQUILIZERS

To date, systematic experimental studies on the physical dependence-producing properties of nonbarbiturate sedatives and minor tranquilizers in man have been reported only for meprobamate[11] and chlordiazepoxide.[12] However, individual case reports, reviewed by Essig,[3] indicate that barbiturate-type abstinence phenomena, both of the minor and major kind, can supervene when not only these agents but also glutethimide (Doriden®), ethinamate (Valmid®), ethchlorvynol (Placidyl®), or methyprylon (Noludar®) are withdrawn abruptly after periods of chronic intoxication at high daily dose levels of these drugs.

All of these agents are central nervous system depressants, and the abstinence phenomena that develop after their abrupt withdrawal under the conditions stated closely resemble the barbiturate abstinence syndrome. It may thus be inferred that to a considerable extent at least, there are common neurochemical mechanisms that underlie physical dependence on barbiturates, nonbarbiturate sedatives, and minor tranquilizers. If so, then barbiturates should substitute readily for nonbarbiturate sedatives and minor tranquilizers both in assaying the degree of tolerance and physical dependence that may have developed in patients chronically intoxicated on the latter two categories of drugs and in the clinical management of drug withdrawal.

This principle was applied by Bakewell and Wikler[1] in a study on the incidence of nonnarcotic addiction in a Southern university hospital psychiatric ward, using pentobarbital exclusively as the drug of substitution in the same manner as already described for the diagnosis and treatment of physical dependence on barbiturates. Inasmuch as the earlier studies of Fraser and associates[10] had indicated that the critical daily intoxication dose level of development of physical dependence on barbiturates is 0.6 to 0.8 gm, Bakewell and Wikler[1] adopted as a criterion for classifying patients as physically dependent on nonbarbiturate sedatives and/or minor tranquilizers the ability of the patient to tolerate (i.e. become stabilized on) 0.8 gm of pentobarbital or more daily.

On the basis of this criterion, they found that 9 of 132 consecutive patients (6.8%) admitted to the psychiatric ward over a fourteen-month period were physically dependent on nonnarcotic central nervous system depressants including glutethimide, meprobamate, chlordiazepoxide, diazepam, paraldehyde, and barbiturates, alone or in various combinations (Table B-III).

TABLE B-III

CASE SUMMARIES

Drugs of Abuse

Patient No.	Sex	(Years) Age	Agent	Estimated Average Daily Intake (mg.)	Daily Pentobarbital Stabilization-dose Level (Oral, mg.)
1	M	36	Glutethimide	2,500	800
2	F	59	Glutethimide	5,000	1,200
3	F	44	Glutethimide	2,000	900
4	M	60	Glutethimide	4,000	1,200
5	F	49	Glutethimide	1,000	800
			Meprobamate	4,000	
6	F	60	Glutethimide	?	800
			Chlordiazepoxide	100?	
7	F	53	Amphetamine-amobarbital (elixir)	?	800
			Pentobarbital (elixir)	?	
			Aprobarbital (elixir)	?	
8	M	61	Secobarbital	?	1,000
			Pentobarbital	?	
			Butabarbital	?	
			Phenobarbital	?	
			Propantheline and phenobarbital	?	
			Diazepam	?	
9	M	29	Paraldehyde	?	800

(Reprinted from *JAMA, 196*:711, 1966, by permission of the editor; see reference 1.)

It is of interest that Ewing and Bakewell[7] concluded from a. chart study that in 7.6 percent of 1,686 patients admitted to another Southern university hospital psychiatric ward over a three-year period, the diagnosis of drug dependence was made either on admission or during hospitalization. In their series, however, the drugs implicated included not only barbiturates, nonbarbiturate sedatives, and minor tranquilizers, but also bromides, amphetamines, alcohol, and narcotics.

Theoretically the testing, stabilization, and slow reduction procedures could be carried out with the nonbarbiturate sedative or minor tranquilizing drug on which the patient had become physically dependent rather than with pentobarbital. But since far less is known about the duration of action of the drugs in the former classes, the pentobarbital substitution method is preferable, at least at the present time.

However, differences in duration of action between pentobarbital on the one hand and certain of the nonbarbiturate sedatives and minor tranquilizers on the other may require some modifications of the stabilization and slow reduction procedures described when pentobarbital is substituted for drugs in the other two categories. Thus, patients physically dependent on glutethimide or chlordiazepoxide may seem to be well stabilized on a given daily dose of pentobarbital, only to have convulsions a day or two later while still stabilized, or after a modest reduction of pentobarbital dosage has been made. In the cases of primary physical dependence on glutethimide or chlordiazepoxide, therefore, it might be well to delay initiation of pentobarbital reduction for a few days after initial stabilization.

PSYCHOTHERAPY AND REHABILITATION

As the series studied by Bakewell and Wikler[1] and Ewing and Bakewell[7] consisted of patients admitted to psychiatric wards, it is not surprising that all of those judged to be dependent on drugs were also found to have antecedent emotional and/or characterological disorders, presumably rendering them addiction prone. However, it is remarkable that 93.2 percent of the patients in the first series and 92.4 percent in the second were *not* drug-dependent.

Whether or not the drug-dependent and the non-drug-dependent populations differed significantly in respect to particular kinds of emotional and/or characterological disorders cannot be decided on the basis of available data. However, it would seem reasonable to suppose that such disorders do play a role—if not a sufficient one—in the genesis of drug abuse. In any case, the existence of emotional and/or characterological disorder calls for treatment of these conditions by whatever means may be indicated.

Generally, psychotherapy of other than the supportive type will be more effective after drug withdrawal has been accomplished. Indeed, "painless" drug withdrawal may facilitate development of a favorable psychotherapeutic relationship between physician and patient. It has also been the author's impression that ignorance on the part of the patient, his relatives, and sometimes his physician of the dangers involved in escalation of dosage and/or frequency of administration of central nervous system depressant drugs has contributed to the development of physical dependence. Appropriate education is certainly indicated in such cases.

A difficult question to answer is the extent to which barbiturates, nonbarbiturate sedatives, and minor tranquilizers may be used in the treatment of addiction-prone patients, especially if they had become physically dependent on such drugs on one or more occasions in the past. Generally, these drugs should be avoided or, if used at all, they should be prescribed in therapeutic doses and for only short periods of time with rigid limitation of prescription refills.

In some cases daytime reduction of anxiety may be achieved with small doses of chlorpromazine, or with imipramine or amitriptyline if depression is a prominent symptom. According to Overall and associates,[15] thioridazine possesses not only tranquilizing but also antidepressant properties, and therefore this phenothiazine derivative may be effective in some cases. Persistence of anxiety and/or depression, however, poses a challenge to the psychiatrist's skills which is not met by resorting to the unregulated use of drugs with physical dependence-producing properties, such as barbiturates, nonbarbiturate sedatives, and minor tranquilizers.

SUMMARY

An abstinence syndrome characterized in its complete form by the appearance of tremulousness, anxiety, insomnia, diaphoresis, postural hypotension, tendon hyperreflexia, convulsions, delirium, and hyperpyrexia can ensue when barbiturates, non-barbiturate sedatives, or minor tranquilizers are withdrawn abruptly following prolonged periods of intoxication at daily dose levels that exceed therapeutically recommended amounts. Regardless of the drug category involved, withdrawal of these agents may be accomplished safely by initial stabilization on pentobarbital alone in amounts and at intervals that suppress abstinence phenomena throughout the day and night and produce mild signs of barbiturate intoxication. This should be followed by gradual reduction in pentobarbital dosage at a rate not exceeding 0.1 gm daily.

If delirium has already developed when the patient is first seen, the immediate aim of treatment is not stabilization but heavy sedation with pentobarbital or phenobarbital, sufficient to suppress agitation, insomnia, and hyperpyrexia. Such heavy sedation is maintained for three to five days with appropriate supportive medical and nursing care, after which the degree of sedation is lightened gradually and slow reduction of the barbiturate is carried out as in the stabilized patient.

Psychotherapy and other treatment of psychiatric disorders associated with drug dependence of the barbiturate type is of course indicated, with due regard for the dangers involved in treating addiction-prone individuals with drugs that are capable of producing physical dependence.

REFERENCES

1. BAKEWELL, W. E., JR., AND WIKLER, A.: Symposium: nonnarcotic addiction—incidence in a university hospital psychiatric ward. *JAMA, 196*:710-713, 1966.
2. BELLEVILLE, R. E., AND FRASER, H. F.: Tolerance to some effects of barbiturates. *J Pharmacol Exp Ther, 120*:469-474, 1957.
3. ESSIG, C. F.: Addiction to nonbarbiturate sedative and tranquilizing drugs. *Clin Pharmacol Ther, 5*:334-343, 1964.
4. ESSIG, C. F., AND CARTER, W. W.: Failure of diphenylhydantoin to prevent barbiturate withdrawal convulsions in dogs. *Neurology, 12*:481-484, 1962.
5. ESSIG, C. F., AND FRASER, H. F.: Electroencephalographic changes in man during use and withdrawal of barbiturates in moderate dosage. *Electroenceph Clin Neurophysiol, 10*:649-656, 1958.

6. ESSIG, C. F., AND FRASER, H. F.: Failure of chlorpromazine to prevent barbiturate-withdrawal convulsions. *Clin Pharmacol Ther*, 7:466-469, 1966.

7. EWING, J. A., AND BAKEWELL, W. E., JR.: Diagnosis and management of depressant drug dependence. *Amer J Psychiat*, 123:909-917, 1967.

8. FRASER, H. F.; ISBELL, H.; EISENMAN, A. J.; WIKLER, A., AND PESCOR, F. T.: Chronic barbiturate intoxication: further studies. *Arch Intern Med*, 94:34-41, 1954.

9. FRASER, H. F.; SHAVER, M. R.; MAXWELL, E. S., AND ISBELL, H.: Death due to withdrawal of barbiturates: report of a case. *Ann Intern Med*, 38:1319-1325, 1953.

10. FRASER, H. F.; WIKLER, A.; ESSIG, C. F., AND ISBELL, H.: Degree of physical dependence induced by secobarbital or pentobarbital. *JAMA*, 166:126-129, 1958.

11. HAIZLIP, T. M., AND EWING, J. A.: Meprobamate habituation: a controlled clinical study. *New Eng J Med*, 258:1181-1186, 1958.

12. HOLLISTER, L. E.; MOTZENBECKER, F. P., AND DEGAN, R. O.: Withdrawal reactions from chlordiazepoxide (Librium). *Psychopharmacologia*, 2:63-68, 1961.

13. ISBELL, H.: Manifestations and treatment of addiction to narcotic drugs and barbiturates. *Med Clin N Amer*, 34:425-438, 1950.

14. ISBELL, H.; ALTSCHUL, S.; KORNETSKY, C. H.; EISENMAN, A. J.; FLANARY, H. G., AND FRASER, H. F.: Chronic barbiturate intoxication: an experimental study. *Arch Neurol Psychiat*, 64:1-28, 1950.

15. OVERALL, J. E.; HOLLISTER, L. E.; MEYER, F.; KIMBELL, I., JR., AND SHELTON, J.: Imipramine and thioridazine in depressed and schizophrenic patients—are there specific antidepressant drugs? *JAMA*, 189:605-608, 1964.

16. SORENSEN, B. F.: Delirium tremens and its treatment. *Danish Med Bull*, 6:261-263, 1959.

17. WIKLER, A.; FRASER, H. F.; ISBELL, H., AND PESCOR, F. T.: Electroencephalograms during cycles of addiction to barbiturates to man. *Electroenceph Clin Neurophysiol*, 7:1-13, 1955.

18. World Health Organization Expert Committee on Addiction-Producing Drugs: Thirteenth Report. *WHO Tech Rep Ser*, 273, Geneva, 1964.

Appendix C

PROS AND CONS OF MARIHUANA
LEGALIZATION

SAMUEL IRWIN

F EDERAL AND STATE drug laws are both irrational and incon-sistent: The Harrison Narcotic Act of 1914 properly lists mor-phine and heroin as narcotics but also includes cocaine, a stimulant. Oregon State law lists marihuana as a narcotic, the Federal Marihuana Tax Act properly does not. Both Federal and state laws declare the mere possession and use of marihuana, a relatively safe drug, a felony—according it the same treatment as heroin. The illicit possession and use of Methedrine and dextro-amphetamine, more dangerous even than heroin when abused, is a misdemeanor in state laws and has no penal con-sequence in Federal law. The laws also do not make distinction between the more serious offense of selling drugs and their possession and use (or mere presence at a location where illicit drugs are found); nor do they distinguish between trivial or extensive trafficking or use. The Federal government is now considering an Omnibus Drug Act to supersede all other drug laws that will make these quantitative distinctions, will take the seriousness of the offense into account, and will have one consistent penality (probably misdemeanor) for the mere posses-sion or use of illicit drugs regardless of drug class or type. The national American Civil Liberties Union recently has taken a position favoring the legalization of marihuana, with regulation akin to our alcohol laws. The issue they raise is a constitutional one, but the problem of drug abuse and the laws developed to deter it encompasses a level of complexity that few have considered.

What follows is an attempt to place the entire issue into

broad, formal perspective. Judgments concerning whether or not a drug should be legalized or whether the penalties for possession and use should be altered require a consideration of the impact of the drug and laws on the entire social system, i.e. the potential hazard from abuse of the drug itself must be considered in relation to the potential or real hazards to society that emerge in response to the laws.

Present Laws

Federal

The Federal Marihuana Tax Act of 1937 makes no distinction between drug traffickers and users. Both charges are regarded as a felony with mandatory minimum sentence of two to ten years imprisonment for a first offense, five to twenty years for a second offense, and ten to forty years for a third offense.

A judge has no discretionary power in adjudicating such a case. The Federal marihuana law is deemed so harsh by the courts and police that it is now rarely enforced.

State

State laws governing marihuana tend to list it as a narcotic and impose misdemeanor-felony or outright felony convictions with sentencing up to life imprisonment. In the State of Oregon it is a felony; no distinction is made between drug selling and use, and marihuana is designated a narcotic. A misdemeanor in Oregon provides for a maximum sentence of six months.   .

General Considerations

General understanding of illicit drug use will be improved if a distinction is made between drug use, misuse, and abuse, e.g., law enforcement officials and physicians tend to designate as drug abuse all drug use outside of legal channels or not as prescribed by a physician. As a guideline, drug *use* is when one takes a drug to achieve desired objectives with minimal hazard to oneself or others; drug *misuse,* when drugs are used inappropriately or in such manner as to increase the probability for adverse consequences or reactions; drug *abuse,* the protracted, compulsive or excessive use that may result in harm to the individual, society or both.

Most illicit drugs seem taken at use and misuse levels; only infrequently at abuse levels.

There is no evidence, for or against, of necessarily greater misuse or abuse of illicit drugs than of legally obtained drugs, no evidence that a person using illicit drugs is necessarily a sick person in need of psychiatric therapy, no evidence that he is necessarily more harmed by such drug taking, and no evidence that he is necessarily more sociopathic than the rest of the population.

The major danger, apart from breaking the law, is that one can never be sure of the composition, purity, and dose of illicit drugs taken.

Illicit drug taking by adolescents is usually exploratory and sporadic, but a special danger when they become preoccupied with drug taking (alcohol or otherwise) at their stage of development. There is considerable evidence to show that regulations for young drinkers have not been and cannot be satisfactorily enforced and frequently may contribute to disrespect for the law. The age at which one begins drinking does not seem the problem. The problem develops when one makes a virtue or sin out of drinking (or drug taking) and does not learn how to drink safely for pleasure.

THE PERSPECTIVES

Enforcement-Morality

Drug-user abusers are seen from this viewpoint as antisocial criminal deviants to be isolated from society, i.e. a police problem. Recommended are legal control over drug traffic aided by legislative and penal sanctions. The strategy for eliminating drug use is to increase the severity of the penalties to discourage drug trafficking and new recruits. Sought is increased police discretionary power; opposed is research that may deviate from or undermine the official view. The attitude is authoritarian controlling; the "scare-mongering" approach to education of both the police and public is not intended to deceive. It stems from the narrow range of contact with drug use that enforcement personnel experience, leading to biased perceptions, uncritical inferences, and a tendency to reject any contrary findings from systematic research.

The drug addict stereotype emerges from this view of the illicit drug user as essentially evil and criminal. A consequence of this view and its propagation has been much public misinformation, hysteria, increasingly punitive legislation, inhumane treatment, resistance to a therapeutic rehabilitative approach, and community antagonism toward the illicit drug user.

Medical-Rehabilitative

Drug-user abusers are here viewed as psychiatrically disturbed individuals in need of therapy and rehabilitation—not a jail sentence. Illicit drug use is seen as a contagious disease necessitating the isolation, quarantine, or control of the offender through civil commitment for therapy. The drug addict is considered a passive, dependent, weak, inadequate or sociopathic personality, often with hedonistic tendencies. Much attention is given to the "unstable personality" and potential damaging effects of drugs on him. Taking a drug without a doctor's supervision is considered drug abuse. Hence, most efforts in writing are biased to emphasize or exaggerate the potential hazards of drugs and to justify their illegal status, i.e. as harmful to the individual and dangerous to society.

The medical view of the drug-user abuser is colored by the type of distressed individuals seen. Illicit drugs may exacerbate or produce the observed pathology, but may also ameliorate it. The pharmacologic, potential therapeutic effects of drugs occur with or without a doctor's prescription. Usually not seen are the drug users that get along without problems or with real benefit.

Sociologic

Drug-user abusers are viewed as emerging from a particular set of social relationships and pressures, the deviancy being within the social structures and processes rather than within the individual. Required for the prevention, control, and real change in the patterns of social drug use is a reorganization of the social setting that evokes the drug using behavior, a point usually stressed by the users themselves. Recommended would be less focus on drug taking as the problem and greater attention to the social environment that breeds it; also, research on the social patterns of drug use (as related to peer groups, subcultures, and adverse or beneficial adaptive effects on individual, group or community functioning).

This view would claim that the sources of strain that generate a drug-using movement can be eliminated by social change, not by legislative drug action per se. One could allow use but control abuse through compulsory treatment.

A consequence of the sociologic view would be recommendations for social change, support for a therapeutic rehabilitative approach to drug abusers, the removal of punitive sanctions against the possession and use of illicit drugs, and the legalization with regulation of drugs for social use compatible with individual and societal goals and needs. It would support legislative control over the trafficking of drugs destructive to individual and societal goals and needs.

Alcohol

Alcohol produces a high level of psychologic and physical dependence difficult to treat. It is highly addicting, the most intoxicating drug used, markedly impairs judgment and increases aggressiveness when immoderately used, and can produce permanent damage to the brain, liver, kidney, pancreas and other tissues of the body when used excessively. As a problem, alcohol abuse in America outranks all other modes of drug abuse. With the possible exception of stimulant or "speed"-like substances (Methedrine or dextro-amphetamine), it is more hazardous and damaging when abused than any other known substance of abuse including heroin.

Alcoholism is the fourth ranking public health problem in the United States, surpassed only by heart disease, cancer, and mental disease. A 1965 nationwide survey showed that 77 percent male and 60 percent female adults drank at least occasionally, 12 percent heavily. There is estimated to be four to five million alcoholics in the United States, representing about 6 percent of the adult population. One in seven newly admitted patients in state mental hospitals are alcoholic, and 0.8 percent of all deaths are from alcoholism. The life expectancy of an alcoholic is ten to twelve years less than the average. Drunken driving accounts for about 25,000 deaths and 200,000 injuries annually. Of all arrests, 60 percent are alcohol related, often involving homicide, assaults, offenses against children and theft. The cost to business and industry from lost time, accidents and the like is estimated at two to five billion dollars annually.

In the State of Oregon, 22 percent of all hospitalized patients are alcoholics or suffering from alcohol related problems; also, alcohol is implicated in about 50 percent of traffic fatalities, 33 percent of pedestrian accidents and 67 percent of police arrests. In the City of Portland, about 50 percent of police time is devoted to alcohol-related problems at a cost of about one third of their budget. It is the most abused drug by adolescents.

Marihuana

It has been estimated that marihuana has been tried or used in the United States by about thirty million people; its use is steadily increasing. In potency (Mexican source) it seems equivalent to that of beer; its effects are dependent on the manner of smoking; about 50 percent of those trying it for the first time experience nothing at all. Marihuana-induced psychosis in this country seems relatively rare, few are hospitalized for reasons of adverse reactions to it, and there seem few recorded instances of criminal problems or driving accidents arising from its use. In Eastern countries where more potent forms of cannabis are available, cannabis-induced physical ailments reported include conjunctivitis, chronic bronchitis, various digestive ailments, impaired physical health from neglect and psychotic reactions; panic reactions are not uncommon among inexperienced users. Excessive use can lead to a social deterioration similar to that experienced with alcohol.

Major concern in the United States is with the possible development of an amotivational syndrome from the constant use of marihuana leading to greater passivity and nonproductivity, but it is not yet known whether marihuana (a relatively weak substance) is the cause of such behavior, facilitates it or may exacerbate it once developed. Many adolescents today not using marihuana exhibit the same behavior. But the more potent hashish (six times more potent than marihuana) frequently increases the activity and drive state of its chronic users more than it decreases it. Marihuana seems to increase reflective thinking and talking preferentially over physical-muscular activity, thus it may increase activity in the former and diminish the latter. Also, marihuana tends to diminish aggressive-competitive behavior, a concern of some who deem this desirable in our society and a boon to others who think we suffer as a nation from too much aggressiveness.

Criminogenic-Legal

A viable criminal law should be one that responds to a real social problem, effectively deals with the problem, and is enforceable. Attempts to legislate personal morality, the area of personal decision making by the individual, have not worked. Such laws have had the greatest deterrent effect on those least requiring them, and least deterrent effect on those most requiring them; all have been relatively unenforceable. Their very existence causes many (particularly adolescents) to flaunt them, to develop patterns of disregard and disrespect for the law, to result in inequitable enforcement, to further burden the courts, to force a major segment of our population to engage in "criminal activity" for indulging personal desires, to penalize them when caught for "crimes without victims" (often more severely than for crimes against victims), and to force narcotic drug addicts into a life of crime (to support their drug habits) resulting in a major assault on the public, e.g. over 50 percent of all petty burglaries in New York City. Such laws are felt to invade the private rights of individuals, have been generally inhumane and cruel, have not accomplished what they were intended to achieve, and thus may have done considerably more damage to society than if they did not exist.

Organized crime in America, originating in the Prohibition Era, has an estimated income from illicit drugs, gambling, prostitution, abortion and other rackets of about forty billion dollars annually—tax free. It has a corroding, corrupting influence at all levels of city, state and national governments, and a vested interest in maintaining the laws that nourish and enlarge it. Without these laws organized crime would be forced into "legitimate" activities, eventually to disappear. The damage to our society from organized crime alone far outweighs any presumed gains from our morality-based laws. Paradoxically, such laws in effect encourage immorality rather than diminish it.

There is no evidence that various legal control systems in the United States bear any relationship to the extent or nature of alcohol use or alcohol problems. Actually, most arrests for illegal delivery occur in those jurisdictions with the most rigid control of distribution, no bars and very few package stores. The regulations concerning adolescents have not been and cannot be satisfactorily enforced. Colleges with formal prohibitions against drinking have fewer students who drink, but of that number, more who drink frequently and heavily than at colleges with more liberal attitudes toward drinking. It is unrealistic to expect that alcohol can be removed from society by legislative decree. No country in Europe or the Americas has yet succeeded in eliminating its use by legislative means. Also, there is no consistent relationship between excessive drinking and availability and sales of alcoholic beverages through state monopoly or private liquor stores. These observations reported for alcohol are likely to apply to all drugs of potential abuse.

THE ISSUES

Constitutional

Whether or not the prohibition of behavior with direct effects limited to the individual is within the function of the state, enforcement inevitably encourages the violation of constitutional guarantees of privacy. United States drug laws have always been an attempt to legislate morality, justified in terms of preventing antisocial acts.

Pragmatic

Marihuana laws are not enforceable and are not a deterrent to use despite their severity (2 to 10 years for a first offense). Their existence provokes disrespect for all laws regulating the use of drugs and produces secondary consequences to the individual and society far more harmful than what the laws are intended to correct.

Symbolic

The marihuana laws symbolize for many the major wrongs in our society, hence superseding the significance of marihuana itself. The following are examples:

1. Misinformation to the public with exaggerated claims of hazard by government officials and professions in attempts to justify the drug's illegal status.
2. Hypocrisy in denying the relevance of alcohol use to the justification for marihuana use, and in severely penalizing marihuana use (a safer drug) while allowing the legal advertising and use of alcohol (a more dangerous drug).
3. Administering more severe punishment for marihuana use (a "crime without a victim") than for crimes of assault or against property.
4. Resistance to reducing penalties (from felony to a misdemeanor) and discrimination against the young in enforcement of the law.

THE PROS AND CONS

1. There are at least medical uses for alcohol; there are none established for marihuana.

   There seems little question but that marihuana is a psychoactive drug capable of producing improved appetite, a sense of well-being, and relaxation. It is taken by users for this purpose as well as to reduce excessively irritable or aggressive behavior. However, the issue of medical utility is entirely nonrelevant to the social use of drugs. Far more relevant from a medical view is the relative safety of the drug. Marihuana produces no physical dependence, significant evidence of tissue damage, or tolerance development and there have been no fatalities from overdosage; its lethal dose is inordinately high and has not been established.

2. Marihuana can nonetheless produce psychological dependence, acute panic, and psychotic reactions; it is still a dangerous drug.

> True, but the psychological dependence liability to marihuana (moderate) is lower than with alcohol (high) and the compulsive, chronic marihuana user can be more readily treated than the alcoholic. Psychotic reactions to marihuana have been reported resulting in hospitalizations, but these seem rare with this weaker form of cannabis. Most remarkable is the relative rarity of hospitalizations for treating adverse reactions to marihuana compared to alcohol and all other psychoactive substances in social use.

3. Still, all writers on the subject refer to the great danger of driving under the influence of marihuana; do we want to impose this greater hazard on the public by legalizing and broadening its use? We have a chemical test to show when a person has been under the influence of alcohol; we have no such test for marihuana.

> These are largely gratuitous speculations with no data justifying this view. There is a long history of cannabis use (usually stronger preparations) in other countries; reported studies do not indicate that such problems exist to anywhere near the degree they do with alcohol. The experimental data available also will argue otherwise. Doses of cannabis even to the point of perceptual change produce no impairment of gait or coordination in regular users (a slight impairment does occur with inexperienced users) and virtually no impairment of reaction time or cognitive function tests exists—alcohol impairs performance on all of these. Significantly impaired performance with marihuana has been reported only after extreme doses producing hallucinatory-like behavior; at the level of social drug use, the data shows marihuana more likely to improve performance. However, there is one point of concern that should be further investigated—the tendency of marihuana to produce a "lapse-dream" state, i.e., to increase the tendency of a person to focus in on a

train of thought and become less aware of the environment during that interval. Many marihuana smokers
claim no difficulty driving under the influence of marihuana, some feel they drive better, while others are
concerned about the possibility of becoming less mindful
of the road and will not drive after taking marihuana.
A danger thus may exist, but marihuana users are less
likely to drive when intoxicated (more likely to go to
sleep) than beer or alcohol drinkers who seem to become
more reckless about driving. It is doubtful that marihuana will pose that much of a problem with driving;
further study is needed to test this.

4. Even if this is true, aren't you concerned about marihuana
use leading people to desire even more kicks and go on to
the use of hard narcotics?

Virtually every leading authority and investigative body
examining this question has rejected this notion. There
seems nothing intrinsic to manihuana effects that would
lead one to experiment with narcotics or speed. Except
for the law enforcement groups who continue to make
such claims, the progression from marihuana to other
drugs is thought to be influenced more by sociologic-
peer influences than by the intrinsic effects of the drug
itself. To document this, marihuana use in this country
has greatly increased in the past five years; heroin use
has not.

5. Still, marihuana is a disinhibiting drug like alcohol. Do we
want another drug that can increase aggressive and criminal
behavior?

Marihuana is a disinhibiting drug, but it seems to dis-
inhibit behavior less than with alcohol. Rather than
increase aggressive and criminal behavior, evidence
shows that it is more likely to decrease it. For example,
juveniles who are most delinquent have been shown to
prefer alcohol, whereas marihuana users tend to be
nonaggressive and to stay away from trouble. It could
in fact be argued that as a society we are too competitive

aggressive for our times and that marihuana use could help diminish this.

6. Our country could not have grown and developed so astonishingly if it were not for this aggressive drive; alcohol use can be justified because it doesn't interfere with it and enables one to compete more effectively. I'm concerned by the increasing reports that marihuana use is leading to inertia and lethargy, to what has been called an 'amotivational syndrome' with diminished productivity and desire to pursue goals. This could be a disaster to our country.

This must be watched carefully. If marihuana does in effect so reduce personal drive, it is a matter for concern. It requires further observation and study. However, if anything, it seems more prone to increase intellective activity and drive at the doses commonly taken, perhaps at the expense of physical muscular drive. Too many adolescents who do not take marihuana today exhibit this same behavior—the causal factor may be sociologic; a reaction of adolescents to society. It is quite possible that marihuana use may reinforce this kind of behavior once it develops; also, persons less goal-oriented and withdrawing from society are the more likely to turn to marihuana use.

7. When advocates for legalizing marihuana claim that it is less harmful than alcohol, they are actually comparing the relatively small effects of marihuana at the low end of the dose-response curve with the effects of alcohol at the toxicity end of the curve. If both drugs were compared at the upper end of the curve, they would see that the effects on the individual and society are highly deleterious in both cases.

True, but overlooked is the greater safety or less deleterious effects of marihuana at the lower end of the curve and of its more potent form (hashish) at the upper end of the curve. Proponents of legalization of marihuana would offer to the public this weaker form of cannabis only, with effects corresponding to those sought by the users. It seems less prone to be abused than the more potent forms of alcohol available.

8. If all controls on marihuana were eliminated, potent preparations probably would dominate the legal market. If the potency of the drug were legally controlled, predictably there would be a market for the more illegal forms.

> True, but it would be the most deviant in our society who would seek such more potent preparations. Marihuana use is increasing because the public is convinced that it is safer. To obtain marihuana they must associate with a subculture of drug users and sellers who have more dangerous drugs available for sale. This could be avoided if marihuana were legalized. Present laws have not prevented adolescents from using marihuana, tobacco, or alcohol; at least they do not have to associate with drug traffickers to get the latter two.

9. Marihuana is relatively new in our society. There is an extensive network of social sanctions related to alcohol usage and many intricate patterns of learning relative to the use and abuse of alcohol. The same cannot be said for marihuana.

> True again, but it is questionable that our learned social pattern of drinking alcohol encourages its proper use. More impressive and illustrative of the greater safety of marihuana is the fact that there seems so few problems attending its use; it is clearly less abused than alcohol.

10. Marihuana legalization would not solve the most serious problem we now have with alcohol. There is no reason to believe that alcoholics would turn to marihuana. Instead, we would add an unknown number of "potheads." Two vices cannot make a virture.

> Also true. Some alcoholics are known to have switched to marihuana use with salutary effects, but there is no reason to believe that large numbers would do so. Prevention of alcohol misuse and abuse is the main argument for legalization; even when abused, the de-

leterious effects of marihuana are less than with alcohol. Take a broader view. The public is now restricted by public decree to the social use of two of the most damaging drugs to man—tobacco and alcohol. In every area of human consumption, an effort is made to develop safer, less hazardous drugs for public use. In the area of social drug use, this is not done. Laws that prevent the social use of safer drugs do not seem in the public interest, nor are attitudes that proscribe the development of safer social drugs as an instrument of government policy. It seems unlikely that drug abuse, alcohol or otherwise, can be eliminated by either education or legislation—only by out-competing them with safer alternatives, perhaps inclusive of all the drug types commonly used and abused. Given safer, cheaper, acceptable options, whose dosage and composition are known and quality controlled, the drug abuser would seem less likely to use illicit sources of drugs and could the more readily come under professional supervision and control.

11. This country is a cosigner of a United Nations treaty regarding cannabis which would be violated if marihuana were legalized.

Not necessarily so. Specifically excluded from that treaty is bhang, a weak form of cannabis that is used in India. Bhang is similar to marihuana in potency, but is taken as a drink. Similar status conceivably could be accorded marihuana.

ADVISORY COMMISSION REPORTS

I. *British Report of the Indian Hemp Drug Commission* (Simla, 1894)

1. "There is no evidence of any weight regarding mental and moral injuries from the moderate use of these drugs."
2. "Large numbers of practitioners of long experience have seen no evidence of any connection between the moderate use of hemp drugs and disease."

3. "Moderation does not lead to excess in hemp any more than it does in alcohol. Regular moderate use of ganja (3 times more potent than marihuana) or bhang (a drink similar in potency to marihuana) produces the same effects as moderate and regular doses of whiskey. Excess is confined to the idle and dissipated."

II. *Mayor's Committee on Marihuana* (1944)

1. "The use of marihuana does not lead to morphine or heroin or cocaine addiction and no effort is made to create a market for these narcotics by stimulating the practice of marihuana smoking." (p. 25)

2. "Indulgence in marihuana does not appear to result in mental deterioration." (p. 186)

3. "Without marihuana only 4 of 14 subjects said they would tolerate the sale of marihuana while after ingestion 8 of them were in favor of this."

4. "In most instances, the behavior of a smoker is of a friendly, sociable character. Aggressiveness and belligerency are not commonly seen. (p. 139) . . . There was found no direct relationship between the commission of crimes of violence and marihuana." (p. 214)

5. "The lessening of inhibitions and repression, the euphoric state, the feeling of adequacy, the freer expression of thoughts and ideas, and the increase in appetite for food suggest therapeutic possibilities." (p. 218)

III. *The President's Advisory Commission on Narcotic and Drug Abuse* (1963)

1. "The Bureau of Narcotics maintains that the present severe penalties act as a powerful deterrent. The Commission does not agree . . . the weakness of the deterrence position is proved every day by the fact that the illicit traffic in narcotics and marihuana continues." (p. 40)

2. "This commission makes a flat distinction between narcotics and marihuana and believes that the unlawful sale or possession of marihuana is a less serious offense than the unlawful sale or possession of an opiate." (p. 42)

IV. *President's Commission of Law Enforcement and Administration of Justice* (1967)

1. "The 1962 report of the President's Ad Hoc Panel on Drug Abuse found the evidence inadequate to substantiate the reputation of marihuana for enticing people to antisocial acts . . . there are too many marihuana users who do not graduate to heroin, and too many heroin addicts with no known prior use of marihuana to support the theory that marihuana leads one to addicting drugs. The most reasonable hypothesis is that some people who are disposed to marihuana are also disposed to heroin use." (p. 225)

2. "The time will come when we will have to determine causal relations and consider the possibility that traditional methods of law enforcement produce more rather than less crime . . . it is difficult to persuade people that they should at least consider whether drugs and crimes are simply the effects of common causes—that delinquents resort both to drugs and to crime for more deep-seated reasons than that the one causes the other." (p. 303)

3. "The Commission believes that enough information exists to warrant careful study of our present marihuana laws and the propositions on which they are based." (p. 225)

V. *Council on Mental Health and Committee on Alcoholism and Drug Dependence* (1967)

1. "No physical dependence or tolerance has been demonstrated. Neither has it been demonstrated that cannabis causes any lasting mental or physical changes."

2. "Most experimenters either give up the drug quickly or continue to use it on a casual basis similar to alcohol."

3. "The prognosis for persons psychologically dependent on marihuana, (and particularly for experimenters, is good in most cases . . . continuous use may be associated with the development of psychiatric illness, although few chronic users are admitted to psychiatric inpatient facilities." (*JAMA*, *201*:368, 1967)

VI. *British Government Advisory Committee on Drugs* (1969)

1. "In terms of physical harmfulness, cannabis is very much less dangerous than the opiates, amphetamines, and barbiturates, and also less dangerous than alcohol."

2. "At this time, the Committee could find little bad to say against marihuana. The worst that reports from the East 'suggest that very heavy long-term consumption may produce a syndrome of increasing mental and physical deterioration.' But it noted dubiously that other drugs may have been involved in those cases, and that the syndrome has never been seen in the West."
(Quotations from *The Oregonian,* Jan. 9, 1969)

REFERENCES

1. Mayor's Committee on Marihuana: *The Marihuana Problem in the City of New York.* Lancaster, Jacques Cattell Press, 1944.
2. *The President's Advisory Commission on Narcotic and Drug Abuse.* Washington, U. S. Government Printing Office, 1963.
3. Task Force Report: *Narcotics and Drug Abuse, The President's Commission of Law Enforcement and Administration of Justice.* Washington, U. S. Government Printing Office, 1967.
4. Council on Mental Health and Committee on Alcoholism and Drug Dependence: Dependence on cannabis (marihuana). *JAMA, 201*:368-371, 1967.
5. ISBELL, H.; JASINSKI, D.; GORODETZKY, C. W.; KORTE, F.; CLAUSSEN, U.; HAAGE, M.; SIEPER, H., AND VON SPULAK, F.: Studies on tetrahydrocannabinol: I. Method of assay in human subjects and results with crude extracts, purified tetrahydrocannabinols and synthetic compounds. Committee of Problems of Drug Dependence, National Academy of Sciences, National Research Council, pp. 4832-4846, 1967. Also in *Psychopharmacologia, 11*:184-188, 1967.
6. Marihuana and society. Joint official statement of the Council on Mental Health and Drug Dependence of the A.M.A. and the Committee on Problems of Drug Dependence of the National Research Council. *JAMA, 204*:1181-1182, 1968.
7. The Dangerous Drug Problem—II. Report of subcommittee on Drug Abuse, Medical Society of the County of New York. *New York Med, 24*:3-8, 1968.
8. Alcohol and Alcoholism. *Pub Health Service Pub. 1640,* 1967.
9. SOLOMON, DAVID (Ed.): *The Marihuana Papers.* Indianapolis, Bobbs-Merrill, 1966.

10. CAREY, JAMES J.: *The College Drug Scene.* Englewood-Cliffs, Prentice Hall, 1968.
11. CHOPRA, I. C., AND CHOPRA, R. N.: The use of cannabis drugs in India. *Bull Narcotics,* January-March, pp. 4-29, 1957.
12. McGLOTHLIN, W. H.: The marihuana problem: an overview. *Amer J Psychiat, 125:*370-378, 1968.
13. KEELER, M. H.: Motivation for marihuana use: a correlate of adverse reaction. *Amer J Psychiat, 125:*142-146, 1968.
14. WEIL, A. T.: Clinical and psychological effects of marihuana in man. *Science, 162:*1234-1242, 1968.

NAME INDEX

SUBJECT INDEX